THE PEARL FRONTIER

THE PEARL FRONTIER

Indonesian Labor and Indigenous Encounters in Australia's Northern Trading Network

Julia Martínez and Adrian Vickers

University of Hawai'i Press

Honolulu

Printed in the United States of America

22 21 20 19 18 17   6 5 4 3 2 1

Library of Congress Cataloging-in-Publication Data
Martínez, Julia, author.
  The pearl frontier : Indonesian labor and indigenous encounters in Australia's
northern trading network / Julia Martínez and Adrian Vickers.
      pages cm
  Includes bibliographical references and index.
  ISBN 978-0-8248-4002-0 (hardcover : alk. paper)
  1. Pearl industry and trade—Australia, Northern—History.   2. Pearl industry and
trade—Indonesia—History.   3. Foreign workers, Indonesian—Australia, Northern.
4. Australia, Northern—History.   I. Vickers, Adrian, author.   II. Title.
  HD9678.P42M37 2015
  338.3'7141209598—dc23

                                                                    2014045925

ISBN 978-0-8248-7517-6 (pbk.)

Designed by George Whipple

Contents

ACKNOWLEDGMENTS

Both the authors wish to acknowledge the financial support of an Australian Research Council (ARC) Discovery Project grant for 2007–2009 without which we would not have been able to embark on the study of Indonesians in a broader geographic context. We began our collaboration on this project while working at the ARC-funded Centre for Asia-Pacific Transformation Studies (CAPSTRANS), at the University of Wollongong (UOW). Andrew Wells, as friend, colleague, and CAPSTRANS director, and then as dean, played a major role in the development and formulation of this project. This book is very much based in labor history, and it was our experience at CAPSTRANS that has shaped this perspective. We have taken an archival approach to the subject, since others have already done much work on the oral history of Asian-Australians in northern Australia.

We owe a huge debt to Susan Edgar and the community members who attended our public talk in Broome. Their enthusiasm about our project was inspiring and has allowed us to better understand the personal dimensions of the materials in the archives. This public talk was organized by the Broome Historical Museum, which welcomed us and provided access to valuable resources, and the work of Kylie Jennings was outstanding. The Museum and Art Gallery of the Northern Territory hosted our public talk on the project in Darwin, where we also benefited from meeting members of the Darwin community formerly involved in the pearling industry.

A number of historians have provided advice, encouragement, and assistance to us both, in particular Jeremy Beckett, whose anthropology set a benchmark for future generations, as well as Peter Boomgaard, Robert Cribb, James J. Fox, Heather Goodall, Hans Hägerdal, and Tony Reid, all of whom made important interventions and contributions and provided inspiration at different stages of the project. We are also very grateful for the help of staff at the Dutch National Archives, the National Archives of Australia, and the Northern Territory Archives Service.

In preparing this book, we both benefited immensely from the major contribution of Hazel Moore, who, in addition to copyediting, provided valuable commentary and support, including on our 2010 trip to Darwin and Broome.

Julia Martínez

My research on the pearling industry began as part of my Ph.D. dissertation on the history of Darwin, completed at the University of Wollongong in 2000. My heartfelt thanks go to my supervisors, Adrian Vickers and Andrew Wells, for encouraging me to pursue the study of Asian-Australian labor history. Thank you also to Regina Ganter, who invited me to present a paper on Indonesians in Darwin in 1999, at one of the first Asian-Australian conferences. Working with Regina on a chapter for her ground-breaking book on Aboriginal-Asian connections, *Mixed Relations* (2006), was a key inspiration for this project.

During the period that Adrian and I worked together in CAPSTRANS, I received financial support from CAPSTRANS; a Northern Territory government History Award; and a UOW University Research Committee grant. I am grateful to the International Institute for Asian Studies (IIAS), Leiden, where I was a visiting fellow on three occasions during 2005–2007. Thank you in particular to historian Manon Osseweijer at the Royal Institute for Linguistics and Anthropology, the KITLV, who shared her experience of writing her Ph.D. on the Aru Islands. Rick van Velden provided invaluable assistance in navigating the Nationaal Archief in Den Haag, and Yoko Harada helped with newspaper research.

I spent many weeks in the branches of the National Archives of Australia (NAA), and I am grateful to the staff in Darwin and Brisbane who helped me to locate and open the naturalization files that were so important to this study. I also wish to acknowledge the staff at the State Records Office of Western Australia and at the Northern Territory Archives Service who helped to fill in local stories from Broome and Darwin. Adrian Cunningham very generously provided access to his M.A. thesis and related materials, some of which have been incorporated into the NAA website. Many colleagues from UOW offered advice and moral support along the way, in particular Christine de Matos, Di Kelly, Lenore Lyons, and Li Tana.

Adrian Vickers

The first debt of this book goes back to the pioneers in the study of Indonesia and northern Australia, in particular Campbell Macknight, who opened up our understanding of the links between these regions. Also influential in shaping my thinking have been Barbara Andaya, Leonard Andaya, Heather Sutherland, David Walker, and Jim Warren, who wrote a number of the masterpieces of labor history in Southeast Asia. Steve Mullins provided materials and expert commentary on the history of the pearling industry. Specific historical details of eastern

Indonesia have been shaped by conversations with and the work of Geneviève Duggan, Arend de Roever, Patsy Spyer, and Emilie Wellfelt, but it was in supervising Syarifuddin Gomang's M.A. thesis at the University of Wollongong that I first gained some insight into the nature of eastern Indonesian history and society.

My father's stories of his experiences of his war service in Morotai and Ambon during and immediately after World War II, including his memories of sharing a military field hospital ward with Jack Wong Sue, were important for my understanding of how much Indonesian history connects to the lives of all Australians. In working on the project, I have benefited greatly from the help, advice, and material of a number of people, particularly George Hilliard and his family; the staff at the Australian War Memorial, especially Karl James; Paul Tickell (not least for sending the valuable document from *Pewarta Deli*); Richard Chauvel who kindly provided material and advice on the *Tiki* expedition and the benefit of his work on West Papua; Jan Lingard; and Fridus Steijlen.

Susan Gilligan helped with organization of the trip to Broome and Darwin, and provided other kinds of research assistance at the University of Sydney. The enthusiasm of a number of colleagues in Australian history at Sydney has also been invaluable. Particular comments and ideas came from Alison Bashford, Catriona Elder, Vicki Grieves, Julia Horne, and Iain McCalman. The Asian Studies Program in the School of Languages and Cultures has also been a great source of support, especially in balancing the needs of teaching and research. Final work on the manuscript was completed while I was a Senior Visiting Fellow at the Asia Research Institute of the National University of Singapore, and I would like to thank all the ARI staff for their support and assistance.

Aboriginal and Torres Strait Islander people are warned that this book may contain images of people who are now deceased.

Abbreviations

AIA	Australia-Indonesia Association
ANOM	Archives nationale d'outre-mer, Aix-en-Provence
AWM	Australian War Memorial, Canberra
CCC	Civil Construction Corps
CMO	Commonwealth Migration Office
CTC	Celebes Trading Company
DEA	Department of External Affairs, Commonwealth of Australia
DI	Department of Immigration, Commonwealth of Australia
ISEAS	Institute of Southeast Asian Studies, Singapore
KITLV	Koninklijk Instituut voor Taal-, Land- en Volkenkunde, Royal Institute for Linguistics and Anthropology, Leiden
KPM	Koninklijke Paketvaart-Maatschappij
NAA	National Archives of Australia
NAN	Nationaal Archief, National Archives of the Netherlands (before 2002, Algemeen Rijksarchive, ARA)
NAWU	North Australian Workers' Union
NEFIS	Netherlands East Indies Forces Intelligence Service
NICA	Netherlands Indies Civil Administration
NTAS	Northern Territory Archives Service, Darwin
QSA	Queensland State Archives, Brisbane
RAAF	Royal Australian Air Force
RIMA	*Review of Indonesian and Malaysian Affairs*
RMS	Republik Maluku Selatan—Republic of the South Moluccas
SRD	Services Reconnaissance Department (otherwise known as "Z Force")
SROWA	State Records Office of Western Australia, Perth

Introduction

The Pearl Frontier

In July 2010, the authors were giving a public talk at the Broome Historical Museum. A sizable audience had gathered to hear our presentation on the history of the pearling industry in northern Australia and eastern Indonesia. The highly regarded Aboriginal elder Susan Edgar (Marjardee) opened proceedings with a welcome to the country and was followed by Adrian Vickers, who provided a general overview of Australian involvement in the industry in Indonesia. Then Julia Martínez took the floor to present some of the personal stories of pearling workers. Julia had reconstructed these accounts from documents she had found in the archives.

As Julia began to tell of these men indentured to work in northern Australia, she was asked by Susan if there were any photographs of her father, whose name, said Susan, was Abdoel Gafoer. Julia smiled and screened her next slide, a photograph of a young and handsome Alorese man who had been indentured in Kupang, West Timor. Susan called out in surprise: "That's my *Bapa* [father]." She wept as she saw for the first time old archival photographs of him. The photographs that Julia had discovered dated back to the time Abdoel Gafoer was first hired to come to Australia, and were part of the documentation relating to his long struggle with the government to obtain the right to stay in Australia with Susan and her mother.

The community hall broke into an excited uproar, as local people of Broome and surrounding areas responded to images of their parents, uncles, and friends, many of whom had long been separated from the community. "Look, there's Uncle Tom The!" yelled one. Three women in front asked for information about their fathers, heroes of World War II, but unrecognized as such. Others in the audience talked about connecting with long-lost family members on the remote eastern Indonesian island of Babar. Seated in the middle of the hall was Ahmat Bin Fadal, one of the last indentured workers, now silver-haired and emanating a quiet air of dignity. History was alive in Broome.[1]

Like most of the workers in the pearling industry, Susan's father, Abdoel Gafoer, moved backwards and forwards on the maritime frontier between Australia and Indonesia. His relationship with an Indigenous woman was not recognized by either government, and he tried for many years not to be sent back to Indonesia. Abdoel Gafoer and his family had been luckier than most in getting official permission to stay in Australia. Others present told heartbreaking stories of being separated forever from their fathers when the men were deported at the end of their contracts.

This book is an attempt to document and explain the context of these relationships, showing how they were created by an industry that sought to move beyond national boundaries in its search for the treasures given up by pearl shells. Despite common views that Indonesia and Australia have always been quite separate, we found stories of Indonesians in Australia and of Australians in Indonesia. Beginning with the north Australian bases of the pearling industry and the central role Indonesians have played in that industry, the scope of our investigations widened to look at how work, culture, and marriage had shaped a whole shared region across international borders.[2] The stories that we found, like that of Abdoel Gafoer, are stories of a frontier in which new connections were formed in a context of hard labor and changing economies, societies, and politics. The story of Indonesian workers in the Australian-dominated pearling industry is a story of mobility against restriction, of blurred borders and personal ties, and it opens up a wider picture of the region in which the Indian and Pacific Oceans meet.

The starting point for our research was Julia Martínez's discovery of a series of documents from the 1950s and early 1960s giving a unique insight into the lives of the last group of Indonesian pearling workers who remained in Australia: These were their applications for Australian citizenship, made at a time when the infamous White Australia policy was beginning to break down. These stories of Abdoel Gafoer and his colleagues led us to uncover a wider, and hitherto almost unknown, picture of the zone that takes in eastern Indonesia and northern Australia. We began by tracing the family relationships that were created by work in the pearling industry. As we expanded the scope of this history of the precious commodities of pearl shells and pearls, we also found stories of Australians who went to Indonesia between 1905 and 1942 to set up pearling businesses. Both sets of stories gave a very different picture from the standard histories of the connections between the two countries, which barely mentioned any relations in the first part of the twentieth century.

For almost one hundred years, Indonesians were indentured into the Australian-based pearl-shell industry. This was an industry that crossed international borders and linked parts of eastern Indonesia to northern Australia. On the Australian side, the industry was based in the frontier towns of Broome and Darwin

SOUTH-EAST ASIA AND AUSTRALIA

PACIFIC OCEAN

PHILIPPINES

MINDANAO

BISMARCK ARCHIPELAGO

Rabaul

Finschafen

Port Moresby

Lae

PAPUA BRITISH NEW GUINEA

GERMAN NEW GUINEA

Aitape

Hollandia

WEST PAPUA (NETHERLANDS NEW GUINEA)

BIAK

CORAL SEA

Cairns

QUEENSLAND

Normanton

Princess Charlotte Bay

TUDU I. (WARRIOR I.)

BADU I. (MULGRAVE I.)

THURSDAY I.

Torres Strait

ARAFURA SEA

ARU IS

KEI IS

TANIMBAR IS

MELVILLE I.

ARNHEM LAND

Darwin

NORTHERN TERRITORY

A U S T R A L I A

WESTERN AUSTRALIA

MOROTAI

HALMAHERA

MALUKU (MOLUCCAS)

MISOOL

TERNATE
TIDORE
BACAN

SERAM

BANDA

BANDA SEA

BURU

AMBON

BABAR

KISAR

LEITI

TIWI ISLANDS

EAST TIMOR

WEST TIMOR

Kupang

ZIMBAWE

TIMOR SEA

Cape Leveque

Broome

Roebuck Bay

Port Hedland

Gantet Bay

INDIAN OCEAN

SULAWESI (CELEBES)

CELEBES SEA

Manado

Zamboanga

SULU ARCHIPELAGO

SABAH

BRUNEI

SARAWAK

BORNEO

KALIMANTAN

Balikpapan

Makassar

BUTON

FLORES SEA

ALOR
ADONARA
SOLOR
LOMBLEN
SAVU
ROTE
SUMBA
KOMODO
SUMBAWA
LOMBOK
BALI

BAWEAN

MADURA

Semarang
Surabaya

JAVA

Jakarta (Batavia)

I N D O N E S I A

THAILAND

VIETNAM

M A L A Y S I A

SINGAPORE

Singapore

PAHANG

Penang

SUMATRA

MERGUI ARCH.

COCOS IS. (KEELING)

CHRISTMAS I.

500 miles

500 kilometres

and in the Torres Strait Islands; in Indonesia, the island of Aru was one of the prime pearling sites. The industry shaped and dominated the societies of these frontier sites.

The importing of workers from what was then the Netherlands East Indies into the Australian segments of the industry was a significant exception to what is generally known as the White Australia policy. The introduction of indenture along Australia's north coast in the nineteenth century helped to shape a unique form of colonial society. This was a society that drew on the models of British and Dutch colonialism in Southeast Asia, while trying to adapt to the expectations of Australia's southern settlement colonies.

When British officials first explored the possibility of setting up colonial outposts on Australia's north coast, they were guided by enthusiastic writings of naturalists and explorers such as Alfred Russel Wallace and George Windsor Earl, who highlighted the natural wealth of the Indonesian archipelago. It was understood that the Netherlands East Indies could provide not only easy access to markets and commodities but also to crucial labor supplies. The British were well aware that the Southeast Asia pearl-shell industry had been established for many centuries and that the fledgling Australian industry would benefit from access to skilled divers and competent sailors and navigators. It was also recognized that they brought with them cultural capital and linguistic ability in local indigenous and Malay dialects.

Historian Campbell Macknight, who in the 1970s pioneered the history of contact across this maritime frontier, emphasized the precolonial connections between north Australia and the port of Makassar, which was home to the fleets of traders and sailors who dominated the trepang (*bêche-de-mer*) trade. Makassar was important, but the pearl frontier as we have described it was far more geographically and ethnically diverse. Diversity of religion was also a factor. Indonesians may have introduced the Muslim faith to north Australia, but the pearling indents, as they were known, also brought with them the full range of religious beliefs, with Christian and animist elements, from eastern Indonesia. And overlaying the diversity of religion was the common culture formed by their strong connection to the sea that joined their island homes to Australia's north coast. The sea and its maritime produce represented both a major source of income and a central arena for cultural and spiritual life. These were understandings that they also shared with the Indigenous Australians, or "saltwater" peoples of the northern coast of Australia.

While white Australians viewed the Netherlands East Indies as a source of profit, the first forays by Australian pearling masters into Indonesian waters were met with suspicion and even accusations of piracy. It was not until the turn of the

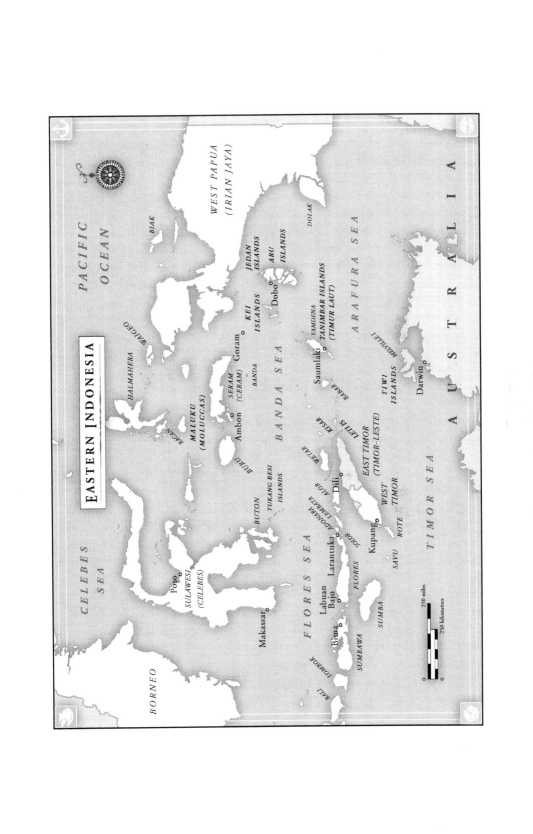

EASTERN INDONESIA

twentieth century that Australian pearling masters were actively welcomed by the Dutch, who were themselves eager to expand their pearl-shell industry. Australians such as James Clark and Henry Hilliard were at home on both sides of the pearl frontier and played an important role in the Netherlands East Indies industry.

On the Australian side of the frontier, pearling masters were at first rather wary of using labor from the Indies, finding that the men were unwilling to serve white masters who often did not understand the cultural expectations of a diverse workforce. Stories of violence and mutiny shaped early perceptions of the frontier. But by the beginning of the twentieth century, as labor was imported by recruiters in larger numbers, particularly from the Timorese port of Kupang, there was a sense that pearling masters viewed Indonesians as the least problematic source of labor. Aboriginal and Pacific Islander labor had, by the late nineteenth century, become more difficult to obtain as antislavery strategies were put in place. The pearling industry was soon dominated by highly skilled Japanese divers. Indonesians continued to make up the majority of the support crew on board pearling luggers, and as divers, they came to be viewed as a precautionary measure to mitigate against Japanese dominance.

The exotic presence of Indonesian men on the streets of north Australian towns was described by most writers who passed through the pearling ports in the early twentieth century. Orientalist imaginings of fabulous pearls, harvested by mysterious and potentially dangerous eastern men, abounded. As the pearling ports began to sustain a slightly larger white population in the 1920s, the tone of writings, particularly by residents, became noticeably less tolerant. There were numerous demands for a stricter regime of racial segregation to keep Asians separate from both the Indigenous and white residents.

It was not until the 1930s that a new wave of internationalism reached both sides of the pearl frontier. The Australian unionists and Indonesian workers who believed in the concept of equality for all workers formed a small but crucial lobby, particularly in the port of Darwin. There, shared social events, such as mixed soccer games, signaled a way of thinking that would eventually lead to the downfall of the Dutch colonial empire.

The advent of World War II along the pearling frontier marked a radical break. For a few years, while the pearling industry was put on hold, Indonesians were able to take on new roles and meet new people. Some traveled south to the Australian capital cities of Melbourne, Sydney, and Brisbane, where they found more like-minded people who questioned the basic social foundations of the colonial world. As the Indonesians took the first steps toward decolonization, many Australians were willing to support the Indonesian workers. But hopes for a new era of fair wages and treatment in the pearling industry were all but crushed in the first years after the war as the pearling masters took steps to return quickly to business as usual. With the Dutch still in control of the port of Kupang it was not surprising that Indonesian protesters in Australia were swiftly deported and replaced with new recruits. It took more than a decade for the Australian government to slowly and reluctantly question its own policies of rigidly controlling indentured labor.

In the new era of international diplomacy in the 1950s, Australia was forced to reconsider not only its labor policies, but also to confront the fact that the White Australia policy was hurting Australia's international reputation. After 1957, Indonesian pearling workers were among the first Asians to become naturalized since the creation of the federated Australian nation. These positive changes were far too long in the making. When we examine the complex processes that were required for Indonesians to gain Australian citizenship, there can be no doubt that as individuals, each naturalized Indonesian was helping to break down an unjust and outdated regime. And there were many in Australia, on both sides of politics, for whom the plight of aging pearling indents from Indonesia spoke to the need for urgent social and political change.

Rather than attempting to trace all aspects of the connections between Australia and its nearby Indian and Pacific Ocean connections, in this book we have chosen to approach social and cultural relations as the outcome of commodity relations. These relations are of two types. The first revolved around one set of commodities, pearls and pearl shells. However, trade in objects requires first the commodification of labor, in this case semi-free labor, and its utilization by capital. So tracing the history of these commodities requires an understanding of the workings of the whole of the industry—hence, a transnational kind of history. Labor's alienation, the conditions under which people worked, the manner of their employment, the levels of exploitation involved, raised people's opposition to being turned into objects in the production process. Men such as Abdoel Gafoer came to Australia with deep histories of seafaring, kinship, and ethnicity, all of which were hidden by the label "coolies." The categories of race involved in their employment were one means to turn them into cheap labor, but could be used by themselves to find alternative lines of power. While the workers in the pearling industry occasionally resorted to direct confrontation with the pearling owners—in calls for better pay and conditions, even strikes—most often they cut across the divisions by which they were governed. One of the most frequent ways they did this was through their relations with Aboriginal people, especially marriage.

The stories of Aboriginal-Indonesian intermarriage shed light on the nature of citizenship entitlement in Australia and the struggles of both Indigenous Australian and Asian peoples to lead their lives free from control by government and capital. Theirs are stories of colonial boundary-marking, wartime disruption, and postwar reactions, which attempted to assert the idea of Australia as a white bastion in Asia and the Pacific. In the often-tragic stories of families of Indonesian men and Aboriginal and Torres Strait Islander women cruelly broken by paternalistic officials, the long wait of workers for citizenship rights also becomes a story of endurance and stoicism.

Beginning with the story of Abdoel Gafoer, we outline the idea of this maritime zone on either side of the Timor and Arafura Seas. We then introduce the worlds of eastern Indonesia and northern Australia (particularly Broome, Darwin, and the Torres Strait), reviewing the various histories of both regions, and demonstrating the importance of understandings based on local perspectives from this fascinating frontier. The early part of this story is based on the idea of mapping it, as national boundaries cutting across the zone were established between 1494 and 1957. People throughout the zone imagined their participation in a variety of ways, calling on notions of ethnicity and race, allegiance and enmity, to help navigate the physical and ethnic complexities of the region. By telling the shadowy history of indenture in the pearling industry from both Indonesian and Australian perspectives, we offer insight into a previously unexplored area of shared history in the Asia-Pacific.

CHAPTER ONE

Border-Crossing on the Pearl Frontier

In its heyday the pearling industry stretched across the Asia-Pacific, but by focusing on Australian-Indonesian connections, we have been able to explore the particular maritime border zone at the heart of the industry. Pearling created the strongest ties between Australians and Indonesians across this zone, despite the fact that a number of other maritime products were important for trade in the region, including trepang, trochus shell, and shark fin.[1] Our study opens up new understandings of the connections between Indonesia and Australia, but it also shows that national categories are not adequate to account for the ways that people moved and worked across what was a single pearling zone, which we call the pearl frontier.

Between the 1870s and the 1970s thousands of Indonesians worked in northern Australia in the pearling industry. The majority of these men came to Broome, Darwin, and Thursday Island as indentured laborers, some only temporarily, others for many decades. The men to whom we refer here as "Indonesians" were classified before 1945 into two broad categories: "Koepangers" and "Malays." The term "Koepangers" referred to men recruited from the port of Kupang in West Timor, but these men were drawn from a number of surrounding islands. The term "Malays" was more confusing as it was used both for men recruited from Singapore—who often originated from the Netherlands East Indies—and for men recruited from other ports such as Makassar, Dobo on the Aru Islands, and Ambon in Maluku (the Moluccas). It was interchangeably used as an ethnic and a racial term. Other more specific terms such as "Javanese," "Ambonese," and "Macassans" were also used to refer to people from what was the Netherlands East Indies up until 1945. Today, many people assume that the "Malays" came from present-day Malaysia, but in fact this country was a source of only a small portion of workers in the pearling industry.

The colonial use of "Malay" was advocated by the British as a racial referent for insular Southeast Asians, displacing the general use of "Javanese" promoted by the Dutch.[2] Indonesia was generally referred to as part of the "Malay archipelago" or "Indian archipelago" in British colonial writing, although it was a British author, George Windsor Earl, who coined the term "Indonesia" in 1850, as a way of differentiating the islands then largely under Dutch control.[3] Peoples of the archipelago have referred to themselves as "Melayu" to denote participation in a coastal, mainly Muslim culture shared in present-day Indonesia and Malaysia (and even in southern regions of Thailand and the Philippines), so their use of "Malay" has been much more specific than the British one. Throughout this book we will use the term "Indonesian" (and "Malaysian" and "Singaporean") where the geographical origins of the workers are clear from the documentation. To use the colonial "Malay" would be to maintain the colonial categories.

What in the Indonesian context were fluid categories of ethnicity became categories of "race" in colonial systems, particularly that of the British Empire. With the term "Koepangers," the pearling industry invented a new version of these racial categories, one meant to accommodate a specific form of labor recruitment in a context where "colored" labor was meant to be excluded by the Immigration Restriction act of 1901. This act, one of the first of the new Australian parliament, was the mechanism by which the White Australia policy was administered, so that any "colored" person might be denied entry to Australia. The pearling industry, however, was granted an exemption from the act.

This pearl frontier largely coincided with a pearl fishery, a single sphere of activity, even though it crossed marine trenches and continental zones. The pearling circuit we describe has its westernmost point in the far north of Western Australia; it then tracked eastward across the Northern Territory to the Torres Strait in north Queensland and from there across to Papua New Guinea. Moving westward from the island of New Guinea, it included the oldest known pearling beds in Maluku (the Moluccas) in eastern Indonesia. The zone covered the Arafura and Timor Seas, and part of the Flores Sea. This was a frontier that attracted men from all around the world. The owners and traders were Europeans, Australians, and Americans working alongside merchants of Chinese and Arab descent, joined by Japanese divers and traders. Workers were brought into the pearl frontier from the Philippines, the Pacific Islands, Singapore, and Malaysia, as well as from parts of Indonesia besides the areas where pearl shells and pearls were found.

The pearl shell distinctive to the region was the *Pinctada maxima*, with its gold- and silver-lipped varieties, but the beds also included the black-lipped *P. margaritifera* and a number of other varieties.[4] These luminous shells were harvested chiefly to make buttons and other products. Those used in the Australian industry went under categories such as "chicken," "light," "medium," "bold," and "grubby" (not to mention "thin medium" and "dead"); but some were also called according to their market, "Bombay," "Egyptian," or "Lingah." Trained sorters and graders of later times, such as late-twentieth-century Donnelly McKenzie, working for Broome pearling company Streeter & Male, had to distinguish between eighteen different types.[5] The shells, of course, were also prized for the pearls produced from sand irritations to the mollusks.

The region where pearl shell was gathered was a frontier in several senses. It joined the areas of Indonesia and Australia that were most remote from their centers of government. The distance from these centers, respectively Jakarta (Batavia) and Sydney-Melbourne (later Canberra), meant that much that happened on the frontier was at the edges of state control, where laws were for stretching and breaking, or did not apply at all. The areas of eastern Indonesia and northern Australia were hard to get to, despite some parts of the pearl frontier being on regular trade routes. Such remoteness bred a frontier mentality, where local power was available to those who took it.

Indonesian Labor Mobility

The story of the pearl frontier is a story of labor mobility. An important part of the story of the pearling industry is the movement of Indonesians between islands, and ultimately outside the national borders of the country. The largest proportion of people moved to find work, although others moved for religious, social, educational, and political reasons. Mobility is built into deep cultural patterns and is a norm of social life. In our research on the movement of peoples from present-day Indonesia to Australia, we have found that patterns of moving overseas began in societies where movement between islands and subregions within current Indonesian borders was well established before those borders came into being. The presence of hundreds, and at times thousands, of Indonesians in northern Australia during the early and mid-twentieth century is an extension of long traditions.

Indonesian mobility is often regarded as a modern phenomenon, but it has a long history. In 2007, the number of Indonesians officially reported working abroad had reached 4.3 million, bringing their home country an income of US$6 billion in remittances.[6] By 2010, the numbers working abroad was well over five million, including the numbers of those "smuggled" across the Indonesian-Malaysian maritime borders.[7] While the scale of movement may be significantly larger, the nature of Indonesian mobility is not at all new.

In recent years, attention to Indonesian migration has produced important studies of workers, particularly women workers. Beginning with studies of Indonesians working in Malaysia,[8] attention has now spread to the wider movement of workers throughout the Middle East and East Asia.[9] One of the major publications on labor migration points out that it is often women from eastern Indonesia, from the poor province of Nusa Tenggara Timur, who form a significant number of these mobile workers.[10] This is the same area from which many of the pearling workers came to Australia.

Compared with the literature on the Chinese, Japanese, and Indian diasporas, there has been little recognition of Indonesians as an immigrant people. More than forty years ago, Craig A. Lockard published a survey of Javanese emigration calling for further research into this neglected aspect of Indonesia's history.[11] Since then there have been a number of specific country studies, but little work has been done to link the different forms of mobility and find common patterns. Australia as a destination country is all but forgotten.

In the Australian literature up until recently, there were only a few studies of Indonesian political refugees overseas; those studies treated mainly the Leftists who contributed to the Indonesian Revolution from Australia.[12] Jan Lingard's work has shown that such a political story opens up a wider set of issues of cultural and social interaction, represented by the marriages between Indonesian activists and refugees with Australian women.[13] In most of those cases, the Australian government did not see these marriages as important and forced the Indonesians to go back home, leaving their wives with the choice to go with them or not.

While there has been an extensive literature on Australian-Indonesian relations, there are major gaps in the narrative of ties between the two nations. The key elements that are usually described are early ties between Indonesian trepang fishers and Aboriginal Australians, Australian support for Indonesia's independence movement, and the diplomatic entanglements of Australia and Indonesia over issues such as East Timor. The first story, documented through stories of fishermen from South Sulawesi coming to the areas around Arnhem Land, is described in the scholarly and popular literature as belonging mainly to the period before 1911, when steps were taken to make border control tighter.

The second series of events, in which left-wing Australian unions and community groups put pressure on the government to support Indonesian independence, took place in the early stages of the Indonesian Revolution, particularly in 1946 and 1947, although its roots lay in the encounter between Australians and Indonesians in the Pacific War. During that struggle, Australian, Dutch, and Indonesian forces were linked first in the attempt to stop the Japanese invasion, secondly in the often-covert operations behind Japanese lines, and thirdly in the defeat of Japan in Southeast Asia. In fighting the Japanese, "Ambon" took on a new meaning as the site where Australian prisoners were massacred by the Japanese naval forces; heroic events such as the sabotage of Japanese ships in Singapore harbor involving passage through Indonesia; and the basing of Australians at Morotai (north Maluku), from where they launched into battle at Balikpapan (Kalimantan) and other strategic sites. The war and the subsequent Indonesian Revolution are regarded as the first period in which Australians ventured into

Indonesia, but our research on the pearling industry shows that this was not the case at all.

A final and more familiar story dates from the end of the 1950s and the 1960s, when Prime Minister Menzies established Indonesian Studies in Australian universities in response to the Cold War, inaugurating a period of mass encounters that oscillated between tourism to Bali and the dreadful threat of violence. By the end of the 1990s, a million Australians per year were visiting Indonesia, but this period at the end of the Suharto regime also saw large riots, sectarian conflict, and general civil unrest. Tourism and violence came together in the Bali bombings of 2002 and 2005, in which over ninety Australians died.

Despite the importance of mass tourism, the narrative of Australian relations with Indonesia over the last fifty years has been more about government-to-government ties, most often presented in terms of prime ministerial and presidential visits. Key events have included Prime Minister Gough Whitlam's assent to Indonesia's invasion of East Timor in 1975, Prime Minister Paul Keating's admiration of the Suharto dictatorship, and Prime Minister John Howard's pressuring of President B. J. Habibie to grant East Timorese a referendum on independence. Agency is clearly vested in political leaders, not ordinary people. A theme running through such a narrative is the idea of "living dangerously," of Indonesia as a threat to Australia.[14]

Strangely, most narratives of Indonesian-Australian relations say little about the idea of an intrinsic connection between the two as countries, and rarely if ever do they present Indonesian movement to Australia as anything more than temporary. Only in 1999 did Julia Martínez put forward the idea that Indonesian migrants have a multigenerational history in northern towns such as Darwin.[15] The period from the early twentieth century until the 1940s remains neglected in Indonesian-Australian historiography, as, to a lesser extent, is the period of the 1950s. The thinking underlying the intellectual separation of the two states is that northern Australia and eastern Indonesia are isolated "outbacks." Seeing both as "outbacks" ignores the Arafura and Timor Seas as a source of connection, a unifying space, as indigenous intellectual Epeli Hau'ofa argues of the Pacific.[16]

The historical understanding of Indonesian-Australian connections and mobility needs to be informed by two dimensions: the cultural norms and habits that make it easy to move between places, and the economic and social forces that have shaped patterns of movement. The majority of Indonesians coming to Australia have maritime backgrounds and have come by sea. Indeed, the continuity of this traffic is shown by ongoing disputes between the present-day governments when Australian authorities jail Indonesian fishermen for what is essentially regarded as poaching. Even more recently, boat crews have been arrested for "people smuggling"—that is, transporting refugees.[17]

A Zone of Movement

The plight of Indonesian fishermen trying to make a living in the twenty-first century shows that modern borders are just that, recent inventions, and Southeast Asian history, like Pacific history, is a history of movement, not of neatly bounded nation-states.[18] By examining the internal dimension of maritime movement, we wish to expand on how Indonesians can understand their participation in global patterns of mobility and migration. We therefore want to show that the fluidity of movement across borders—not only Australia and Indonesia, but also Timor Leste, Papua New Guinea, and into the Pacific Islands—means that the region should be viewed in terms of a shared history. It is no longer good enough to maintain the false dichotomy between the West as shaping Australia's history and Asia as determining its geography, as Australian political leaders do.[19] Such a dichotomy relates very closely to the way Australian nationalism promotes an Anglo-Saxon identity, a whiteness in which Asia is a threatening outside element.[20]

Many factors have influenced Indonesian mobility, but trade and maritime movement are closely linked as part of a movement involving Indonesian agencies. The peoples who are now Indonesians have been linked into regional and global systems for a very long time. Their contact with Oceania goes back to early prehistory and to the movement of peoples down from Asia across the Pacific. According to A. M. Jones, the geographical range of seafaring Indonesians extended as far as the coasts of Africa.[21] He argues that Indonesians arrived in Madagascar not later than 400 CE and continued on by sea to the west coast of Africa to Ghana and the Congo. Using as evidence the prevalence of xylophones and other cultural factors, Jones concludes that there was an Indonesian colonization of coastal parts of Africa no later than the eighth century.

International trade in Southeast Asia is very ancient. Its earliest evidence is the transmission of bronze drum types, traced back to Dongson in Vietnam, but found in Bali and other parts of present-day Indonesia, probably having arrived after 500 BCE. Sea trade with India and China may have already existed at that time, although the earliest evidence for that comes some five hundred years later. Certainly the ninth-century depictions of large ships on the Borobudur temple in Central Java demonstrate the strength of Indonesian boat-building technologies. By 1000 CE, large-scale trade was already taking place, and by the time that Europeans had established a presence in Southeast Asia, after 1511—when the Portuguese conquered the great city-state of Melaka—the region was already a major focus of global commerce.[22]

Although the eastern part of Indonesia is regarded now as a remote area, it was in fact the focus of much of the early international trade. The islands of

Maluku (the Moluccas) were the source of spices—nutmeg, mace, and cloves—and the spice trade was also accompanied by other forms of commerce, such as bringing Indian textiles and Chinese porcelain into Indonesia, and other commodities, such as sandalwood and trepang, which were to the large market of China. Thus not just Maluku, but islands farther south, notably Timor, were important global centers, leading in the latter case to the division of that island, first between the Netherlands East Indies and the Portuguese empire, and then between Indonesia and Timor Leste or Timor Loro Sae.

In discussing trade, writers have tended to look at the mobility of traders from outside—namely, the Chinese, Indians, Arabs, and others who have been both temporary and permanent settlers in major and minor ports.[23] Caught up with trade mobility, however, has been a set of other movements of Indonesian people, from aristocrats to slaves. While this movement is now primarily associated with urbanization, it has broader roots, and broader implications, particularly in relation to maritime movement.[24] Trade depends on work—that is, production—so a history of trade across the frontier is a history of labor as well as of the consumption of a commodity.

Australia in Asia and Asia in Australia

The published histories of Australia have been inclined to underestimate the depth and continuity of Asian connections. While acknowledging trade connections to India and China in the early days of the Australian colonies, many still believe that the traffic with Asia was shut down at the beginning of the twentieth century as a result of isolationist policies. The literature revising this view of Australia's Asian history began in the 1970s with particular case studies, for example, of Chinese traders who dominated Darwin, the Japanese women working in the brothels of Cairns, or the Japanese divers in the pearling industry.[25] Only recently have studies begun to look at Asians as collections of groups that have made a significant contribution to the north of Australia.[26] Regina Ganter and Henry Reynolds in particular have highlighted how Asian migration shaped a unique poly-ethnic culture across north Australia. But while stories of Japanese and Chinese migrant experiences are embedded in the homes they left behind, there has been little sense of home when discussing Indonesian migrants.[27] The islands to the north of Australia remain vague shadows, despite the complex connections that existed between northern Australia and eastern Indonesia.

One important connection to Indonesia has been the exception. Writing in the 1970s, the archaeologist and historian Campbell Macknight described the industry of trepang, which took off in the eighteenth century, and involved temporary settlements in the top of the Northern Territory of people from South Sulawesi, mainly from the Makassar ethnic group. This industry created interaction between Aboriginal people and Indonesians, including intermarriage, and some Aboriginal people travelled back to the port city of Makassar. The industry is largely seen as having wound down in 1911, when Australian authorities began to try to enforce national boundaries.[28] The contacts led to integration of Indonesian cultural elements into Aboriginal cultures, and following Macknight's lead, a number of scholars began to examine Asian-Aboriginal contacts, including the influence of Indonesian languages on northern Australian languages. Although such contacts are given the label "Makassan," in fact people from a range of ethnic groups, including the so-called Sea Gypsies, or Bajau, were involved. A series of articles in the journal *Aboriginal History,* beginning with anthropologist Jeremy Beckett's documentation of contact in the Torres Strait, opened up this field of inquiry.[29] Nevertheless, even when showing that there was extensive traffic between northern Australia and eastern Indonesia in the nineteenth century, Macknight wrote about it as a thing of the past, only slightly more current than the prehistoric links among the Aboriginal, Indonesian, and Pacific peoples.[30]

Commodifying Indonesian Workers

The field generally called labor history should be better considered as a series of histories of production and consumption, in which Asia-Pacific mobility has played a significant part since precolonial times. The first examples of such mobility were related to slavery. Trade and maritime economies are also linked to forms of forced migration. The same sites that were important for trade were also important centers of piracy, including slave raiding.[31] The stratified societies of Indonesia had a variety of forms of slavery, bondage, and dependency, and these were combined in both precolonial and colonial times into international slave trading.[32] There was overlap between indigenous forms of maritime migration and the colonial slave trade. In the seventeenth century, the preeminent Dutch multinational company, the United East India Company (VOC), stimulated the slave trade in order to find labor for their new ports from Desima in Japan to Batavia, the capital of the VOC empire, and for their colony at the Cape. The export of slaves to Africa resulted in, among other things, forced migration of Indonesians (20 to 30 percent of whom were women) to present-day South Africa, creating the mixed community called "Cape Malays." The slaves were joined by political exiles, including Javanese princes and Makassar sultans, creating complex new communities. In Sri Lanka, the new community found a very different social role in the colonial military.[33] The comparison between the South African and Sri Lankan cases is revealing. In both, Dutch colonies were taken over by the British, and the Indonesians there were subsumed into the race-based category of "Malay."

The slave trade was abolished by the Dutch in 1860. Unofficially, however, it continued into the twentieth century, overlapping with the period when labor migration was supposed to be undertaken only by nominally free indentured laborers. Thus, peoples of Flores, Sumba, Solor, and Alor were subject to slave raiding up until recent times.[34] Likewise, the smuggling of slaves, coolies, and sex workers backwards and forwards from Indonesia and China into present-day Malaysia and Singapore continued across the "porous borders" of the South China Sea into the early twentieth century.[35]

The late nineteenth century thus saw a slow transition from slavery to indentured labor, with a blurring of the distinction between the two in many cases. After the Dutch abolition of slavery in 1860, Indonesians were sent on contracts of indenture to work in Australia, in the German colonies in the Pacific, and for the British in Singapore, North Borneo, and elsewhere in Malaya. Precise figures for this period are difficult to ascertain, but as later chapters will show, for the pearling industry, those sent to Australia numbered in the thousands. This was the same period that Australian companies were importing indentured laborers from the Asia-Pacific, through means that often turned into kidnapping in the so-called blackbirding of Pacific Islanders from the New Hebrides (Vanuatu) and other islands.

The constant movement between western Indonesia and the Malay Peninsula makes it very difficult to date the presence of Indonesian workers across present-day borders, but the numbers were significant by the beginning of the twentieth century.[36] This followed on from Indonesian migration to Singapore between 1825 and 1881, when the "number of Javanese in Singapore increased from 38 to 5,885."[37] By that time, Javanese were in the majority, but there were also Makassar, Bugis, Boyanese from Bawean Island, and Balinese and Madurese.[38] The Straits Settlements (Singapore, Penang, Province Wellesley, Dindings, and Malacca) stopped the use of contract labor in 1916, while in the Federated Malay States workers were imported up until 1932, during which time Indonesians were employed on rubber plantations. North Borneo (Sabah) also employed Indonesian laborers in larger numbers after 1907, when the Dutch officially permitted plantations to recruit Javanese workers. By 1911, the population of Javanese in Sabah was 5,511. After 1915, numbers of Indonesian workers remained high, peaking at 8,714 in 1927.[39] Maureen De Silva estimates that some 1,490 Indonesians, mostly women, remained in Sabah. Throughout the indenture period approximately 31 percent of recruits were women. Her work shows how indenture, initially seen as a system of importing labor for plantations in Indonesia, has been important as the basis of exported labor as well.[40]

For the most part, indentured labor migration, which was fixed by contracts of two to five years duration, was imagined as a temporary form of migration. But it was not always the case that people returned home after the expiration of their contract. In many instances, the migrants included both men and women who were willing and able to remain overseas and form an ongoing community. These communities differed according to the laws of their new homes and according to the degree of intermarriage with other peoples. Most Indonesians who travelled overseas did so because of poverty and limited employment opportunities in the Netherlands East Indies, and in many cases it was these same factors that inspired Indonesians to remain overseas where they were able to secure a better standard of living.[41]

The Dutch had made various attempts to limit labor movement, including placing a ban on free migration in 1887. The ban, however, was eased in less than a decade. It took some years before the official indentured migration trade commenced, and this occurred on a country-by-country basis as the Dutch tried to ensure that contracts would be enforced. The negotiations were concerned in part with establishing appropriate wages, holidays, food, and accommodation, but there was also an understanding that providing so-called coolie labor to other colonies during a time of labor shortage could be a profitable business.

Not surprisingly, the first shipments of indentured labor went to the Dutch colony of Suriname in 1890. Some 32,962 Javanese workers and their families were brought there between 1890 and 1939 to provide labor on sugar plantations.[42] Rosemarijn Hoefte noted that between 1902 and 1910 alone, a total of 5,433 Indonesians left Batavia and Semarang for Suriname. Although some returned to Java, the descendants of these workers form a significant part of the current population of Suriname, and seek links back to Java.[43]

The plantations of Indochina, particularly of southern Vietnam, then known as Cochinchina, also imported Javanese workers, particularly after the Dutch agreed to allow immigration on five-year contracts in 1909.[44] Little is known about the total numbers of Indonesians in Vietnam or when recruitment ceased, but in 1928 there was still a demand for their labor.[45]

The French government was quick to secure labor for New Caledonia soon after 1896. New Caledonia became home to the second largest Javanese community outside Indonesia, with some twenty thousand immigrants sent between 1896 and 1955.[46] Javanese going to New Caledonia were sent on five-year contracts, after which they had the right to seek either repatriation or an alternative employer.[47] A range of other imported workers, including Vietnamese, Réunion Indians, Japanese, and Pacific Islanders, were also brought in to New Caledonia. Javanese were favored for work on coffee plantations and as domestic servants in rural areas.[48]

In the mines, Javanese were employed alongside Vietnamese. The main reason for considering Javanese as an alternative to Vietnamese was that the wages set for Javanese workers were one-fifth of those of Vietnamese.[49]

The Indonesian government began to be concerned with colonial labor links soon after independence and set up a consulate in New Caledonia in the 1950s. This played a part in sustaining Javanese culture and arts, as R. S. Roosman noted when writing about the revival of Javanese culture as a postwar phenomenon. He argued that before World War II, there were few Javanese communal groups apart from a Muslim funeral association known as *marabou,* a *gotong royong* (mutual assistance) system, and a soccer club. In comparison, in the 1970s there were many formal celebrations of Indonesian heritage and activities organized by social clubs in Noumea, suggesting that the consulate had played an important part in sustaining culture and the arts.[50]

According to Marie-Jo Siban, founder of the Association Indonésienne de Nouvelle-Calédonie, a resurgence in historical consciousness was prompted by the centenary celebration in 1996 of the arrival of the first Javanese in New Caledonia. It was, she claimed, a commemoration of "their courage, their sacrifice, their perseverance."[51] In that year, Fidayanti Muljono-Larue published a history of Javanese migration to New Caledonia.[52] Marcel Magi organized the association Asal Usul three years later to record the memoires of "*des anciens*" and to restore interest in Indonesian traditions. Magi was born in Noumea of a *niaoulie* (New Caledonia-born Indonesian) mother and an Indonesian father who had arrived from Yogyakarta in 1938. When Jean-Luc Maurer published his history of the Javanese in New Caledonia, his work became an important part of this process. He wrote in collaboration with Magi and with a contribution by Marie-Jo Siban.[53]

The study of Indonesian indentured workers to Australia is less developed. Lockard, in his survey of Javanese emigration, made no mention of Australia other than in relation to migration to Papua New Guinea.[54] The Queensland sugar industry was best known for its use of Pacific Islander labor, but, as tighter regulations governing Islander employment were introduced, the sugar growers turned to alternative sources. In 1885, sugar growers introduced several hundred workers from Banten and Sunda in the Netherlands East Indies. They came on three-year contracts of indenture with free passage home at the end of their contract, and the expectation that they would not stay.[55] One newspaper report expressed the opinion that Javanese were "a docile and industrious people accustomed to agricultural work in a country nearer to the Equator than the Johnstone River or any part of Queensland."[56]

While Vincent Houben refers to Indonesian workers in German New Guinea and Queensland, he regards the Queensland case as marginal, involving only a few hundred immigrants.[57] In discussing Queensland, Houben does not include the Torres Strait, but rather focuses on the sugar industry, better known for its use of Pacific Islander labor. The Immigration Restriction Act of 1901 effectively banned non-white labor immigration; subsequently, the numbers of Indonesians on sugar plantations dwindled.[58] Tracing the descendants of Javanese immigrants in Mackay, North Queensland, Houben suggested that the fourth-generation Javanese had "nearly lost their specific cultural characteristics," thus implying a degree of intermarriage and acculturation.[59]

Australia is firmly based in the Asia-Pacific, historically as well as geographically. Our story is about how intertwined Australian and Indonesian history have been in the period since the 1870s. Thus we also contribute to the stories of Indonesian history, most importantly the deep history of mobility across borders in Southeast Asia, which goes beyond a cosmopolitanism based on the adventures of members of ruling elites. The cosmopolitanism of ordinary people from the nation that is now called Indonesia has long been a feature of the region's history, with each village and island full of tales of epic voyages back and forth across the waters. These are stories that connect Australia intimately to Southeast Asia and the wider Indian-Pacific Ocean world.

CHAPTER TWO

The Birth of the Pearling Zone, 1860–1890

The history of the pearling frontier is bound up with the intrusion of Europeans into northern Australia and eastern Indonesia. The whole overlapping area operated as a shared zone open to economic exploitation. In the nineteenth century, the zone was mapped both literally and figuratively as it was explored and reimagined as a frontier, a place of adventure full of pirates and headhunters. The establishment of the modern pearling industry on this frontier was caught up with processes of marking boundaries and claiming ownership, including claims of control over the workers, who in the 1870s began to be recruited in eastern Indonesia for the new pearling centers of northern Australia. Such claims were part of attempts to restrict the relatively free movement that was characteristic of the pearl frontier.

When Abdoel Gafoer came to Australia from Alor via Kupang, he followed a very well-worn path. Like other young men who travelled from island to island seeking work, his encounter with Europeans armed with indenture contracts had a degree of familiarity attached to it. The eastern islands of the Indies had seen heavy traffic of Europeans since the Portuguese first sought to profit from the spices there. In the nineteenth century, parts of the eastern islands of the archipelago were still independent of Portuguese and Dutch control, and whalers, traders, and carpetbaggers from all nations passed through. The predecessors of the Australians who recruited Abdoel Gafoer usually had little respect for the laws of either the Netherlands East Indies or the British colonies, since their first consideration was profit. Entering into a zone they considered to be full of piracy and poaching, they themselves were not averse to either if they could get away with it. This chapter will outline the deeper history of the formation of the pearl frontier.

European Claims over Eastern Indonesia

The earliest mapping of eastern Indonesia began with the first European expeditions in search of the valuable clove, mace, and nutmeg of the Indies. The first maps of the Spice Islands of Maluku resulted from Antonio Pigafetta's account of the

Abdoel Gafoer in his application for registration as a diver's tender, 1941. National Archives of Australia, K1331, INDONESIAN/ABDOEL G.

Magellan expedition's visit there and to Timor in 1520–1521, after Magellan himself had been killed in the Philippines. These were hardly reliable navigational aids but they extended the claims of the 1494 Treaty of Tordesillas by which the Portuguese and Spanish attempted to divide up the world into areas that they could control. Portuguese claims to the Spice Islands, leading to colonization in Southeast Asia, were soon challenged by the Dutch. By the first years of the seventeenth century, Dutch expeditions had mapped out the islands around Timor, and then moved onto northern Australia. Such claims followed the 1605–1606 voyage of the *Duyfken* under Willem Janszoon, which went from Banda, through the Kei Islands, to Papua and the Cape York Peninsula. By the late 1640s, Abel Tasman's maps filling in extensive details of the Indonesian, Papuan, and related Australian coastlines began to be published.[1]

It remained for James Cook, over one hundred years later, to claim the South Land for Britain by separating it from the Dutch Indies, although his voyage necessitated stops in Savu, near Timor, and Batavia, the capital of the Dutch company that ran the Indies.. Cook was not the first English traveller in these waters; the privateer Sir Francis Drake had preceded him in the Indies. The pirate, William Dampier, left detailed descriptions of his travels to the coast of northwest Australia and the eastern Indonesian islands, which provided among other things the precedent for the founding of the settlement of Broome.[2] Following Dampier's voyages at the end of the 1690s, Kupang in Timor became known as a stop-off point for voyagers, although the Dutch authorities there had been reluctant to let Dampier land, since they had been subject to attacks by other pirates, notably the French.[3]

In 1803, Matthew Flinders produced the map that would define the continent as "Australia," drawing on the knowledge of Indonesian seamen he had met on the way.[4] After Flinders' voyage, it suited the British colonizers to play down any connections with what was then called the Netherlands East Indies, Portuguese Timor, and the various independent polities that existed to Australia's north.

The independence of the various sultanates, kingdoms, and tribal domains of Southeast Asia was eroded throughout the nineteenth century. For the British, their new colonies on the Malay Peninsula and Singapore were important points of contact for travel to and from Australia. The East India Company official George Windsor Earl argued in his 1837 book *The Eastern Seas* that a trade emporium was needed in the region of the eastern islands of the archipelago to match that of Singapore. He considered the north coast of Australia to be suitable as it was "immediately to the southward of the largest and richest islands in the eastern portion of the Archipelago."[5] He pointed out that the Aru Islands of South Maluku, whose inhabitants were "comparatively unmolested by the Dutch," were only 250 miles from the north coast of Australia. His plan was to transfer Aru's commerce, which involved Chinese, British, and Bugis traders, to northern Australia. In addition, he remarked that the rich pearl beds between Aru and New Guinea were hardly disturbed and were "more productive than any to be found in the East."[6] He was concerned, however, that any port would require an increase in maritime security to guard against pirates and to keep the Dutch at bay.[7]

It was Earl's insistence that led to the establishment in 1838 of Port Essington on the Cobourg Peninsula on the north coast of Australia. A few years later, Earl travelled on the *Britomart* from Port Essington to Aru. He remained enthusiastic about its potential, noting that there were Dutch, Chinese, and some three hundred Bugis traders in Dobo, Aru's main port. Again, he mentioned pearl shell as an important trade item. The Bugis, he noted, were taking their trade goods to Singapore and making excellent profits, but the Dutch were trying to shut down their trade. He had spotted an official Dutch notice in the town ordering the Bugis to depart from Dobo. On his way home, the ship passed through Timor-Laut (Tanimbar) where he saw local men who, he suggested, would make ideal immigrants for Port Essington. The return voyage from Tanimbar to Melville Island, close to present-day Darwin, took only one day, and his report reminded readers that these eastern islands were within easy reach of Australia.[8]

There were already European castaways and beachcombers in this area. A report reached Port Essington in 1839 of a young English seaman living in Tanimbar. Joseph Forbes had travelled to Melville Island and then had continued on, sailing around southern Maluku. When attempting to go ashore at Laruan in the Tanimbar islands, he and his crew-mates were shipwrecked, with only Forbes and a crew-mate named Edwards surviving. Forbes was only seventeen years old at the time, but managed to escape to the larger island of Yamdena. The famous Owen Stanley expedition to map and scientifically document the area to Australia's north had failed to locate Forbes, but a later expedition led by a Captain Watson brought him back to Sydney, where he was very unhappy, having grown accustomed to island life. Apparently his companion, Edwards, had left descendants on the island, but there is no information about why he did not return with Forbes.[9]

The story of early nineteenth-century British colonialism in Southeast Asia is largely one of attempts to determine the economic utility of the region, as well as to control the piracy for which the area remained famous. The Malay sultans of what is now the southern Philippines, especially the Sulu sultanate, made their name and power as slave raiders and pirates, as did the people from the neighboring Ilanun ethnic group on the island of Mindanao, who roamed throughout Southeast Asian waters.[10] These Sulu and Ilanun pirates were found in the waters around Timor until the 1860s or 1870s.

Science and Colonization

British mapping and scientific expeditions in northern Australia and New Guinea often began from bases in Asia, as was the case with Owen Stanley's expedition of 1846–1850. This expedition on the *Rattlesnake* was under the auspices of the British Navy, but like Cook's voyage to Australia in the previous century, naturalists, including Thomas Huxley, were on board. Following Stanley, other expeditions included those by Augustus Gregory to northern Australia and eastern Indonesia in the 1850s.[11] The voyage of the *Rattlesnake* was an important basis for Alfred Russel Wallace's travels in Indonesia in the 1850s, which led to his co-formulation with Charles Darwin of the theory of evolution.

Wallace relied on Stanley's material, particularly in the islands of Kei and Aru in present-day Maluku, where Wallace was stuck for six months in 1857 due to the activities of Sulu pirates.[12] Part of his intellectual legacy is the Wallace Line, marking the difference between "Indonesian" and "Australian" flora and fauna—

except that most versions of the line locate it squarely in the middle of Indonesia, running between Bali and Lombok, and Kalimantan (Borneo) and Sulawesi (Celebes).[13] The Wallace Line in fact joins eastern Indonesia and New Guinea to Australia as an ecological zone.

Wallace, however, was also concerned with dividing the peoples of the archipelago into racial categories, by emphasizing, for example, the difference between "Papuan" and "Malay" races. At the same time, he recognized that it was impossible to make clear racial distinctions in places like Aru, where there was long-standing intermarriage. "The varieties, however, are so numerous and puzzling, that a person unacquainted with their origin would be apt to conclude that no line of demarcation could be drawn between the Papuan and Malay races. In Arru there are evident signs of the admixture of Malay, Arab, and European blood, and that so extensively and for so long a period, that the mixed races perhaps preponderate over the pure Papuans." His categories of "race" were quite complex, but struggled to cope with the varieties of ethnicity and mixing found in Aru:

Everywhere are found natives of Macassar, Javanese, Ceramese, and Amboynese, who have native wives, and have settled permanently in the country. In the Mohammedan districts a lighter skin, and finer features, indicate the infusion of Arab blood, while the discovery of many Portuguese words still in use in Arru, though unknown to the Malays, enables me to account for some decided South European characteristics which I had previously observed. That enterprising nation had evidently discovered these remote islands, and commenced the trade with them during the short period they held the supreme dominion of the Eastern seas.

In Wallace we also find racial stereotyping at work. "The character of the natives of Arru is very different from that of the Malay races. They are less reserved and apathetic, they speak louder, laugh more, and are altogether a much noisier, merrier set of people. The difference is, in fact, so very marked and striking, that it alone would suffice to separate them completely from the Malays."[14] In the decades after Wallace, European scientists attempted to establish more refined definitions of the characteristics of the region's different races, partly by ignoring Wallace's discovery that ideas of "pure" race were a long way away from the realities of life in the Asia Pacific.[15]

Luigi D'Albertis completed three voyages in the 1870s. In the first, he sailed from Singapore to Maluku and on to New Guinea. The later expeditions approached the island of Papua via Somerset at the tip of Queensland. From there he sailed up the Fly River, which is currently part of the border between Indonesia and Papua

New Guinea. Around the same time, Sir William John Macleay mounted a major scientific expedition to New Guinea which involved extensive collection of materials in eastern Indonesia.[16]

Wallace, D'Albertis, and many of the other naturalists relied on Dobo as an important stopping-off point on their journeys. They did so particularly because it was a major trading center where both supplies and local knowledge could be gained.[17] Aru and Seram (Ceram) were known for the trade in birds of paradise, thus contributing to naturalists' collections, but Wallace also observed trade in pearls and pearl shell there.[18] Strangely, many of the later studies of the voyages of explorers such as D'Albertis omit any mention of this Indonesian connection in the explorations of Australia and Papua.[19]

D'Albertis travelled from Ambon to Kei and Aru on the Italian vessel *Vittor Pisani,* and his observations give a sense of how Europeans perceived the region. Although he was mainly interested in Papuans, he spoke Malay, and his initial dealings were with the raja of Kei, who was a Muslim and followed Malay cultural practices. The naturalist commented on the fact that the rajas of eastern Indonesia were under the authority of the sultan of Tidore as well as that of the Dutch,

Dobo in 1912. From a Netherlands East Indies Government expedition photograph, National Museum of World Cultures-KIT-TM 10002850.

although he interpreted Dutch rule as token. Of particular concern to him was the slave trade in the region, which contributed to its image as a wild and despotic zone, but one that nevertheless might have been attractive to those in search of cheap labor: "Who does not know that there are slave markets in Ternate, in Misor [Misool, Papua], in Ke[i], and in Arru? If the negroes of Africa inspire so much interest, why should those of New Guinea be forgotten?"[20]

D'Albertis observed that Kei was at that time already trading in mother-of-pearl, as well as trepang. When he arrived on Aru, he was told that the Dutch were ridding the region of pirates, but that the people of New Guinea were cannibals.[21] There were already strong stereotypes of the peoples of the region as cannibals and headhunters, dating back at least to Dampier's voyages, and D'Albertis' subsequent documentation of headhunting in New Guinea did much to further the image of savagery in this region. This was an image that came to permeate much of the popular Western imagination of the pearling zone during the late nineteenth and early twentieth centuries.

The European scientists who ventured into the eastern archipelago were often careful to provide precise information about the places they visited. D'Albertis, despite his sometimes violent experiences in New Guinea, was at pains to write down only "What I Did and What I Saw," as he subtitled his book. Likewise Wallace's sojourn on Aru, despite his search for racial types, made him appreciate local lifestyles:

> With the exception of the short visit of the commissioner, there is no law or government in Arru; yet the motley population, all striving to get what they can, live very peaceably together. Every one minds his own business, and, although he "does that which is right in his own eyes," takes care not to injure his neighbour. Gambling quarrels occasionally arise among the Bugis, and a few deaths by the creese [*kris,* Indonesian dagger] may occur, as they do in Macassar; but on the whole, considering the mixture of races and religions, the competition in trade, and the crowding together of a population of about a thousand in such a remote spot and so far removed from the civilised world, a degree of good feeling and charity is shown which I am very much afraid would not exist in an equally miscellaneous assemblage of Europeans for similar purposes.[22]

This vision of peaceful commerce was being challenged by European attempts to exert control, leading to the claims staked by rival nations in the 1880s that delimited the pearl frontier.

European Competition and Boundary Marking

By 1885, the Dutch were suspicious that Australian activities in northern waters might be connected to British imperial designs on some of the islands of the Indies and the Pacific. This was a sentiment shared by their German neighbors who had laid claim to New Guinea. Parts of the present-day Indonesian archipelago were still independent at that stage. Indeed, it was not until 1910 that the Dutch consolidated control over the whole region, and not until 1922 that they finalized control over the western part of Papuan Island. Australian gold miners remained active across the borders in Papua New Guinea. In 1886, these miners had attempted to establish direct relations with one of the local rajas at Poso in Sulawesi, but were rebuffed by the Dutch. The Dutch also feared Australian interest in East Timor; Australian business leaders had actively advocated purchasing the colony from the Portuguese.[23] The British formally annexed Ashmore Island, near Timor, in 1878, moving to forestall the United States' interests in acquiring the area, and in the same year the Queensland government moved to annex Papua.[24]

The Dutch attempt to ban labor recruitment in the eastern islands in 1885 was followed by an Australian being accused of piracy in Maluku. John Carpenter, captain of the *Costa Rica Packet,* had been one of the first to complain to Queensland newspapers about labor recruitment bans. American-born, but a British subject, Carpenter had been whaling in Maluku since the late 1850s and was trading out of Ambon between 1880 and 1885. By 1886, Carpenter was whaling in Ambon again on the *Costa Rica Packet,* a barque belonging to the famous shipping company, Burns, Philp & Co.[25] He was arrested on November 1, 1891, in the port of Ternate and accused of having stolen the cargo of a local vessel off Buru Island three years earlier. While Carpenter claimed this was a matter of salvage, the Dutch claimed theft. The major item in question was a case of local spirits, *arak,* which Carpenter had sold in Bacan.[26]

When Carpenter was taken to Makassar for trial, his case became a major international incident, with complaints from the British governor of Singapore about lack of consular access, and a New South Wales (NSW) government Select Committee of Investigation established to report on the case. Newspaper reports about Carpenter's imprisonment, designed to scandalize the Australian population, included such details as his having to share a cell with a "sick native" (in other accounts a "sick soldier") and being under the control of a "half-caste" jailer. The charge was eventually dropped, and Carpenter was released on November 28.[27] When the Select Committee report was tabled in the NSW legislative council, it recommended that the Netherlands government pay compensation of £25,000 to Carpenter, Burns, Philp & Co. and the crew. They also found that "the whole of

Australia has suffered from the attitude assumed by the Netherlands-India Government, as further enterprise by our fellow-colonists has been checked when the field of the proposed operations has been the Malayan seas or islands, even though not subject to the Netherlands-India Government, from a fear that should the operators be forced by necessity to enter a port subject to that power they might be subjected to outrage of similar character as unjustifiable as in the case of Mr. Carpenter."[28] After complex negotiations and what one analyst has called "carefully orchestrated bluster" involving the British Foreign Office, and in which the Canadian High Commission and the court of the Czar were involved, reduced costs were paid. Of these Carpenter ended up with £2,700, and his crew £600.[29]

Not coincidentally, the British had backed up the Queensland colony's claims to the nearby territory in 1888 by formally taking control over the part of New Guinea now known as Papua.[30] Carpenter went on to found a pearling company, as will be discussed in chapter 4.[31]

Between the 1870s and the 1920s the Dutch, British, and Portuguese finalized a set of land and maritime boundaries that formed the basis of present-day borders between Malaysia, Singapore, Indonesia, Timor Leste, Papua New Guinea, and Australia. British New Guinea became Australia's Papua in 1906. The Germans had acquired the northeastern part of New Guinea, along with surrounding islands, but lost them to Australia (under a League of Nations mandate) during World War I; the transfer was not completed until 1921.[32]

Even after 1921 some anomalies remained. Present-day Sarawak and Sabah in Malaysia were still under private control, the former under the famous "White Rajah" family of the Brookes, the latter under the British North Borneo Company until World War II. Two sets of islands just south of Java, Christmas Island and the Cocos-Keeling Islands, had been claimed by British adventurers in the nineteenth century. One of these, the Clunies-Ross family became the lesser White Rajahs of the region when they settled on the Keeling Islands, mainly a stopping-off point for whalers. American whalers, Herman Melville included, worked in Indonesian waters from Sumatra to the Timor Straits.[33] While *Moby Dick* portrays the whalers in these waters as American and European, distinguished anthropologist Robert Barnes' decades of research in the region shows that Sydney was a key base for nonindigenous whalers coming to Kupang, where they would have recruited local labor.[34]

Wallace's meeting Clunies-Ross on Lombok,[35] which was still independent from the Dutch in the 1850s, demonstrates the high degree of traffic around the region at the time. The Cocos-Keeling and Christmas Islands were administered from Singapore as part of the Straits Settlements, but in the lead-up to the 1957 independence of the Federation of Malaya and the subsequent separation of

Singapore from Malaysia, these colonies became Australian "external territories." Some of the "Cocos Malays" on that island were moved to Sabah (North Borneo) while others chose to remain. The Australian government, declaring that there were no indigenous inhabitants on Christmas Island to consult, refunded the British government Malaysian $20 million paid in foregone income from the island's phosphorous deposits.[36]

Establishing the Pearling Zone and Recruiting Labor

There was a significant shift in the pearling world in the 1860s and 1870s, when the north coast of Australia was opened up as a new frontier for pearling exploitation. Trade in pearls already existed in eastern Indonesia, and the references to that trade by midcentury scientists must have caught the attention of pearlers when their scientific accounts were published in Britain.

In this period, the London jeweler Edwin Streeter and his son Harry were pearling in the hazardous Sulu waters and trading in Singapore and Sri Lanka. Sometime during that period, they sent the *Sre Pas-Sair* (Sri Pasir) from Singapore to Solor in eastern Indonesia via Sulu. The ship was largely crewed by ethnic Malay recruits from Singapore, with the younger Streeter accompanying Captain Edward Chippindall. They shipped seven men in Sulu, then recruited sixty-one divers from Solor, "and signed them on before the Dutch Governor at Koepang."[37] From there they went to the Admiralty Gulf and Darwin, moving up to Aru, and then on to New Guinea. The divers had a rough time. Many of the crew developed the deadly thiamine deficiency known as beri-beri, and sixteen died, after which the rest were returned to Solor and paid off. Despite the dire nature of these conditions, the Streeters continued to travel between a new Australian base at Cossack Bay (in northwest Western Australia), Makassar, and Sulu.[38] Other pearlers travelled even further afield, to the Mergui Islands off southern Burma (Myanmar), where Australian pearlers were still examining possibilities as late as 1895.[39]

The industry was a profitable one. In 1870, Britain imported around 1,500 tons of mother-of-pearl.[40] As Steve Mullins, the major historian of the Australian industry, notes, most of this was re-exported to France and Austria to be made into buttons. Sources for the mother-of-pearl were Ceylon (Sri Lanka), the Sulu zone, and Aru, and then Streeter added Australia to that list. The price up to that time varied as widely as £35 to £85 per ton, although the first shell to come from Australia was reported to have realized between £200 and £250 per ton, according to Frank Jardine, a Torres Strait magistrate and cattle station owner. Jardine clearly saw the opportunities, since he was to become a leading figure in the Torres Strait pearlshell industry.[41] The pearls were also of great value. One that Streeter obtained in

Western Australia, with a weight of 45 grams, sold in London in 1884 for £900. Streeter bought it back for £1,500 two years later so that it could be incorporated into a pearl necklace that was later sold to Tiffany & Company in Paris for £10,000.[42]

Edwin Streeter's book on pearling remained frustratingly vague about the business details of what became a crucial event in the establishment of a pearling industry that encompassed eastern Indonesia and northern Australia. Streeter had registered two new firms in London to consolidate his pearling activities, the Australian Pearl Shell Fishing Company (Limited) in 1888, and the Aru-based Pearling and Trading Company Ltd., in 1889. Streeter also had interests in Sri Lanka.[43] With these companies Streeter bought out smaller owners, establishing the model of using a large fleet of luggers and adopting the latest technology of copper helmet and full diving dress to replace "naked" skin-diving. These companies provided the basis for the establishment of a permanent settlement in Broome, which came to be dominated by the firm Streeter & Male. Streeter himself retired from pearling after setting up these businesses, but Arthur Male, his partner in Broome, kept the original partnership name.[44] In Streeter's first trips, the links between Broome, the region around Kupang, and Aru were firmly established. The pearl frontier was now fully formed.

Knowledge of pearl shell in the Broome-Roebuck Bay area went back to Dampier, who had mentioned pearl shell in his 1715 visit. It was not until 1861 that the first commercial event in the industry occurred, when the expedition by surveyor Francis Gregory collected £300 worth of pearl shells and some pearls.[45] Aboriginal people were encouraged to continue their traditional practices of obtaining pearl shells, this time for the Europeans, leading to a virtual slave-trade in Aboriginal labor. The Aboriginal people of the area, especially the Yawuru and Djuleun peoples, were the ones most heavily affected by the new work regimes, which became part of a long story of dispossession and marginalization.

In Western Australia, the pearling industry favored unpaid Aboriginal labor up until 1871, when new legislation imposed stricter conditions. Labor from the vicinity of Timor had already been recommended by George Windsor Earl in his 1863 publication, *Handbook for Colonists in Tropical Australia*. He expanded on his earlier recommendation of Aru by describing the island of Rote, not far from Kupang, as being the nearest to the Australian continent and having a population of some twenty thousand, most of whom were Christians of the Dutch Reformed Church. Rotenese men worked in agriculture during the rainy season but would migrate to Kupang for work once their crops were planted. Earl explained that he had "ascertained that many of them would willingly accept employment in Australia during the eight months in which their labors at home are suspended, if a passage each way is provided for them." He argued that this would suit the fisheries of Australia, which suspended work during the rainy season. Apart from Rotenese, he also recommended labor from Savu and emigrants from Tanimbar who came in their own *prahus* (proas or boats) to Banda. Colleagues of Earl had also described the maritime professions of other eastern Indonesians, especially the Bajau, or "Sea Gypsies," with whom the pearlers of the Sulu Sea would have been familiar. The Sulu pearlers had brought Bajau and eastern Indonesians north as slaves for the pearling industry. Despite the way the embarkation port of Kupang came to represent the source of eastern workers for Australian pearlers, Earl argued against using ethnic Timorese, noting that as slavery was rife in Timor, it would be difficult to obtain Timorese labor.[46]

Henry Taunton, who spent time in the Western Australian pearling industry in the late nineteenth century, described the process of recruiting crews. Earlier writings, such as those of Earl, had established that captains would sail to Kupang to pay a security of £20 per head to the Dutch and subsequently sail to one of the islands of Solor, Adonara, or Alor, where the captain "would have to bleed freely to the local rajah or chief before he would allow any of his people to engage as divers." Tauton complained that the Malays expected wages paid in rupees and food "of their own kind."[47]

The Australian employment record was rather dubious during the early years of recruitment. One of the most famous of Australian captains was Scottish-born Francis Cadell. He became famous for his steamship navigation, mapping out some of the unknown islands of the region.[48] He became involved in whaling, trepang-gathering, and pearling in the 1870s, including labor recruitment. Cadell had been accused of cruelty to his pearling workers, although this brought outraged defense of his name from someone who had worked with him.[49]

Allegations of mistreatment were made first in Western Australia in 1873. Captain Cadell's crews complained to Magistrate Laurence that they had been detained in Australia beyond the lawful term of their contract and against their wishes. Laurence recommended that Malays should be obliged to register their agreements with some authorized person. He noted that they were "almost as helpless to enforce their agreements as the natives and are as liable to ill usage."[50] Darwin-based pearlers reported that it was Cadell who was giving Australian labor recruiters a bad name in Timor, and he may even have been the cause of the Dutch recruitment tax, which some pearlers found too exorbitant.[51] Cadell was murdered by some of his crew in the Kei Islands in 1879. He had been sailing from Ambon and Banda, transporting crew and divers between islands, including crew from "Bardo" (Badu Island in the Torres Strait, also known as Mulgrave Island), but at the time was alleged to be under warrant from the Queensland government for illegally transporting Indigenous people from Darwin.[52]

The evidence suggests that the work of pearl diving itself was also very arduous, but potentially profitable for Indonesian recruits. The Dutch resident at Kupang reported in 1873 that a Mr. Adams had arrived in Kupang from Australia, bringing home pearl-shell divers from Alor:

> In the beginning of June, the abovementioned Mr. Adams came here [to Kupang] from Australia with the *Clarisse,* in order to bring some people from Allor back there; who in the preceding year had been taken from there as divers for the fishing of mother-of-pearls. These people declared that they had been well treated and each of them had saved more than 100 Guilders, one even 200 Guilders; while Mr. Adams placed 225 Guilders with the Posthouder on Allor to hand out to the relatives of six Allorese who had died during their service. However, they declared that their work at length was too heavy, and Mr. Adams also did not succeed in gaining new divers.[53]

A Netherlands East Indies government document claimed that despite the Australian recruitment in Solor and Alor, no complaints of ill-treatment had been heard.[54] As the industry expanded the Dutch took steps to regulate recruitment.

The compensation money of *fl.*225 was a substantial sum, even a fortune—at the time a *picul* of rice, or 60 kilograms, was worth *fl.*10.[55] Throughout the colonial period, *fl.*12 were equivalent in value to approximately British £1 Sterling (which was equal to Australian £1 up until 1929). That Alorese could bring back small fortunes was even more extraordinary, particularly since the economy in the region must, at that time, have been largely one of gift exchange (as we will demonstrate in chapter 3).

Other accounts suggest an even more hostile relationship between Australian pearling masters and their crew. Captain George Roe of the schooner *Gift* lost his vessel when his crew mutinied. The *Gift* had arrived from Kupang on October 20, 1872. On board were the master, Christie, the owners, Roe and Passey, and thirty-seven Indonesian divers, thirteen of whom were "Macassar men," engaged for collecting, shelling, and curing of trepang. Apparently these men were experienced, being described as "useful as sailors and fair divers."[56] Three weeks out from Kupang, they called in at the Lacepede Islands. That night Passey was attacked by the *serang* (head man), and a battle ensued between the crew and the white masters, leaving Christie and six Indonesians dead and Passey lame.

The mutiny against Cadell and the attack on Roe and his men were not the only cases of rebellion against the pearling conditions. On October 19, 1899, the brigantine *Ethel,* sailing from Broome to the La Grange pearling grounds, was

hijacked by its "coloured crew." The "three whites" on board were murdered—
Captain J. A. Reddell (aged sixty), his son John, and another man named James
Taylor (the ship's carpenter), along with "one Japanese" and "one native"—and the
vessel was taken north toward "the islands of Macassar or Manilla." The ship was
scuppered and the crew arrested at Timor Laret (Laut/Tanimbar) and taken to
Makassar.[57] The "native" turned out to be "an aboriginal named 'Tommy'" (later
called "Jimmy" in the same report), and the crew were "Manilamen" (Filipinos),
hence their suspected destination. The main testimony in their trial at the Perth
Police Court came from the surviving Chinese cook, Pooh Ah King.[58]

Large-Scale Recruitment: Broome

Maritime labor from Kupang was originally engaged under a Netherlands East
Indies regulation, promulgated in 1835, which permitted seafarers to be taken overseas to be engaged before the harbor master. This act was amended in 1862, but
the new regulations mentioned above were put in place in 1875, with a series of
amendments between 1876 and 1903.[59] An official Western Australian government
report on pearling of 1875 describes how there were 989 designated as Malays
and 493 Aboriginal people employed on the 57 vessels licensed out of the port of
Cossack on Roebourne Bay. Estimates for this and the smaller landing spots in
Western Australia suggest a total of 1,800 Malays were employed. Of the 548 Malays who had signed on for that year, 33 had died, and many were sick.[60] It is not
clear how many of these Malays came from present-day Indonesia, and how many
from the Malay Peninsula and Singapore.

The growth of the Southeast Asian population of the area around Roebourne
Bay was a very rapid one. In 1870, a population of 100 Malays (a suspiciously round
figure) is given for the workers in the pearling industry, and the 1875 number of
989 was actually the highest figure for that century. The following year, 228 Europeans, 344 Aborigines, and 800 Malays are recorded. In 1878, only 24 Malays
are recorded.[61] Such figures simply indicate the highly fluid nature of the industry. It depended on seasons, was subject to the forces of nature, particularly the
cyclones that batter that part of the coast on an almost-annual basis, and was operated by people who probably did not want much of their information officially
recorded.

The Dutch authorities formalized the bond at *fl.*200 (later reduced to *fl.*100),
which seems an unrealistically high amount of guilders per diver, to be forfeited
by the pearling master if the Indonesian died or was not returned to his home-
port within thirteen months or was not paid stipulated wages. The pearling masters were also liable to a 300 guilder fine if they took on people without making

an agreement before the harbormaster. In protest over these stricter regulations, only 72 Indonesians were employed in 1883.[62] That was also the year that the Western Australian government decided to formalize the growing settlement in the region by establishing the town of Broome.[63]

By 1887, the nature of the pearling industry was changing with the advent of diving suits, leading to the more dangerous practice of deep-water diving. Aboriginal and Indonesian divers were used less and Japanese divers were brought in and would come to dominate the industry.[64] The attempted Dutch ban of free migration from the East Indies in 1887 did not extend to recruitment from Kupang. Two years later, recruitment was clearly continuing, with the Streeter schooner *Undine* sailing from Kupang to Cossack in Western Australia with 150 men on board to be signed up as pearling crew.[65] The largest pearler at this time was T. H. Haynes, operating under a London registration with two schooners, fifteen luggers, and 150 men.[66] Captain Haynes had worked for Streeter with Captain Chippindall until Chippindall's death in 1886.[67] He lobbied the British Foreign Office for official support against any restrictions levied by the Netherlands East Indies government.[68]

Not until the beginning of the twentieth century do the gaps in statistics start to fill in, and then they show that between 1903 and 1906 there were between 1,031 and 1,235 Malays working out of Broome. By that stage new categories had appeared in the lists: Japanese, who came to outnumber Malays; Chinese; "Manilamen"; and later a new category of "Koepangers." The explanation for these changes is pursued in chapter 5.

Pearling in Port Darwin

Port Darwin was named in 1839 by John Stokes, during a survey of the Timor Sea. Stokes named the port after his old shipmate Charles Darwin. After the failure of previous settlements such as Port Essington, Darwin was established as a settlement by the South Australian government in 1869, and was a majority Chinese town in its early days. Some colonial planners with experience in India and Malaya took up Earl's vision from thirty years earlier of making Darwin a second Singapore to capture some of the growing Asian trade.[69]

In 1873, in an early attempt to locate pearl shell in Port Darwin, the *Victoria* moored in the harbor and a diver was sent down. He was able to bring up pearl shell but was prevented from working properly by the strength of the tides. The pearlers knew that the local Larrakia Aboriginal people were bringing in good quality pearl shell to trade, but they did not know where they were finding it.[70]

Mother-of-pearl shell was first discovered in potentially profitable quantities in Port Darwin harbor in 1884, prompting a rush of pearling boats from the Torres

Straits. The muddiness of the water, however, hindered the divers, and the industry was abandoned within three years, the local authorities supposing that the beds were depleted.[71] In these early days, the seas around Darwin were still frequented by the Makassar trepang fleets. In 1885, when the pearling lugger *Minnie* was lost off Melville Island, just off the coast of Darwin, the "Macassar men" swam ashore where they were welcomed by the local Tiwi people and permitted to stay for seven months until they were rescued by a passing "Macassar proa [*prahu*]."[72]

Darwin's pearling industry eventually revived after a Japanese diver known as "Charley Japan" found shell in 1892. Three years later, there were enough Japanese, Indonesians, and Filipinos in the town to be causing unrest. Reports of a fight in 1895 indicated that between thirty and forty Japanese and an equivalent number of Southeast Asians were involved. On the night of January 6, 1897, eighteen pearling luggers were destroyed in a cyclone, but by 1902, when Government Resident Dashwood made a report on the economic state of the outpost town, the pearling industry in Port Darwin was thriving.[73]

Indonesians in Queensland's Torres Strait

In 1869, pearl shell was found on Tudu (Warrior Island) in the Torres Strait, and during the 1870s and 1880s, thousands of Asian men came to work there. Pearling stations were established on the islands adjacent to Thursday Island, traditionally the territory of the Aboriginal Australian Kaurareg people.[74] In 1874, when Western Australia started recruitment of Indonesian workers, the pearling masters in the Torres Strait employed labor from the Pacific Islands.[75] But the recruitment of Pacific Islanders was becoming difficult. The antislavery movement had made accusations of kidnapping against the recruiters, who became known as "blackbirders" for their underhand practices. Britain had responded by imposing the Pacific Islanders Protection Act 1872.[76] The pearlers of Torres Strait now looked north in search of a new labor supply, taking their lead from their colleagues to the west. J. W. Tyas, following in the footsteps of Wallace, describes the first failed attempts to recruit divers from the vicinity of the Aru Islands in 1873, indicating that perhaps word had spread from Kupang of the nature of the work involved, or that the reputation of Cadell and his like had already spread. "We could not account for their evident fear of us. Wherever we had gone we had treated the natives with great kindness. . . . We had at last a strong suspicion that our friends at Dobbo had something to do with this matter by spreading false reports, by means of their small boats of our intentions. The terror of the natives was evidently real, and we supposed that they took us for pirates from the neighboring islands, or for kidnappers."[77] On finally meeting men from the pearling island of Vorkay (perhaps Barakai?), they were able to enter into negotiations, but despite offering a range of trade items, they were unable to finalize an agreement to recruit divers. Eventually the Torres Strait pearlers began to recruit Malays from Singapore, while other men were brought directly from the eastern islands of the Netherlands East Indies, from Timor, Ambon, and then the Aru Islands.

The recruitment of Indonesians led to the establishment of a "Malaytown" on Thursday Island, and a second Indonesian settlement, or *kampong,* on Badu. There was, however, a second large presence of Indonesians farther south. In the sugarcane fields of North Queensland the restrictions on hiring Pacific Islanders had also resulted in labor shortages. As a result 1,100 workers were brought in from the Netherlands East Indies. These were mainly Javanese, predominantly from Sunda, West Java, although there were some Malays from Pahang in present-day Malaysia among these workers.[78] These workers were described in racial terms as being suited to working in the tropics, but it was also clear that their stay in Australia should only be temporary. This was an experiment. The British consul in Batavia, N. McNeill, did not anticipate that many men would remain in Queensland, because, he argued, "the difficulty experienced in obtaining women to accompany them would be a strong reason for their returning"[79]— even though the terms of their contracts provided wives with free passage and board. This recruitment for the sugar industry was affected by a Dutch attempt to ban indentured labor, and was suspended in the 1880s.

As the historian Paul Battersby observes in chronicling the problems with recruitment, the harsh conditions and ill-health of the workers coincided with a series of newspaper reports about the savagery of "the Javanese." Such reports, drawing on the popular colonial literature of the region, described Javanese as having a tendency to "run amok." Incidents like the 1888 murder of three Europeans in Normanton (on the Gulf of Carpentaria) by a Javanese named Sedin were, however, more likely to have been the result of cruelly exploitative conditions than innate savagery.[80] In reporting the subsequent riot by the European population of Normanton, Brisbane's *Boomerang* magazine showed a burly white man defending Australia—depicted as a terrified woman—from a mixture of Chinese and Malays. Sedin was hanged in 1889. The incident was part of a series of events that eventually led to the restriction and then banning of Indonesian and Malaysian indentured workers from the cane fields. More importantly, it led to the establishment of policies designed to keep out "colored" labor, and the first coining of the term "White Australia policy."[81]

The first census taken at Thursday Island (popularly referred to as TI) in 1885 indicated a resident population of 139 Europeans, 77 Malays, 49 Filipinos, 20 Cingalese (Sinhalese from Sri Lanka), 16 Aboriginal people, and a handful of Chinese, Japanese and Arabs. Torres Strait Islanders are grouped among those described as "Aboriginal" in official reports. In that same year there were 257 "Malays" engaged in the marine industry and this peaked at 270 in 1886.[82] The pearl-shellers still employed Pacific Islanders, specifically Rotumans and New Caledonians, as well as "Manilamen" from the Philippines.[83] However, the Torres Strait fleet was diminished in 1886, after the powerful pearling master, James Clark, and others took their luggers across to Western Australia ostensibly because the pearl shell was more plentiful there.[84] Their arrival in the West meant that they were caught up in the cyclone of 1887 that claimed many luggers and the lives of 126 "colored" and 14 white men.[85]

It was not until 1891 that the luggers began to return to Thursday Island, by which time the depleted pearl-shell beds had recovered.[86] In 1896, the population of Thursday Island was 1,354 and very diverse: There were 626 Europeans, 233 Japanese, 119 Filipinos, 115 Malays, 84 Chinese, 70 Pacific Islanders, 65 Aboriginal Australians, 30 Cingalese, and 2 Javanese. Already at this time there was a small second generation of those described as "Malays," with the census recording 3 Malay women and 14 children. The number of Malays on fishing vessels was much the same, with 270 Malays employed.[87] By 1902, this number had dropped to 172 Malays, compared with 397 Pacific Islanders and 246 Torres Strait Islanders.[88]

Australian employers were generally in favor of Indonesian labor. In 1897, a Brisbane newspaper suggested that Malays and Javanese were regarded as appropriate servants, particularly as "hewers of wood and drawers of water to the whites."[89] Writing in 1898, Fred Hodel, a resident of Thursday Island for eight years, argued further for "Kanak" and "Malay" labor, stating that unlike the Japanese, "they do not drain the wealth from the country, but marry and settle down in the colony."[90]

Race and Borders

The attempts to create borders and control movement went hand in hand with the creation of a new federation of the Australian colonies, one whose population came to be based on the idea of the white race. Just as the naturalists had sought to divide the "Malay" East Indies from "Papua," the colonial powers wanted to segregate both from Australia. In the second half of the nineteenth century, such theories of race were at odds with the practices of the pearling industry.

Racial thinking, however, helps to explain the ruthlessness of labor regimes. The cheap labor of the East Indies was seen by white recruiters as having innate characteristics. Given the dehumanizing effects of these attitudes, it is not surprising that the recruiters had no qualms about subjecting the Indonesians to harsh and dangerous working conditions. There was also no thought given to any roles for Indonesian women in these regimes, nor to the relations that were to develop between Indonesian men and Aboriginal women.

The official and the popular views that were emerging among white colonizers and pearling masters showed little understanding of the complexities of the various peoples indigenous to the pearl frontier. Even the naturalists' attempts to create a distinction between "Malay" and "Papuan" peoples were not usable in practice. The racial images used to keep eastern Indonesians separate from British Australians were confused and were also infused with linkages between race and gender. The histories and cultures of the Indonesian participants in pearling show that they entered the industry with very different understandings.

CHAPTER THREE

Maritime Mobility in Eastern Indonesia

Who were these men from the islands of the Indies who chose to join the Australian pearling masters? Scant details were recorded in Australian archives about the early life of Abdoel Gafoer, except that he was born on Alor in 1897. His family knew very little about his background; his daughter thought that he might be Timorese, since he had been categorized as a "Koepanger." Once in Australia, Abdoel Gafoer had become the first Indonesian in Broome to undergo initiation as an elder of the Australian Aboriginal Yaruwu people. Perhaps with this new status he symbolically left behind his previous life of poverty in Alor. In the late nineteenth and early twentieth centuries such cross-cultural contacts were facilitated by the rising traffic of people across the seas. Direct transport between northern Australia and eastern Indonesia ceased in the 1950s, so the present-day descendants of Abdoel Gafoer and the other pearling workers in the Indonesian Aboriginal community of Broome have become estranged from their families in the tiny eastern Indonesian island groups such as Alor, Babar, and Solor.

Indonesian pearling laborers were drawn from a diverse range of backgrounds and ethnicities. These were people who before the coming of Europeans moved around the eastern islands, particularly to engage in maritime activities. In order to explain how the pearling workers may have viewed their participation in pearling, this chapter surveys the rich variety of ethnic and linguistic groups in eastern Indonesia. It focuses particularly on the way that the long history of the sea peoples of Alor and surrounding islands led them to create networks of alliances that ultimately connected with the centers of Portuguese and Dutch power in the region. Such networks provided channels for those familiar with sea work to come to Kupang to seek employment. Despite their economic function, these networks were based on mythical connections to ancestors, which were reproduced through rich symbolic traditions. Nevertheless, the changing nature of interactions among peoples of the islands, Europeans, and other more recent arrivals created a variety of maritime industries from whaling, to pearling, to hunting for shark fin.

While we cannot fill in the details of Abdoel Gafoer's motivations and experiences, we can at least say something about why so many Indonesians chose to travel to Australia, and how they viewed the maritime world. Those who have the greatest movement across Indonesia's current international boundaries are the people whose everyday activities belong to the sea, the fishing peoples of the archipelago. Indonesia is still the world's largest producer of South Sea pearls; the Southeast Asians who participated in the pearling industry were continuing involvement in a trade and industry that stretched back beyond recorded time.[1]

Alorese Culture in the Wider Indonesian Context

Despite the fact that the term "Koepangers" refers to Kupang, the port in West Timor, the pearling laborers were recruited from several of the surrounding islands of eastern Indonesia, including Rote and Savu near Timor, as well as Solor, Flores, and Alor. Men from Alor had in early years been recruited from Makassar in Sulawesi, which lies just to the north, as part of the large slave trade channeled through that port.

Tracing the island origins of pearling workers is not an easy task. We know that Abdoel Gafoer came from Alor, but this location was home to a number of different peoples. His name tells us that he was Muslim, and this is the first clue as to where, more precisely, he came from, and how his religion linked him to wider networks that stretched throughout the Indonesian archipelago. His Muslim background was an important element in the cultural mix that makes up eastern Indonesia, where people are highly adaptable and able to move easily between different ethnic and religious modes.

The coastal or maritime cultural complex of Southeast Asia of which these Indonesian islands have been active participants was traditionally associated with the idea of "Malay" ethnicity, an ethnicity associated with Islam and the courtly culture of Islamic sultanates. Converts to Islam were said to *masuk Melayu,* to enter the Malay cultural and social world.

At first "Malay" seems identical with the closed ethnic category that the British employed, but further investigation shows that it was an open cultural matrix allowing for mixing of religions and ethnic identities. Throughout the islands of Southeast Asia, specifically Malay cultural elements, such as styles of sarong or *keris* (kris) handles, have been found in combination with elements from Javanese culture, like gongs, shadow-puppet imagery, and even use of the Javanese language. This mixture shows that the concept of *Melayu* coexisted and combined with one summarized by the term *Jawa,* or *Jawi,* meaning the civilization originating from Java, although in the Middle East, *Jawi* has been used to refer to Southeast Asia in general. The adapted form of Arabic script used to write Malay is also called *Jawi*. The combination of these concepts made up a wider cultural matrix, that of the coastal, or *Pasisir*, culture of Southeast Asia.[2]

The *Pasisir* cultural mix was furthered by traditions of moving outside one's area of origin to find work or to make one's fortune, which was well entrenched in most Indonesian societies. The most famous example is the *merantau* of the Minangkabau of Sumatra, by which young men went out into the world, leading to large-scale chain migration into other parts of Indonesia and Malaysia. In earlier times Malay and Javanese peoples spread their influences in a variety of ways, particularly because they had been the centers of large kingdoms, including the medieval and early modern kingdoms of Sriwijaya in Sumatra, Majapahit in east Java, and Melaka on the Malay Peninsula.

Malay and Javanese power centers were not the only sources of the coastal cultural matrix. An important contribution to the *Pasisir* came from the seafaring peoples from South Sulawesi, usually referred to as Makassar (Makassarese or Macassans) and Bugis (Buginese), but who also included peoples from Mandar and the boat-building island of Buton. The Makassar and Bugis ethnic groups intensified their movement throughout Southeast Asia as a result of local conflicts and feuds in the sixteenth and seventeenth centuries. While the peoples of south Sulawesi are now best known as ships' captains and traders, in earlier times troops of Bugis and Makassar people served as mercenaries as far afield as Thailand. Their more regular regional movements extended out to neighboring islands in the Philippines, to Singapore and the Malaya Peninsula, and to northern Australia and New Guinea. These maritime migrations were often described as "visits" by fishing fleets rather than as permanent migrations, and yet we know that such visits resulted in intermarriage and cultural exchange, as in the case of the fleets that visited the north coast of Australia. This historically formed coastal culture provided an important basis for the economic life of the region, which flourished as a center of global trade.

Local Networks

It is hardly surprising that Alorese were recruited in Kupang. Historically, the island of Timor, and the port of Kupang in particular, had been the hub of regional social, political, and economic links. Local Alorese versions of the *Pasisir* cultural matrix included a set of connections that linked the many different nearby ethnic groups. Although the Alor Islands are relatively small and obscure, they have been the focus of academic attention because of their rich ethnic and linguistic diversity. Alor, which lies to the north of Timor, is made up of the larger islands of Alor and Pantar, and includes the smaller islands of Buaya, Ternate, Kepa, Pura,

Tereweng, Ata, Kangge, Lapan, and Batan.[3] The peoples of these islands are grouped in a large number of ethnicities. Estimates of the number of languages spoken give a figure as high as thirty. Most of these languages are of the category generally known as "non-Austronesian" (or "Papuan")—that is, belonging to a family of languages that stretches throughout northern and eastern Indonesia and takes in the Papuan languages, but not part of the Malayo-Polynesian family of languages that stretches from mainland Southeast Asia across the Pacific. Many of the non-Austronesian languages are spoken by inland peoples. A major anthropological study of the inland people of Alor was undertaken by Cora Du Bois in the 1930s, at a time when classifying such people in the category of the "primitive" was still a major focus of a form of anthropology that turned away from the idea of modernizing societies.[4]

Accounts such as those of Du Bois gave a picture of isolated peoples. This at least was a development from the orientation toward theories of race of earlier ethnographies, or the stereotypes of Alorese as warlike "cannibals," which appeared in some of the European travel literature. All such images of the Alorese denied the fact that eastern Indonesia had been interacting with the rest of the world for centuries.[5] Alorese themselves recognized a distinction between peoples of the land and peoples of the sea, but both groups were bound together by complex systems of alliance, furthered by oath-taking and marriage.[6] Nevertheless even "land" people such as the Abui people of the village of Atimelang, among whom Du Bois worked, had foundation myths based on fishing and taboos concerning sea turtles.[7]

Just off the main island of Alor, near the capital of Alor Besar, is an island called Ternate, not to be confused with the other Ternate, the famous spice sultanate in northern Maluku. The people of Alor's Ternate are Muslim, as opposed to the inland peoples who mostly converted to Christianity in the colonial period, while still retaining elements of animist beliefs. The people of Ternate speak an Austronesian language, actually a dialect of Lamaholot (Solorese), and thus closer in relation to the Malay language (a dialect of which became Indonesian) than the Papuan languages.[8] It is highly likely that this is the group from which Abdoel Gafoer came.

The bifurcation of ethnic groups and subgroups on Alor into inland or upriver (mountain) and coastal or downriver (sea) peoples has been typical of the *Pasisir* cultural matrix, but was extended into a further grouping of sea peoples. Syarifuddin R. Gomang, a senior Alorese leader and anthropologist, explains that this division was part of the way that ethnic groups of Alor formed themselves into sets of allies and enemies, based on the long history of political competition in eastern Indonesia.

There were two major formal sets of relationships facilitating political links between groups regarded as kingdoms (*kerajaaan*), which were sometimes also referred to as "domains": the Galiyao Watang Lema (the five coastal domains of Alor-Pantar) and the Solor Watang Lema (the five coastal domains of Solor, the islands between Flores and Timor). These were enduring sets of relationships, and are still relevant for explaining ethnic relations in present-day eastern Indonesia.[9] These networks have existed for a long time and connected members to as far away as Java. Reference to these eastern networks is found in the fourteenth-century Javanese text of the Majapahit kingdom, *Negarakertagama*, which mentions Java's connections with the Galiyao and Solor systems of clan or group alliances.[10]

These sets of relationships were commemorated in oral history poems that were performed ceremonially. The alliances determined relationships with the other Indonesian ethnic groups from Maluku, Sulawesi, and Timorese in both West Timor and Timor Leste. Such patterns of alliance, along with mirroring ones of enmity, also existed in Maluku and other parts of eastern Indonesia. These facilitated movement by people from Alor, Pantar, and the Solor islands to neighboring islands. When Australian labor recruiters arrived, they were entering into a complex political situation of which they had very little understanding.

Kupang as a Center for Trade and Politics

The Galiyao and Solor alliances seem to have come about in an intricate set of conflicts stimulated by competition for the spice trade. The big players in that wider history were the twin sultanates of Ternate and Tidore in north Maluku and the sultanate of Makassar (along with various other ethnic groups of South Sulawesi). By the sixteenth century new players were regional powers; the first of these were the Portuguese—particularly the ethnic subgroup usually called the "Black Portuguese" or "Topasses"[11]—and then in the seventeenth century, came the Dutch.[12] The Solor alliance was initially identified with Portuguese interests, and Galiyao with the Dutch, although things were never so straightforward. In practice only the inland-oriented Demon domain remained under the Portuguese as was the Catholic Larantuka kingdom after 1619.[13]

Solor was the original European base in the southeast islands of Indonesia, established by the Portuguese and then taken over by the Dutch. The Dutch, however, shifted their fort to Kupang on Timor in the seventeenth century to take advantage of the sandalwood exports of the island, and this in turn encouraged a strong presence of Larantukans of Solor in this trade and warfare. The Larantukans and other troops from Solor, led by the families of the Solorese-Portuguese

Kupang ca. 1925. A crowd gathers at the dock to await the arrival of a KPM ship. Leiden University Library (KITLV Collection) 55656.

"Topas," or *Larantuqueiro,* adventurers Antonio de Hornay and Matheus da Costa, were then involved in conflicts between the Dutch and Portuguese in Timor.[14] These conflicts integrated the Larantukans into the Timorese kingdoms, and led to the division of the island between the European powers. Even after the sandalwood trade declined because of over-exploitation, Kupang was maintained as a strategic center, controlling southern access to Maluku.[15]

The Galiyao alliance became the basis of Dutch claims in 1847 that Alor and Pantar fell within their territory, despite counterclaims from the Portuguese, which helped the Alorese and others to maintain their independence. It was only in 1916 that Alor and Pantar were formerly incorporated into the Netherlands East Indies, and as late as 1918, the Alorese were waging armed resistance against the Dutch. Direct colonization brought Dutch education to Alor, along with colonial administration.[16] The colonial link later brought political parties, especially the Sarekat Rajat (People's League), which in the 1920s had both Muslim and radical Communist wings. This league was followed predominantly by Muslim and Christian political parties. Such political connections also strengthened ties to Kupang and other centers.[17] This was the world that Abdoel Gafoer left behind when he was first recruited to work in Australia in 1921, at the age of twenty-four.

Since Kupang was the administrative center for the Dutch, Alorese and other eastern Indonesians continued to visit this major trading axis. Kupang became the principal meeting place for a variety of ethnic groups, especially the Rotenese groups, who had played a key role in eastern Indonesia since Portuguese and Dutch times. Social anthropologist James J. Fox has documented the role of the Rotenese in Kupang, where they came to prominence as Dutch allies in the eighteenth-century conflicts against the "Topasses." Increasingly in the nineteenth century, people from Rote and other nearby islands came to dominate the west coast of the island of Timor.[18]

Rote has been one of the major sources of fishermen still coming to Australia today, although many of those based on Rote have been Bajau (Bajo) or Sama-Bajau, the so-called Sea Gypsies, who trace their immediate origins to the Tukang Besi Islands south of Sulawesi.[19] According to an early nineteenth-century account by J. H. Moor, Solor was a home to "Bajau Orang Laut" (a Moro sea people) who acknowledged the Dutch authority of Kupang and provided *prahus,* small boats, to transport people from Rote and Savu to Timor when they were required.[20]

The Bajau concentrated around South Sulawesi to get access to the trade going through Makassar, and they specialized in marine produce, notably tortoise-shell.[21] While the Sama Bajau originally came to Sulawesi from the Sulu zone, their legends of dispersal go back to the fall of the Malayan kingdom of Johor, the heir to the great regional power Melaka. Other related sea nomads still live in the Andaman Sea, off Thailand and Myanmar. The Sama Bajau are still found throughout eastern Indonesia, and as their Sea Gypsy nickname implies, they have been a people continually on the move. The Bajau provided their navigational knowledge to seafarers from Sulawesi and neighboring islands, and probably pioneered the sea routes into Australian waters. They still fish today in their traditional zones around Ashmore Reef, despite the continued attempts by Australian authorities to stop them, and of Indonesian authorities to end their nomadic lifestyles.[22]

Symbolic Links

The ethnographies and historical accounts of Alor and its neighbors show that the Alorese have complex hierarchical societies, many of which incorporate the sea into their practices and worldview. The orientation to the sea is part of a long history of maritime connection with not only the rest of eastern Indonesia, but also the wider international trading world.

The Indonesian cultural forms of interaction have resulted in rich symbolic traditions expressive of the ocean and trade. The traditional societies of eastern Indonesia have a typically gendered division of labor, with women producing the stupendous diversity of woven textiles for which the region is famous. Throughout these islands woman weave *ikat* cloths, so called because they are made by tying (*ikat* means to tie or bind) groups of threads into a design before they are dyed and woven. Most ethnic groups have their own distinctive sets of designs and styles, and the nuances of style help to define clan and ethnic groups or domains. These cloths then enter into the complicated relationships of exchange that govern social relationships and connections to the ancestors, usually as bride wealth or dowry. Most famous in the region are the huge cloths of Sumba, but Flores, Savu, Rote, Lembata, Timor, and even the more eastern islands of Babar and Tanimbar have rich traditions. It is the weavers of Lamahalot who produce textiles for the non-weaving Alorese.[23]

In addition to textiles, bride wealth and dowry included animals and other objects with both economic and cultural value, including hugely expensive luxury trade items such as elephant tusks, double-*ikat patola* textiles from Gujerat in India, and ancient bronze drums. The symbolic systems in which such valuable objects were enmeshed connected people to their ancestors through connections made in marriages. As the anthropological studies of the region show, being able to exchange bride wealth and dowry in marriages that joined clans was what made indigenous social systems work. For young men seeking to marry and fulfill other social obligations, finding sources of money to buy the valuable exchange items was important for becoming a mature member of society, and would surely have been a major incentive to join the Australian recruiters.

Many of the textiles have used maritime imagery, from sea creatures to ships. The wives of the traditional whalers of Lamalera, for example, showed their husbands' vessels in action, while larger junks, along with sharks, rays, prawns, and crocodiles, feature in other cloths.[24] Ship symbolism has been a vital part of most Indonesian societies, particularly those of the eastern islands, and ships or boats are representative of the whole social order. Thus, for example, in Babar, descent groups belong to a single house, but the house community is spoken of as a boat, with the members of the community as the crew, and the clan house is constructed with a prow, representing how it is "sailing" from east to west.[25]

As elsewhere in Indonesia, ships have also been vehicles between the mundane world and the afterlife. Beautiful stone and wood carvings demonstrate this symbolism, particularly on Tanimbar, which once specialized in intricate interwoven patterned carving, a tradition that largely disappeared with Christianity. A colonial-era description of Alor records how *prahu* were constructed for the dead to carry their souls into the afterlife.[26] In Tanimbar and Kei the house-as-boat metaphor extended to both larger and smaller social groups, as, for example, in a marriage where the bride was the sailing vessel and the groom the captain, or in village organization, where the whole village has been laid out according to the boat pattern, with key village rituals involving travelling for trade.[27]

While the textile art of eastern Indonesia is distinctively indigenous, it is simultaneously cosmopolitan in its symbolism. The *Pasisir* cultural matrix has employed the same kinds of ship symbolism as the animist cultures of Tanimbar and Kei, thus showing that there is no clear line between peoples of tribal systems and those belonging to larger civilizations. Supplementary-weft *songket* fabric, woven with silver and gold threads from the sultanate of Bima in Sumbawa, Balinese paintings, north Javanese batik made under Chinese influence, and cloths from the pepper-growing region of Lampung in south Sumatra all relied on this same kind of maritime imagery.[28] This cultural complex could readily incorporate elements of the European cultures in eastern Indonesia, as in the garb of the region's sultans, which made use of Portuguese hats and Dutch military uniforms. The elements of indigenous animist beliefs were maintained and even strengthened within *Pasisir* culture.[29]

Anthropologist Sandra Pannell, commenting on symbolic systems around the islands of Leti-Luang, argues that such representations link islands and water into a single "landscape." The stories that people tell of movement across this space are parts of mental maps of the region, and in her case study of Luang, people narrate how the original six polities of the island moved out to settle in Seram, Tanimbar, Kei, Sermata, Timor, Kisar, Lakor, Teun, and Damer. Their origin stories connect all of these locations into a single cosmological and moral order.[30] Claims to ownership and connections are established through this sacred order, which is "mapped" by legends that describe, for example, how a mountain and a *prahu* became fused together on the island of Luang or how the dangers of a nearby reef stemmed from a promiscuous, siren-like, female spirit.[31] Such beliefs are in accordance with a general Indonesian recognition that certain places are charged with power. Through such beliefs, the sea is imbued with agency and power for those who risk its hazards to make a living.

Studies of Indonesian ethnic groups frequently demonstrate that mobility is built into cultural views and that "foreign" elements are easily incorporated. Many societies have "stranger-king" myths, similar to those of Pacific cultures. These kinds of myths have a number of forms. In some, such as those found among peoples of Savu and Tanimbar, whole ethnic groups originate from neighboring islands.[32] In others, it is royal or chiefly lineages, or at the least their titles and symbols of power, that come from legendary centers such as Makassar, Sumbawa, or Majapahit (or Java in general). The Atoni people of the Belu domain or kingdom on Timor give their origins as *Sina Mutin Malaka,* the White Chinese of Melaka (Malaysia).[33] Such symbolic forms include recognition of affinities with an outside "Other," the sense of some kind of ancient linkage. The Mambai of Timor Leste, faced by complex sets of colonization and conflict, narrate their origins as cosmopolitan:

> *White and black*
> *Timorese and Portuguese*
> *Australians and Germans*
> *Dutch and Japanese*
> *They have one mother*
> *They have one father*
> *[Who] gave birth to white and black*
> *Gave birth to the Malaila and the Timorese.*[34]

Within the eastern Indonesian context, then, there is no clear bifurcation of Europeans versus indigenous populations. Eastern Indonesians could incorporate newly arrived white Australians alongside the Portuguese and Dutch who had long been part of the social world of their islands, just as they accommodated trading groups such as the Chinese and Arabs. The mixed descent and multisided political origins of the current social orders in the various islands have created ways by which "outside" and "inside" have combined and interacted.

It is easy to see how Indonesians might have extended this open interaction to the various northern Australian Aboriginal groups, and why Abdoel Gafoer would have embraced his role as a Yaruwu elder. For the Makassar peoples living for periods of time in northern Australia to harvest trepang, the Bajau "Sea Gypsies" travelling from Rote to the islands in the zone between Indonesia and Australia, or the pearling workers settling in Broome, the journey to Australia was an extension of their existing form of interconnection.[35] For their part, the majority of Aboriginal peoples responded in kind. Aspects of Indonesian culture were assimilated via their personal relations, most notably the use of a form of Malay as a lingua franca in earlier times, and the incorporation of words into their own from Indonesian languages such as that of the Makassar ethnic group. The Bardi and Jawi peoples, from north of Broome, are just two of many who make extensive use of Malay loanwords in their languages. We can speculate that the name *Jawi* may even come from reference to Indonesians.[36]

Work from the Sea

While the pearling owners may have viewed Indonesians as "coolies," men such as Abdoel Gafoer came from societies with long maritime traditions, and working out to sea was part of a proud maritime heritage. Ancient reliefs from the ninth century on Central Java's Borobudur temple show that Indonesian ship-building skills were already highly developed over one thousand years ago, to the point where large war vessels from Indonesia sailed to India. These were the larger vessels called *jong* in Malay, a word that has erroneously been linked to the very different Chinese sailing ships known as "junks."[37] These *jong,* ranging in size up to one thousand tons were built without iron nails and had multiple-layered hulls, two lateral rudders, multiple masts, and a bowsprit.[38] Smaller-scale indigenous boat-building skills and traditions developed throughout the archipelago along the same lines, with such boats serving a range of functions from fishing to war-raiding. The two-masted fishing vessels of Madura and the outrigger canoes of Bali, as well as the *kora-kora* war-raiding boats of Maluku and the famous *prahu penisi* or Bugis *Perahu* of South Sulawesi that ranged over the whole of Southeast Asia, illustrate the range of technologies found throughout Indonesia.[39]

The coastal peoples of Alor have long made a living from diving for pearl and trochus shell, as well as trepang. Emilie Wellfelt, the only anthropologist to carry out recent research on little Ternate, reports that at present "men are mainly sea oriented, while women to a greater extent are land-based. Men from Ternate specialise in diving for shells containing mother of pearl and for sea cucumber. For weeks, sometimes months in a row, the men live on boats, 8–15 meters long, going all over Eastern Indonesia. However, during the wet season, November–March, the rough western monsoon winds limit these possibilities so it is considered farming season and the divers only go on short trips."[40] Of necessity, the peoples of eastern Indonesia have cultivated a range of livelihoods, since these are islands that are subject to regular famines when the monsoons fail to reach them.[41]

Such patterns have been typical of the sea peoples of most parts of Indonesia. They involve a seasonal reliance on what local metaphors call the "gardens of the sea," but are also complemented by reliance on land crops at other times. In eastern Indonesia, the chief crops are sago and other palm products (especially those of the *lontar* palm, including palm wine, *tuak*), as well as cassava and other root vegetables. The rice farmed so intensely in western Indonesia is much rarer. As Wellfelt and others make clear, catching fish has been expanded by different ethnic groups into specialization in harvesting other sea creatures, such as trepang, as well as varieties of shells, including pearl shell. Before the Europeans came, there were already long-established pearling practices, and it was the indigenous pearlers who informed newcomers of the possibilities of undersea wealth.

The Timor Straits became a focus of international whaling from the beginning of the nineteenth century, but the industry was pioneered locally, particularly by the traditional whalers of the island of Lembata (Lomblen), one of the few areas in the world still to practice nonmechanized hunting. These whalers came principally from the villages of Lamalerap and Lamakera (on Solor Island), although traditional whaling was also practiced on Kei.[42] These whalers have travelled to Kupang since at least the 1740s, and while American whalers worked in the Timor Straits and visited Alor, it is unclear whether they influenced the whaling of the region, or whether hunting sperm whale developed indigenously as an extension of the hunt in other sea creatures, such as dugong and rays.[43]

Aru as a Trade Center

Regional ports developed through these different forms of maritime activity. Alongside Kupang, one of the other centers of maritime trade that became important to the Australian pearling industry was the Aru Islands, particularly their trading town of Dobo.

Despite the decline in Timor's trade in the eighteenth century, Kupang remained one of the significant local hubs, while the larger subregional hub was Makassar, which continues to operate today as the gateway to eastern Indonesia. In the east, Ambon had been a major center, but smaller seasonal trading posts such as Dobo were significant, as the European accounts quoted in the previous chapter showed. The smaller ports of each island operated only seasonally, being closed by strong monsoon winds for part of each year.[44]

In analyzing the trading systems from a Moluccan point of view, Roy F. Ellen identifies levels of nested "trading spheres" for Maluku: that of Ternate and Tidore in the north (taking in Halmahera and Northeast Papua), Ambon in the west (including east Seram), and Banda, East Seram, and Southwest Papua in the east, the latter being a sphere in which the traders of Seram Laut dominated, though Aru was a major subcenter.[45] Extrapolating this model to the south would mark locations such as Solor and Rote as the intermediate-level foci of trade oriented to Kupang.[46]

One aspect of the changing nature of labor and commerce important to eastern Indonesia was the slave trade. The hierarchical nature of eastern Indonesian societies fostered the existence of a class of dependents who were regarded as slaves—that is, as the property of their masters. In the forms of slavery that operated within most societies, referred to as "closed" slave systems, slaves were servants who would either be inherited or enter into relations of dependency because of debt bondage.[47] As Hoskins notes of Sumba, "hereditary slaves were never sold, sacrificed, or used for hard labor." They had a high status connected to that of the noble families to whom they were bound.[48] These slaves were very different from war captives, who could either be sacrificed, as in some of the local Sumbanese practices, or sold in "open" slave systems.

European colonial expansion created a larger market for slaves and increased the scale of this trade in people, leading some ethnic groups, such as the Sulu pirates, to specialize in slave-raiding.[49] In eastern Indonesia, local centers of the slave trade developed initially to provide labor for the spice plantations of Banda, and Aru was one such source of slaves.[50]

When the Dutch first established themselves in the area, the Spice Islands of Maluku provided labor for the administrative capital of the east, Ambon (Amboina). Subsequently, the slave trade was to cater to the markets of Batavia in particular, and specific peoples such as Papuans became the objects of slave raids, although reports of slaving connections between the sultans of Maluku and the "Papuan Rajas" of the coastal regions go back to the sixteenth century.[51] Makassar and Bali developed as the major entrepôts for the sale of slaves collected from eastern Indonesia. Coastal groups often raided the "inland" or interior peoples.[52] Both the Makassar and Bugis ethnic groups played a major role in slave-raiding, and peoples from Sulawesi made up over 30 percent of the VOC slave population in the 1680s.[53] Reports throughout the eighteenth and early nineteenth centuries speak of raiding fleets of up to one hundred vessels in eastern Indonesia, selling to markets as far afield as Mauritius and Bourbon (Réunion).[54] When the Dutch finally decided to ban slavery in 1860, they were intervening in local slaving politics.[55] In Maluku between 1860 and 1863, an estimated 1,255 slaves were emancipated by the Dutch, and this coincided with the opening of the Australian pearling industry. In these early days, the legacy of these forms of slavery, dependency, and bondage would have shaped the expectations of eastern Indonesians who entered into indenture contracts with Australian pearling masters, despite their free choice to do so.

Aru, in the islands of Maluku, thus also grew on the back of slave and subsequently indentured labor. Its chief port, Dobo, had long made use of local and imported workers for a variety of industries, including pearling. While Maluku was principally famous for the spice trade, the harvesting of mother-of-pearl shell had played an important part in its international trade, at least since the eighteenth century. Although there are few early records, European knowledge of pearls in Aru dates to 1660, and a 1797 British account mentions pearls being imported from Aru to Banda, in the heart of the Spice Islands.[56] More detail on the pearling of the Aru islands comes from 1851, when it exported *fl.*15,000 of pearl and *fl.*130,000 of mother-of-pearl. Those exports were also via Banda.[57]

European visitors described a busy and wide-ranging trade, as this vivid account from Alfred Russel Wallace shows:

> The trade of Arru is very considerable, and is all carried on with the port
> of Macassar and with the islands of Goram and Ceram. In the present year

(1857) fourteen large prows, of from fifty to one hundred tons, and one brig arrived at Dobbo from Macassar. The owners are Bugis, Chinese, or Dutch, and the gross value of their cargoes about 20,000 l. Besides these, not much short of two hundred boats and prows of small size arrived from Ké, Goram, and Ceram, the whole value of whose cargoes may be 7000 l. or 8000 l. more. The Macassar traders bring rice, tobacco, gambir, muskets, brass cannon, gunpowder, gongs, swords, knives, choppers, axes, English and Chinese crockery, calicoes and cottons, Bugis cloth and arrack. The prows from Goram and Ceram bring principally sago-cakes, which are there manufactured for the supply of all the eastern part of the archipelago. The Ké islanders bring boats and prows for sale, wooden bowls, native earthen vessels, cocoa-nuts, and plantains. The produce obtained consists of pearl-shell, pearls, tripang, tortoiseshell, edible birds'-nests, and birds of paradise. Of these, the tripang, birds'-nests, and I believe most of the pearls and tortoiseshell find their way to China, the mother-of-pearl shell principally to Europe.[58]

As anthropologist of Aru Patricia Spyer observes, Aru's "entanglement" with international trade, particularly through the trade in luxury items such as birds of paradise, tortoiseshell, pearls, and later shark fins, has meant that these islands were and still are subject to "boom and bust" cycles. The sea peoples of these islands became enmeshed in modern patterns of commodity circulation over many centuries.[59] When the "busts" came, these people had no choice but to link themselves to the next most lucrative commodity and to travel farther afield in order to gain a paid income.

The people of Aru were oriented toward the outside world in their belief systems, and incorporated maritime activities and trade into their symbolic world. Aruese believed that they originally migrated from another island that was destroyed by a flood, and the different territories of Aru were defined by the boats in which people came. But the same people's legends have it that the two ancestors of the different groups took the forms of a whale and a shark, respectively, to shape the people's paths to the sea.[60]

In Aru, the indigenous pearl divers believed that success as a diver was related to a man's ability to maintain a successful relationship with his "sea wife," an undersea spirit. Men brought to these sea wives white porcelain plates purchased from Chinese shops, along with other more common traditional gifts, such as tobacco and betel nut and even imitation gold jewelry. Such a relationship with the spirits ensured the men's success as divers, and kept them safe from the dangers of their work, including sharks.[61] Spyer, studying this belief in the context of a "boom" in pearl shell in the 1980s, argues that the belief evolved within the modern context of capitalist indebtedness, both to restrict the seductions of monetary indebtedness, and also as part of a wider ambivalent engagement with a globalizing system.[62] Spyer even notes that the Arab traders, who dominated Aru before the current generation of Chinese Indonesian storekeepers, had special knowledge of prophets, or *nabi,* governing the layers of the undersea.[63] The spiritual associations with diving go back at least to before the middle of the nineteenth century when Dutch anthropologists were aware of a version of this belief. It is apparent, then, that the process of incorporating Chinese and Arab traders, commercial relations, and trade goods within local cultural systems was dynamic.[64]

The people of Aru, like those of Alor, brought a long history of maritime movement, complex beliefs, and a rich symbolic world to their work in the pearl trade. For the mobile peoples of the eastern Indonesian islands, the establishment of borders dividing Dutch, Portuguese, and British territories, and subsequently separating Indonesia, Timor Leste, and Australia, made very little sense. These boundaries cut across their sea "fields." The lure of wealth and travel was attractive to young men. If the reality of life on board a pearling lugger or ashore at Broome was less than they had hoped, this did not stop hundreds of "Malays" and "Koepangers" signing up every year to come to northern Australia. The twin attractions of cheap skilled labor and the rich pearling beds of Aru in turn drew Australian pearlers north.

CHAPTER FOUR

Master Pearlers on Both Sides of the Frontier

In 1901, the parliament of the newly federated Commonwealth of Australia passed the Immigration Restriction Act, the legislation that became commonly known as the "White Australia policy." That Australian pearlers expanded their activities into eastern Indonesia at the same time was no coincidence; with Australia threatening to exclude "non-white" labor from its shores, some of the biggest pearling masters wanted new ways to increase their profits. They saw how rich the beds of the Netherlands East Indies were. One of these pearling concerns, owned by the Clark family, brought the pearl frontier to its next stage of development.

The Australian master pearlers were eager to escape the stifling regulations that accompanied the transformation of the north from untamed frontier to part of the new Commonwealth of Australia. Operating in the territories of the Netherlands East Indies offered the chance to avoid official scrutiny of hiring and working conditions, as well as to minimize taxation. This chapter looks at the changes that took place within the industry between 1901 and 1940, and at the role of the pearling masters in that change.

Official voices pushed toward the Indies as well. The resident magistrate of Broome, M. S. Warton, advised the Australian government that it should retain an Asian workforce or risk losing the industry to the Netherlands East Indies. He wrote: "There is a Dutch port Koepang in Timor and I need hardly point out that the Dutch authorities there would gladly welcome the golden harvest, running into tens of thousands of pounds yearly."[1] Welcome it they did: by 1901, the Dutch authorities were actively encouraging Australian pearling masters to move their base to Kupang. They offered to remove the tax levied for each worker, stated as equivalent to £30, if pearlers would set up their headquarters in Kupang instead of Broome.[2] Australian pearlers already had considerable experience in the Indies, and they understood the value of what was on offer. They used this incentive to set up bases in the Indies, at the same time using them to recruit labor for northern Australia, thus creating a constant traffic of people and goods across the national boundaries. These pivotal changes that took place at the beginning of the twentieth century shaped pearling for the next fifty years, creating the context of Abdoel Gafoer's hiring in Broome in the early 1920s.

The Clark family and their associates made the Aru Islands in the Netherlands East Indies a major regional hub of their Celebes Trading Company (CTC). Soon to become legendary, the company operated between the Torres Strait, Darwin, and Indonesian waters. Among its associates was the Hilliard family, who worked as labor recruiters in Kupang, but then built up the Flores Cooperative Company in the area east of Bali. Henry Hilliard, the founder of the family pearling enterprise, took advantage of Dutch incentives to work in their colony, but kept up his ties to Broome, where his wife remained. It may even have been the Hilliard family business that put Abdoel Gafoer onto the steamer the *Gascoyne* for his first voyage to Broome in 1923.[3] The Clarks were ruthless in their attempts to maximize profits, manipulating the world market at one end of the spectrum, while devising ways to find cheaper labor at the other. Under the Clarks' influence Aru became the heart of the pearling industry, but it was a strange and distorted part of the frontier. The Hilliards, and a few smaller operators like them, worked differently, finding that accommodating local interests and establishing good relations with Indonesians was important for survival in business.

The Australian Pearl King

The name most closely associated with pearling in the north of Australia was that of James Clark (1857–1933), who began his pearling career in 1881 at Somerset on Cape York Peninsula.[4] He went to the northern-most part of Queensland initially to work for Frank Jardine, the local magistrate and founder of the pearling industry there, but eventually became Jardine's partner. Jardine had been the first representative of state power in one of Australia's most remote areas, "the savage frontier," as one chronicler called it. He had attempted to control the blackbirding, or forced importation of labor from the Pacific, that was rife in the industries of the area. Although questions were asked about conflicts of interest between his role as local magistrate and his land-owning and other entrepreneurial activities, the latter certainly boosted his power and influence in the area.[5] Jardine's fleet was based at Somerset and at Naghir Island in the Torres Strait. His influence was also helped by his association with Robert Philp of the Burns, Philp & Company shipping line, who later went on to become premier of the state of Queensland. Although many of the pearling masters disdained government regulation, they were not averse to attempts at influencing government where they could.

Clark and Jardine divided the partnership in 1882, and the former established himself on Friday Island in the Torres Strait. Three years later, Clark moved his fleet to Darwin and then to Broome the next year. As discussed in chapter 2, Clark allegedly relocated because the Torres Strait pearl-shell beds had been

Main Street, Thursday Island, ca.1917–1920. National Library of Australia PIC/8808/10
LOC Album 1055.

depleted, but in fact he later argued that if it were not for the strong winds, he
and his men would have been able to locate new shell with further exploration.[6]
This comment hints at how Clark was already experimenting with ways to expand the industry, as well as his intention to stay outside the control of local
authorities.

Clark returned to the Torres Strait, basing himself at Thursday Island in 1891,
but like the other Queensland pearlers was severely affected by the March 1899
cyclone. The cyclone wiped out a significant part of the pearling fleet in Princess
Charlotte Bay and killed 307 men. It was described as "one of Australia's worst
maritime disasters."[7] Clark's *Admiral* was one of the boats lost with all hands in
this cyclone.[8] Six years later Clark's company, which by this time included as partners E. E. Monro and Reg Hockings (who had come to Thursday Island in 1897),
moved its seven fleets of 115 vessels from Thursday Island to the port of Dobo in
the Aru Islands, a location that offered direct access to pearl-shell beds.[9]

Aru's reputation for having the "richest pearl oyster beds" and higher-quality
shell meant that a number of Australian operators were following the leads of
nineteenth-century adventurers, such as Carpenter and Cadell, in going there. Before 1890, the Dutch had permitted a foreign firm, De Bourdes & Company, to
operate near the Jedan Islands, the northern islands of Aru. Worried about the

effect of such operations, the Netherlands East Indies government set out an ordinance in 1893 prohibiting nonindigenous pearlers from collecting shells within three nautical miles of the shore, which, according to some interpretations, meant a depth of five fathoms. This ordinance was intended to guard the rights of Aruese. It meant that only though superior diving technology could foreign firms survive. De Bourdes & Company folded quickly because it lacked such technology.[10]

Between 1891 and the coming of Clark's company, Australian-based pearlers had been active around Aru, with individual operators seeking out new pearl-shell beds, and Streeter setting up the Pearling & Trading Company in response to increasing legislative restrictions in Queensland and Western Australian waters. Like the Australian authorities who sought to regulate the industry and its exploitation of divers, the Dutch were not impressed with the newcomers. In 1893 Baron van Hoëvell, resident of Ambon, who controlled the Aru area, threatened one newcomer, Alexander Mackellar, with cutting the air hoses on his lugger if he did not cease activities. It took high-level negotiations between London and The Hague for the Dutch to agree to license the operations of Australian pearlers out of Dobo.[11]

James Clark was forced by Netherlands East Indies legislation to establish a consortium, which he did in 1904 by including his partner E. E. Monro, and his brother, John Clark, in the Celebes Trading Company. Clark paid approximately £7,000 at auction for the lease to fish in eastern waters.[12] When the shell was collected in Aru, the Celebes Trading Company's steamship, *Praetoria*, transported it to Australian waters. Dutch trade statistics did not acknowledge the extent of pearl-shell sales because the shell was sold via Queensland, with some pearl shell exported directly to the United States.[13] The consortium made use of the cross-border traffic to minimize the excise and taxes payable to both Australian and Dutch governments. Clark's status was such that he became Queensland's consul for the Netherlands in 1905, indicating how quickly he had been able to legitimize his extension of the industry.

The Indonesian Pearl King

A major competitor, Sech Said bin Abdullah Baadilla (also spelled Shaykh Sa'id 'Abdallah Ba Adilla), joined the Celebes Trading Company consortium in 1906. Baadilla's father had already established a shipping line between his eastern base of Banda and Gresik, near Surabaya on Java. The forced marriage united two pearl kings, one Australian, the other Indonesian of Arab and Chinese descent, and created a powerful new entity. By 1908, this fleet of 150 vessels had a capital of £100,000 and was registered in the Netherlands East Indies.[14]

Said Baadilla, along with his brothers, Abdul Rahim and Salim, had formed the Baadilla Brothers Company around 1873, after their father died. Their family was of noble Arab lineage, *sayyid,* or descendants of the Prophet, and fitted the role of "stranger kings" in the archipelago. The family had expanded its interests into eastern Indonesia during the seventeenth and eighteenth centuries.[15] The pattern of expansion was similar to that of Chinese families in business in Southeast Asia. Unusually, however, Said's father had married into one of the powerful Chinese families of the eastern part of the Indies, the Tay family of Banda. This strategic marriage united Chinese and Arab trading networks in the region.

Said Baadilla was commonly known by his Chinese name, Tjong, and otherwise as the "pearl king" (*raja mutiara*) of eastern Indonesia. Baadilla began his pearling business in 1880, operating, according to his grandson Des Alwi, between the Sulu Seas, Maluku, and Papua. His brother, Abdul Rahim (Nana), made strategic marriage alliances with the ruling families of Buton, Maros in South Sulawesi, and Kokas in Papua. Their youngest brother, Salim (Tjotjo), commanded the fleet of thirty-three schooners and ninety-nine motorized vessels. The family also had extensive nutmeg plantations.[16] In 1895 Said Baadilla was granted a pearling permit to operate in Aru, and within seven years had expanded from six to forty luggers on those islands, although this was still only a portion of his fleet. The rest were operating in the northern Maluku islands, around Halamahera, where there were other pearl beds. Said Baadilla paid *fl.*130,000 to buy his share of the Celebes Trading Company.[17] The alliance with Baadilla would have given the Clarks access to very powerful trading networks, as Baadilla soon became the *Kaptein,* or head of the Arab community in the east.

Des Alwi, historian and community leader in eastern Indonesia, remembered his grandfather as a very religious man, who had made his first pilgrimage to Mecca in 1880, and had married Halijah, the daughter of a Muslim leader from the old trade center of Tuban in Java. As a Said, Baadilla had high standing in the wider Muslim community of Indonesia. Baadilla also travelled to the Netherlands in 1896, where he presented the regent, Queen Emma, with a giant pearl; later, he also presented her daughter, Queen Wilhelmina, with a large pink pearl when he was made a knight of the Order of Oranje Nassau.[18]

Linking with Clark also gave Said Baadilla access to the London markets, and to the new rationalization of the industry that Clark was setting up. As we shall see, however, this was an industry prone to fluctuations in prices, and one affected by fashions, political events, and a host of other factors. Des Alwi complained that with the coming of Great Depression and the advent of Bakelite as a replacement for mother-of-pearl, his maternal grandfather went from being one of the richest men in eastern Indonesia to bankruptcy in 1933. In that year the Baadilla pearling fleet was bought for a song by Chiu, a Chinese wharf master of Dobo.[19]

Controlling Workers, Controlling the Market

In Clark's relentless search for profits, the expansion into Aru was just one of a number of innovations, which were carried on by his calculating nephew, Victor. Such was James Clark's desire for maximum economic benefits that he advocated finding a market for the pearl shell's edible oyster meat, so that nothing would go to waste. The secret of Clark's success was his ability to connect production and distribution. He had already come up with the innovation of "floating stations," by which numbers of small vessels worked around a larger schooner. This meant that the fleet could operate more consistently, since it did not have to call into port for repairs, and diving could be monitored more closely. Scrutinizing the divers and instigating more rigorous working schedules had the bonus of allowing Clark to keep for himself some of the pearls that previously had been the reward of the divers who found them.

Steve Mullins, the historian of Clark's operations, observes that the Queensland government attempted to restrict the floating stations by limiting the number of licenses on offer. Mullins quotes Clark's expression of frustration at such restrictions, and his clear intention of moving to Indonesian waters in order to provide better returns. "I sent my boats out to work, and the men, instead of working took cases of grog and engaged in drunken sprees in the lee of an island. . . . Divers got anything from £100 to £300 advance, and they kept all the pearls. If I am to remain a pearler I have no time for this system. It was to this cause that we left for West Australia in 1885, and not to the depletion of the beds."[20] Clark was very straightforward about the fact that he had to pay men in Thursday Island £2.5 a month, when he could "get better men at £1 a month" in Aru.[21] Clark was, as Mullins explains, ruthlessly pragmatic, a very "astute and creative entrepreneur."[22]

The industry went through major fluctuations throughout the period 1890–1940. Low points came with the depressions of the 1890s and 1930s, slow-downs with World War I, and high points were reached in the first and third decades of the twentieth century. The pearling masters responded as best they could to the fluctuations by shifting production—from the Torres Strait to Broome and Aru, and then to Darwin and Aru—but had to contend with changing markets, international events, and eventually competition from other parts of Asia.

These fluctuations in the industry had a significant effect on working conditions. When prices and profits went down, the pearling masters tried to find other ways to squeeze out more money farther down the line, including attempting to pay less, and laying off crews. Rarely, however, did wages go up if profits increased.

The 1890s saw a downturn in the pearling industry in Australia, but the broader Australian-Indonesian pearling zone proved to be a rich one that could survive depressed prices. In 1906, the Celebes Trading Company supplied 37 percent of London's imports of mother-of-pearl shell and also provided significant amounts to the U.S. market.[23] Another one-third of production came from Western Australia, which had recovered economically by this time, and the majority of the rest from the Torres Strait. Burns, Philp & Company, in discussion with Clark, gave an overall assessment of the 1906 London market, valuing it at £500,000 per year.[24] These were rich stakes, equivalent to approximately AUD$60 million (US$50 million) in present-day currency.

Not content to increase profits at the expense of his lugger crews, Clark also wanted to control the prices his company received for their shell in international markets. He responded to what he believed was a buyers' cartel that beat down the prices at bimonthly London auctions. Dubbed "the trinity," the cartel was run by New York–based Albert Ochse & Company and two other major buyers, Otto Isenstein and M. Myers. Clark attempted to set up a pearling cartel to put a floor on the price of pearl shell, but other pearling masters were content to negotiate competitively, until the price of shell dropped from its height of £200 per ton in 1902, to a low £110 in 1904.[25] This led Broome master pearlers Hugh Norman and Herbert Bowden to approach Clark. They waited until 1906 to act, when the price went up to £140 a ton, just above the level that an Australian government commissioner calculated was profitable.[26] The associations of pearl-shellers of Broome, Thursday Island, and Aru met in Sydney in February of that year and agreed to suspend production, a move designed to control the London market.[27] However, their efforts were unsuccessful because Burns, Philp & Company would not participate. In 1907, there was a further downturn in the market attributed to changing fashion, but probably the result of buyer manipulation in response to a monetary crisis in New York.[28]

Another rise in prices led Clark to sign a 1909 agreement to sell all his shell to Albert Ochse & Company at £170 per ton. The normally canny Clark had failed to read market fluctuations, and by 1912, Ochse was selling shell for almost £500 per ton, making a profit, according to Clark, of £42,000.[29] It is highly likely that Ochse was taking advantage of a rapid but temporary spike in pearl prices that began in May 1912, when Australian pearl shot up over the £300 mark. This increase came from a combination of the Italio-Turco War, which cut off shell sources from Turkey and the Red Sea, and a trend in women's fashion toward larger buttons.[30] Clark may not have revealed the full story of his finances since Aruese shell was also exported to France and Japan. Of the Celebes Trading Company exports that went through Dutch customs, official estimates put the value at fl.1.5 million (£125,000) in 1909, declining to fl.600,000 by 1914.[31]

Clark, however, no doubt chastened by the experience with Ochse, went back to Burns, Philp & Company, and in a series of negotiations, they set up the Pearl Shell

Convention. The signatories to the convention agreed in April 1913 to supply 1,300 tons of pearl-shell to London at a fixed price. The shell was a substantial part of the world output of 2,400 tons.[32] The new convention included major players in the industry, such as Hugh Norman and J. B. Carpenter & Sons. Through the agreement, Ochse and the other members of "the trinity" agreed to buy shell with a minimum price of over £220 per ton, with a higher reserve of £267.10 at the London auctions.[33]

World War I disrupted the sea lanes and led to a downturn in the market. Clark himself withdrew from the industry. Mullins argues that Clark's demise was accelerated by Australian government antagonism, particularly its antimonopoly legislation, but Clark brought a portion of his pearling fleet, including thirty-two luggers and one schooner, from Aru to Broome in July 1915.[34] Although James Clark left the industry, his nephew, Victor, remained an important figure, and it may be that what appears to have been the 1916 sale of the rest of the Celebes Trading Company to the Makassar firm of Zahid and Jeandel was in fact a restructuring, given that James Clark was just coming out of a lawsuit against him by Burns, Philp & Company in the wash-up of the consortium's losses on the London market.[35] The Makassar firm later became Schmidt and Jeandel, and remained the capital behind Celebes Trading Company, as well as the license holders, but the CTC was essentially still an Australian-run firm.[36] The wily Clarks would outlive any downturns.

It appears that James Clark sold his vessels to Victor while Schmidt and Jeandel took over the concession since the Celebes Trading Company, still under Australian management, remained the largest Aru pearling concern. Before selling his vessels, Clark cornered the market in shells—and gems, for good measure—through his London agents, thus ensuring that he carried his wealth into his retirement.[37] The Australian pearl king left competitors and the officials of two governments foundering.

Clark's move to shift the risk in the industry had come just in time, for pearl shell was to undergo further massive price fluctuations. In 1925, shells from Darwin fetched an average price of £233 per ton in London ("being £15 per ton more than the average price at the same sales for Broome and Thursday Island shell").[38] The Broome pearlers complained that the New York buyers, Otto Gerdau Company, to whom 90 percent of Broome's production went by this time, were restricting the tonnage. Gerdau was a commodity dealer who sought out the most profitable of international goods, from Indian jute to Indonesian cassia bark. He realized that pearl shells, even in a declining market, were important, and sought footholds in the eastern islands and Broome, emerging as Osche's major competitor for the Australian pearl shells.[39] Just as with Clark's agreement with Ochse, the Broome pearlers had agreed to supply shell for four years at a rate of £180 per ton in order

"Chum" Jardine (seated, right) and
Mr. Martinez (left). Courtesy of
Kim Ivey.

to stabilize prices (which ranged from £130 to £220 per ton). However these pearlers did not have Clark's foresight. Changing fashion had led to an over-supply, and the pearlers realized that their position was becoming difficult, as "there were now only about 90 boats at work, compared with 300 in 1914, and 280 in 1920."[40]

As we will see, Broome's misfortune was Darwin's profit, particularly as the Celebes Trading Company increasingly linked the Northern Territory port to Aru. Prices kept rising between 1925 and 1929, when the Depression caused a massive drop in consumption. There was some subsequent fluctuation in profitability, but 1932 seems to have marked the endpoint in the postwar cycle of pearling prosperity. Aru, nevertheless, continued to be lucrative: in 1936, 149,526 tons of pearl shell was collected in the inner (three-mile) zone of Aru, 158,159 in the outer, while 316,722 tons from Darwin waters were processed through Aru, at a total value of fl.444,165. The amount from Darwin alone was approximately 90 percent of the value of 1928 Aru exports.[41]

The World of Aru

The social world of Aru must have been a strange one. The Dutch had placed a low-ranking official there in 1893 to keep control of the multinational population and report back to the resident in distant Ambon. In 1907, the standing of the local official was upgraded from *posthouder* (postholder) to *controleur*, which was more or less equivalent to a district officer in British systems. These officials clearly struggled to enforce any regulation over the mixture of Aruese, Japanese, Australians, and others on the island, as one lamented in a 1916 report.[42]

Aru's population was oriented around production; there was essentially a shifting population, which also tried to take advantage of the indigenous Aruese. The pearlers arrived during the Aru season of the west monsoon, between September and May, and worked on the east side of the island, known as the "Back Wall." They could move back to the safer Australian waters during the east monsoon from April to October.[43] Typically, a lugger collected about one ton per month, as in 1914, when the Celebes Trading Company had ninety-two luggers and five schooners as well as its steamship with a minimum of five men crewing each lugger.[44]

Approximately 13 percent of the 950 tons of shell coming from Aru in 1906 was from local divers, who exchanged their catch for *arak*, or palm spirits, but also for Dutch gin, cloth, tobacco, and gunpowder.[45] It appears, however, that local workers were not enough for the industry, particularly as the Dutch authorities attempted to keep the indigenous divers separated from the Australians. The Celebes Trading Company brought in workers from the Philippines as well as the main part of Maluku (Ambon and Banda) and the islands around Timor, but these largely played a secondary role to the Japanese divers. The 1916 *controleur*'s description of the population of the islands also talked about Fijians and Samoans working there. The diverse population caused problems for this Dutch official: Europeans paid income tax, "foreign Orientals" paid a business tax, and "natives" paid a poll tax, but he did not know into which category to put the Christian Pacific Islanders.[46]

The Celebes Trading Company was a big employer, reported in 1906 to be employing "over 1,000 coloured men."[47] When World War I seriously disrupted access to markets, many of the eastern Indonesian workers in Aru had to be sent back to their various places of origin, although the Japanese were kept on since divers were so hard to find. After 1918, the Dutch stepped up control by attempting to ban the sale of *arak* to local people since it had become an important currency. The Australians were exempt from the *arak* prohibition, but the Japanese were not, and had to set up a Japanese club to get around it.[48]

There had already been Japanese in Aru since the 1880s, when ten Japanese were diving for an Englishman. The Celebes Trading Company encouraged more to come from traditional fishing and whaling villages. According to one source, these villages were in the Ryukyu and Kyushu Islands, although a Japanese report gave the more precise information that they came from Kishu (now Mie and Wakayama Prefectures). With the increase in Japanese fishermen came Japanese women, known as *karayuki-san,* to work as concubines and in brothels; as a result, the number of Japanese grew from ninety to around five hundred.[49] The same villages in Japan served as recruiting grounds for Japanese who came to Broome, so it is likely that they travelled between Broome and Aru with the Australian pearlers. Once at Broome, they needed to stay because it was so hard to get work permits. The only medical practitioner in Dobo in 1916 was Japanese, although he did not have a license to practice in the Indies.[50]

Diving was always the best-paying occupation, but that was because it was the most dangerous. According to Japanese reports, the divers worked at a depth of 45.5 meters, and could make between 500 and 600 yen (Netherlands *fl*.400–800). It is a measure of the prosperity of Aru's port of Dobo that Japanese prostitutes were paid twice as much there as anywhere else in the eastern islands (*fl*.20 for Japanese and Westerners, *fl*.15 for Chinese and Natives). The lay-off season saw an increase in the number of working women. In 1913, there were ten inns or boarding houses, three general shops, two barbers, one bath-house, eight eating places, and nine brothels employing twenty-two women during the regular season, but as many as 120 at other times. According to a detailed 1915 Japanese report on the island, there were also nine Japanese "concubines," including two of mixed descent who were attached to Europeans (Clark being one of them).[51] We do not have any other information on the kinds of relationships involved, but in all likelihood these "concubines" had the status of wives, albeit temporary ones, in accordance with Indonesian custom. The prostitutes and "concubines" appear to have been almost the only women living in Dobo.[52]

Most of the social life of Aru was centered in Dobo, which had an exclusively nonindigenous population, with the multinational pearling workers, Chinese shops, and a *kampong bugis,* or quarter for the Makassar and Bugis. The currency was the English pound, a tribute to the dominance of the Australians, and everything was expensive compared to the rest of the Indies—another problem for Dutch officials posted there, who could not afford to keep their families on their civil service salaries.[53] The Indonesian population of Dobo wore European clothes, even shoes and hats, which was almost scandalous to the *controleur*.[54] One of the only entertainments besides drinking, gambling, and visiting the brothels seems to have been soccer, at which the Aru crews gained some skill. Fighting among ethnic groups also seems to have been frequent: The 1916 Dutch official's report recorded a large battle between the Buton and Makassar ethnic groups—more than one hundred a side—as well as a fight between Filipinos and Japanese over an assault on one of the *karayuki-san*.[55] Subsequent Celebes Trading Company managers set up plantations on some of the small islands that make up the Aru group, and so lived apart from the mixed community of Dobo.[56]

Life was hard and dangerous, and days were long in the pearling season. "To become a pearler . . . you don't live, you just exist. For eight months you go after pearls in luggers, probably landing at towns once or twice," recalled one old Australian hand.[57] Besides the ever-present threat of sharks and deadly sea-snakes, there was the bends, or diver's paralysis, which killed many Japanese in particular. Storms and other disasters also took their toll on the workforce.[58]

Victor John Clark and the Aru-Darwin link

James Clark's nephew, Victor, remained in Indonesia after the original concession concluded in 1915. Victor Clark was born in Brisbane in 1881 but had been on Aru since 1904, and at some stage set up a household on Seram, the larger island of the northern Moluccas. The Seram property, *Awaya,* had originally been established by James Clark in 1899, and grew cocoa, coffee, sago, and rubber. Newspaper reports say it was maintained until 1942.[59]

Victor seems to have taken on his uncle's sharp business practices. Some correspondence between Victor Clark and local officials has found its way into the Dutch archives, and despite the testiness of some of the responses, it provides tantalizingly few details of what must have been a "White Rajah" lifestyle. In a letter of February 25, 1919, to the *gezaghebber,* the local Dutch official, Clark asks for the return of a piece of furniture, a bed, given to the civil servant in what seems to have been an alleged act of bribery. Clark's denial only deepens suspicions that he was trying to gain influence: "It is not my custom to make presents to Government officials & I hope in the interests of good and fair government it is not the custom of officials to receive presents."[60]

Clark's letter came at the end of a lengthy investigation into a dispute involving his "coolie," called Ali, to whom Clark had been meting out his version of justice for attempted theft. Clark had been accused of "pre-emptorily depriving Ali of his personal freedom." Clark was also supposed to have assaulted coolies. In his report, the official provided information that a secret dossier had been made on Clark in 1914 for abuse of coolies. He added that in his investigations, Clark had been "compliant," but had not really told him what had happened with the coolies. The clash went on until 1920, when the courts in Makassar banned Clark from importing Javanese workers to Seram.[61] Nevertheless, the assistant resident, the *gezaghebber*'s superior, decided that any action might lead to an international incident, since Clark had emphasized that he could bring pressure to bear from the British government.

Victor Clark himself did not remain living in Seram, for by 1926 he was a major player in the pearling industry in Darwin. But his high-handed attitude towards his workers sat uneasily with the more regulated labor culture of Darwin and gained him a reputation for exploitation, as we will see in the next chapter. Clark's move south linked the pearl beds north of Darwin, especially those around Melville Island, into the larger Aru-based zone. This shift moved the focus of the Australian industry away from Broome, making the Aru-Darwin region the crux of pearling.

Clark travelled back and forth between the Dutch colony and northern Australia, recruiting workers on the way. Reports from 1927 indicate he was one of only two pearlers in Darwin (the other being Captain H. C. Edwards): "Each had four boats operating, keeping employed 2 Europeans, 11 Japanese divers, about 15 other coloured men and 6 aborigines," with Clark recruiting indentured workers from Kupang and operating around Melville Island and Shoal Bay.[62] By 1928, he had moved most of his family's boats from Broome to Darwin, and persuaded others to follow. As director of the Territory Pearling Company, he was president of the Darwin Pearl Shellers' Association in the early 1930s, but the fact that he was still operating in the Indonesian islands is attested to by his obtaining a "perfect" pearl of seventy-two grains from Aru in 1934 reported to be worth £1,400.[63]

Clark's fleet moved from Darwin to Aru every year around January to April, stopping off at Bathurst Island on the way back and transporting workers across the international boundaries with little restriction, and other pearlers followed his lead again. Belatedly, the Australian government attempted to regulate this movement, imposing catch restrictions in 1934 to stabilize the price of pearl shell during the Depression years. Moving fleets to the Arus meant that pearlers were able to work the beds north of Darwin, particularly around Bathurst Island, without any restrictions. The Australian government took the view that fishing the Bathurst Island beds from Aru was "poaching," while fishing the Aru Islands beds from Darwin was quite legitimate.[64]

Newspaper reports from the 1930s show that Clark's associates and competitors kept up a regular traffic in this area. "Mr. R. J. Stevens, the new manager of the Kepert pearling station [owned by Darwin master-pearler V. R. Kepert]," reported Darwin's *Northern Standard* in 1936, "cleared the harbour on Thursday last for Aroe Islands with crew boys and to pick up fresh boys for the coming season."[65] Victor Lampe, special magistrate in Darwin and a Clark associate, is described in 1939 as being on his way from Darwin to Kupang on his schooner *Eileen* to pick up divers and crew. Also on the *Eileen* were Herbert Cross and "two Japanese and one native" when the vessel sank; all on board were saved. Cross, aged fifty-five, was reported to have been "brother of Stan Cross, one of *Smith's*

Weekly's cartoonists" and a "well-known pearl buyer." The "buying trip" in which he was engaged seems to have been a regular occurrence.[66]

In Australia, Victor Clark had been declared bankrupt in 1936, but the case proved to be very drawn out, and Clark continued to operate, finding ways to evade Australian authorities.[67] In his somewhat (and perhaps deliberately) confusing court testimony, Clark stated that in 1930, he valued his fleet at £15,000. The case seems to have gotten bogged down over whether he or his wife, Eileen, was the owner of the Territory Pearling Company, and the relationship between this entity and the profitable Northern Territory Pearling Company.[68]

The bankruptcy was a minor setback. Clark was still in business in Aru in 1937, when the *Northern Standard* reported on moves by the Dutch to restrict his activities:

> On the 1st January, 1937, the Dutch Government enforced a new law, whereby it is forbidden for any foreigner residing in the Netherland East Indies, to own any sailing, motor vessel, or lugger, over 20 cubic meters, unless it flies the flag of the nation to whom the vessel belongs. In other words a foreigner will not be allowed to register his vessel under the Dutch flag.
>
> Rumour has reached here that V. J. Clark of the Territory Pearling Coy., is making arrangements to send a lugger over to the Aroe Islands in order that extensive repairs and alterations may be carried out.[69]

As always, Clark pushed the boundaries of authority, and encouraged others to do so as well. Throughout the 1930s, the master pearlers had to negotiate between both Australian and Dutch attempts at regulation.

Australians in Southern Maluku

Following James and Victor Clark, others associated with northern Australian pearling and the Burns, Philp & Company line extended their activities in the eastern waters of the Indies. Most pearling masters, like Clark, were attempting to circumvent Australian government restrictions. While there were many companies operating in the area, they mostly collaborated within the cross-border region established by the Clarks. The Clarks had created the rules of the game, and the others followed their lead. Although these other companies wanted to find an alternative base to Aru, the quality and quantity of Aru's pearl shell meant that they had to return there, and submit to the influence of the Celebes Trading Company.

One case of official Australian interference involved the first and only Japanese Australian pearling master, Jiro Muramatsu. Muramatsu was born in

Shizuoka, Japan, in 1878, but was a naturalized Australian and a Roman Catholic. He had first arrived in Australia in 1893 as a teenager, to join his father in business at Cossack Bay. Subsequently educated in Melbourne, he set himself up in pearling in 1899, despite losing his citizenship under the 1901 Immigration Restriction Act. Nevertheless, he was able to travel to and from Australia, thanks to a special exemption from the "Dictation Test," a language test that required the hapless potential immigrant to be knowledgeable in whichever European language an immigration official chose. This arbitrary device was used to enforce the act's exclusionary intention. Muramatsu's exemption meant that he was able to consolidate his business in Western Australia and then become a leading Darwin pearler. He transferred a portion of his fleet from Darwin to Aru under the management of E. J. McKay in 1932.[70]

McKay's first port of call was Saumlaki, the Tanimbar Islands' equivalent to Dobo. It seems that McKay had wanted to compete with Aru. Along with another pearler, Mark Aitken, McKay had met with the resident of Saumlaki and reported, "The Resident . . . was pleased to see our boats here in the Harbour, and [sees] that we were helping to bring the Port of Saumlaki into prominence. He also said that if many more boats came here, he would recommend that Saumlaki be an open port, the same as Dobo."[71] From Saumlaki, McKay went to Makassar to see the manager of the Celebes Trading Company. McKay told the Darwin *Northern Standard* that another Australian company based in Makassar, the Flores Cooperative Company, had eight boats "working at high speed" and fishing about twenty-three tons per boat. McKay claimed that the Australian government had urged the Netherlands East Indies government not to give him shelter, but that he had gone to the governor (that is, the resident) in charge of Saumlaki, and explained that he was fishing legally as the beds were eighty miles off the Australian coast. His headquarters in Saumlaki, he argued, were 190 miles from the pearling beds, while Darwin was 170.[72] The British consulate in Batavia kept track of McKay's movements in Indies' waters, advising the Australian government in July 1932 that he still flew the British flag, even though he discharged his pearl shell in Dobo.[73] That McKay needed to go to Dobo indicated that it was hard to compete with the Celebes Trading Company's established position, and the efforts to establish a base at Saumlaki had little impact.

McKay had drawn Mark Aitken into the Saumlaki experiment because Aitken was the employee of another canny pearler, Singapore-born Walter Randolph Carpenter. Carpenter had worked for Burns, Philp & Company in Sydney and Esperance in Western Australia before moving to Thursday Island in 1896. With three luggers he set up in 1899 what became J. B. Carpenter & Sons, Limited.[74] The company was in the name of his father, John Bolton Carpenter, the same captain who had been arrested by the Dutch in 1891 for smuggling *arak*. The company was a significant one; in 1936 Walter was knighted, an honor that James and Victor Clark never received. In the 1930s, Carpenter's fleet shifted to Maluku and was active around Aru, where Mark Aitken recruited pearling workers for Carpenter throughout the 1930s. Aitken had previously worked for the Celebes Trading Company under Clark. While remaining based in Maluku, Aitken fished off the coast of Darwin under an Australian flag.

Aitken advised Carpenter that he was pleased with the availability of crew in both Dobo and Saumlaki, but that he was not yet convinced about employing Indonesians as divers. Most locals worked for the Celebes Trading Company: "They are at present all working for C.T.C. Jardine is getting all information for me re these men. C.T.C. pay their men *fl*.7.50 per month & tucker & this year the divers are getting *fl*.150 per ton."[75] By 1936, Aitken was back in Australia, fishing the Aru pearling beds from Darwin. He died in Aru of "heart cramp" in January 1936.

The "Jardine" of Aitken's report was the Celebes Trading Company's regular manager on Aru, Cholmondeley ("Chum") Jardine, the eldest son of Clark's original partner, Frank. Chum went over to Aru to work "as agent for several Thursday Island pearling interests" sometime around 1918.[76] A handsome man and great athlete, Chum was a genial figure, and with the dark complexion he inherited from his Samoan mother, he must have blended in well with the cosmopolitan population of Aru, except for his "huge" figure. Chum set up one of his four plantations on Pulau Babi, inviting his sister, Elizabeth (Jaki) Sheldon, and her Queensland-born husband, Charles, to come and help him around 1925. Jardine also hired a Javanese overseer, Wongso, and was in a relationship with his "very attractive" Javanese housekeeper, Mina.[77] Chum was also acting for several Darwin concerns, and, as the *Northern Standard* describes Charles Sheldon as the Celebes Trading Company's manager, it appears he took over this role from his brother-in-law.[78]

Charles Sheldon had been an army officer stationed in the Torres Strait during World War I. Chum's invitation to his sister to join him in Aru was welcome since Australia did not have much to offer in the way of employment at that time. The Sheldons had two children, Pamela and young Chum, named after his uncle, who lived an idyllic if somewhat isolated life on the plantation, where they grew their own food and kept cattle, pigs, goats, and chickens. Native deer also roamed around. They imported clothing, tinned food, stationery, and medicine from John Little's shop in Singapore, and Elizabeth had a piano brought over for entertainment.[79] The family travelled seasonally to Darwin on the big pearling vessels, such as the *Aroetta*, that sailed between the two centers.[80]

Chum died of "a clot of blood on the brain" (or "heart cramp" or "blood poisoning" in other reports) in January 1936, almost at the same time and in the same way as his associate Aitken. "All the natives in the town and adjacent islands went into

CTC Employees on Aru, 1931. National Museum of World Cultures-KIT-TM 10013600.

mourning for him as a father or chief," recalled one old pearling hand.[81] Sheldon then worked with a Danish Australian, Carl Monsted, who had come over to carry out Celebes Trading Company business and became Australian consul to Aru. Carl's nephew, Niels, was also involved in Celebes Trading Company activities.[82]

Other Clark associates had been visiting Indonesian waters regularly, showing what a tight network the pearlers were. James Clark's former pearl-shelling partner, Reg Hockings, seems to have moved from running his Wanetta Pearling Company on Thursday Island to Aru, then back to the Torres Strait before establishing teak and coconut plantations on the island of Buton. There, with the help of two of his Indonesian workers, Batcho Mingo and Thomas Loban of Banda, he led espionage operations for British Naval Intelligence in the Netherlands East Indies during World War I. Hockings sent his men as far afield as Sandakan (Sabah), Deli (Sumatra), Humboldt Baai (West Papua), Batavia, and Bali. In Bali, Loban was attacked by a pair of tigers. Among other things, they succeeded in "foiling a plot to destroy the oilfields of Sumatra." At the time, the Netherlands East Indies was Australia's main source of oil. For these services, the Order of the British Empire was bestowed on Hockings. Batcho Mingo and Loban were recommended for permanent exception from the provisions of the Immigration Restriction Act. In Loban's case, this meant that he became a resident of the Torres Strait. Hockings, living what is described as a "bachelor" lifestyle, travelled constantly between the Strait and Buton, with business side-trips to England to watch Test Cricket. Hockings is remembered in the Torres Strait for his kind support of the Indonesians against the authorities. After he died in the Indies in 1932, his nephews, whom he had invited up to Buton, continued to operate his business interests in Buton and the Torres Strait.[83]

Japanese Competition

The strengthened Australian presence in the eastern waters of the Netherlands East Indies was matched by an increasing Japanese interest, and the Australians found competition on the pearl frontier difficult to deal with. Japanese firms had followed the Japanese divers to the Netherlands East Indies, so that by 1913 the *zaibatsu* (conglomerate) Mitsubishi was already in Aru. It was then joined at the end of the 1920s by the Japanese conglomerates or *zaibatsu*, Okura and then Mitsui, operating with a consortium established by Mitsubishi corporation, Nanyo Kohatsu or Shinju Kabushiki Kaisha (South Sea Pearl Corporation Limited), to compete with the Australians.[84] The Japanese pearlers had an annual "lay-up" station at Palau, and operated around Zamboanga and other parts of the Sulu zone.[85] Buton was apparently one of the Japanese bases, producing 8,000–10,000 pearls per year in 1928–1932, then 36,000 in 1933–1936, for the Nanyo Shinju Kabushiki Kaisha.[86]

In 1933, the Makassar manager of the Celebes Trading Company expressed anger at how the Australian government was allowing the Japanese operating in Indonesia and the southern Philippines to undersell the Celebes Trading Company by restricting the output of pearl shell. The Japanese boats were already regarded as competitors because they worked on a share-system payment for the crew, and were thus able to undercut the Celebes Trading Company by £50 a ton.[87] As newspaper reports show, Japanese based in Aru were operating as far south as Darwin and Torres Straits waters.[88] Regular reports, probably written by Charles Sheldon, were coming to the Australian newspapers from Aru by the late 1930s. In these the correspondent repeatedly expressed anxiety about the intensity of Japanese competition and called for action by the Australian government.

By 1936, the north Australian newspapers were writing of a "Japanese invasion," with talk of a Dutch company in Maluku losing over one thousand tons of pearls due to fleets of fifty to sixty Japanese luggers.[89] Carpenter made similar complaints. His agent, Aitken, had already observed in 1934 that there were twenty-four mostly Japanese-owned vessels between Darwin waters and Dobo, one of which, registered in Zamboanga in the Philippine Islands, flew an American flag.[90] A report from three years later states that there were four boats on Aru owned by a Japanese resident there, but another 120 fishing in the waters around the area.[91]

By this stage, the Japanese had really overtaken the Celebes Trading Company, and by 1937 there were only 250 pearling workers on Aru, a quarter of the workforce of the Celebes Trading Company's heyday.[92]

At the beginning of 1938, the Mitsui Company, the largest of the Japanese concerns, attempted to create an embargo on Japanese pearling because of overproduction. However, nature soon reversed that problem because in early 1939 an outbreak of disease affected the mother-of-pearl, setting the industry back.[93]

The Hilliards

As if the extensive operations of the Australians at Aru were not impressive enough, another Australian family, the Hilliards, had also settled in eastern Indonesia and prospered there. Just as Victor Clark had found it was not always possible to control conditions in the Netherlands East Indies, and in the same way that Chum Jardine thrived by working with Indonesians, this smaller pearling concern also saw that local conditions required flexibility.

In the 1890s, Henry Hilliard, who was from Broome, had extended his labor supply activities to establish a fleet that was fishing in the reefs between Broome and Kupang, with a refueling base at Rote. Hilliard was joined by other "beachcombers" who were obtaining turtles, trepang, and fish in traditional Indonesian fisheries such as Ashmore Reef.[94] Henry Hilliard, a strong man with a full beard in the fashion of the day, realized the advantages of the area. In 1914, he and his son Robin, along with Alex Chamberlain, who was originally from Fremantle, had a Kupang-based company involved in pearling and collecting turtle shell. Their fleet included vessels owned by local Chinese and Dutch companies, such as the boat *Joker* owned by Ah Kit.[95] Henry Hilliard's wife, Martha, remained in Broome where she became a prominent citizen of Western Australia.[96] They had married in 1884 but lived initially on the schooner *Annie Taylor*.[97] Their son, Robin, was born on this schooner in 1888. The Hilliards kept their Broome base at the northern end of the main street, not far from the Streeter Jetty.

The Hilliard's Flores Cooperative Company[98] was based in Makassar, the regional trading hub for the east of Indonesia, the Celebes Trading Company's capital, and the main port from which Japanese worked. Henry Hilliard's original partner, Alex Chamberlain, went bankrupt in 1927, admitting in the Bankruptcy Court that, "the pearling industry made a big appeal to the gambling instinct." He had been in partnership in Broome with a man named Kennedy but had also invested heavily in a cattle station.[99]

Henry Hilliard continued his multiple fishing and labor-recruiting activities until his death by food poisoning in Kupang in 1924.[100] Two years later his son,

Henry Hilliard. Broome Historical Society.

Robin, went into business in the same town as a pearler and labor recruiter along with another regular visitor to Aru, Herbert S. Cross, the pearl buyer whose misadventures in the wreck of the *Eileen* have already been mentioned. Cross was described as the owner of a fleet of four luggers in which Robin Hilliard sailed to Kupang in 1929 to establish a pearling station, "having severed his connection with Broome." This station was also the major labor recruitment base of the region, and Hilliard recruited for Victor Clark.[101] Cross had ten boats in Dutch waters, "where the remarkable cheapness of labour and the absence of duties on gear, rice, etc., makes possible a greater return from lower-priced pearl shell."[102] Some reports indicate that Hilliard worked for Cross, but the relationship seems to have been more of a partnership. The Flores Cooperative included the Dutch merchants of Makassar, Gros Kamp & Drofmeyer, and had fourteen luggers selling shell to Ochse & Company.[103] Alex Chamberlain at some stage returned to working with Hilliard, despite or perhaps because of his bankruptcy in Australia, and they were together when captured by the invading Japanese in 1942.[104]

Labuan Bajo on Flores, their base in the late 1930s, was and remains the main port of access to Komodo Island, and naturalists who wanted to see the famed "dragons" and passed through the port stayed with Hilliard and Cross, the only white residents. One naturalist, the American Lawrence Griswold, met the pair around 1933 or 1934, when the industry was still recovering from the twin effects of the Depression and the collapse of the market under competition from Bake-lite and changing fashion, and later described their meeting:

> They helped us up onto their rickety wharf, told their boys to tie up the *prau* and look after our crew, and then escorted us to their house. Here we were offered rocking chairs to sit in and gazed at a room that might have been lifted bodily from Cape Cod. It was clean and small. Religious pictures were on the walls, sharing honors with a K.P.M. [the Dutch shipping line] calendar, a dining room table occupied the center of the room and the corners held, variously, a sewing machine, a lowboy, and a whatnot. Even our rocking chairs were topped with antimacassars. Only the gasoline light, around which large white flying ants were fluttering, and a bottle of Scotch were contradictions.
>
> Cross and Hilliard were cheerful hermits. Spare and rather hard-bitten in appearance, they were gracious hosts. Although it was well past midnight, Cross sent for his native cook and we had some fresh vegetables and eggs while we heard about the pearling business. It seemed that since women gave up wearing pearl buttons on their clothing there had been a depression among pearlers. Four luggers with Japanese divers barely returned expenses, even with full cargoes of shell and normal expectancy of pearl finds. Consequently, Cross was able to charter us his largest lugger to take our dragons back to Bima.[105]

When they got up mid-afternoon they found their crew had been cross-questioned by the local sultan "practically into hysteria." The sultan had thought they were going to raid the safe in Cross' office.[106]

Between 1934 and 1939, Cross seems to have left a lot of the actual pearling to Hilliard and Chamberlain. By the time of his mishap with the *Eileen* in 1939, Cross was described only as a buyer and a representative of the emergent New York firm, Otto Gerdau Company, which was at this stage trying to control Broome's pearl shell, as mentioned above.[107]

Naturalist Griswold's translation of Hilliard's base at Labuan Bajo as "Pirates' Anchorage" hinted at the source of Hilliard's success.[108] The Bajau, or "Sea Gypsies," held vital knowledge about fishing, navigation, and the ways of the waters. Thanks to Natasha Stacey's oral history interviews with the Sama Bajau of region, we know that they were persuaded by Hilliard to work with him. Bajau such as Si Bilaning and Si Mbaga recalled their friends and family going to *Marege,* the local term for Australia, with "Tuan Robin." The Bajau already had substantial fishing fleets catching turtle and trepang in the waters between eastern Indonesia and Australia, so it was mutually beneficial to work with Hilliard to identify pearl beds.

Labuan Bajo was one of a number of bases that Hilliard used throughout the archipelago, and it seems that he had learned the lesson of the Torres Strait experience many decades before, that beds can easily be fished out. By moving between beds, he was able to let them recover. Besides Labuan Bajo and Kupang, he also operated out of Alor and the islands to the south of Sulawesi known as Tukang Besi, close to where the Japanese and Reg Hockings were working off Buton. Since the Bajau regard these islands as their "home," their relationship with Tuan Robin would have given him full access to these beds.[109] The Flores Cooperative Company did not need to operate in Australian waters, and so did not attract the same Australian attention as the Clarks.

Robin Hilliard seems to have been much more interested than Victor Clark in building up good relations with his local workers, and having local networks was also important for labor recruitment. Hilliard's wife, Sara Nale, was from Rote. Like many Indonesian women, she managed the household budget, and by all accounts quite astutely. She was no doubt an invaluable intermediary for Robin, who is reputed to have paid his workers well and looked after their families in the mode of an Indonesian patron. Some of those families, such as the Manafes, used the support and access to the modern world that Robin provided to educate their children, who became important figures in postwar Indonesia.[110]

The Australian pearlers had gone to Indonesian waters seeking cheap labor, and that remained a significant element in the relationship. However, the pearling industry of the Indonesian islands was more than just a labor source. At times the industry run by Australians settled in Indonesia was more significant than that of Western Australia, the Northern Territory, and Queensland, but it also has to be seen as an organic whole with the north Australian pearling beds. The Australians moving back and forth across the pearling zone were recruiting Indonesians in large numbers and managing their workforce in a variety of ways that ranged from familial patronage to ruthless exploitation. The Australian government was forced to follow the pearlers' expansion into the Indies and offer labor concessions to keep the Australian industry viable, as we will see in the next chapter.

CHAPTER FIVE

Labor Migration to North Australia, 1901–1941

When Abdoel Gafoer first arrived in Broome in the early 1920s to work in the pearling industry, he was one of a growing number of workers coming to Australia who had been recruited specifically from Kupang. From 1923 onwards, the Western Australia Fisheries began recording the employment of "Koepangers" as a separate category, with 294 men listed for that year. By 1925 there were 520 Koepangers and 169 "Malays." With the population of Broome being little more than two thousand in total, at least one in four of those living there were Indonesian, meaning that Abdoel Gafoer would have felt quite at home. The 1925 statistics also record that there were 720 Japanese employed in Broome in that year, which, as we will see, represented a significant drop in the number of Japanese, and meant that the pearling masters were trying to regulate the ethnic mix of the northern pearling industry towns. This chapter examines the relationship between labor and ethnicity, looking particularly at working conditions and the ways that labor organized.

Workers' Indenture

The industry had recovered from the downturn in prices before the end of World War I, and by 1923 the movement of men from Kupang to northern Australia was sufficiently established that the Dutch government sought to regulate their transportation. The Dutch were prompted by a report from the Batavia-based British consul to the Netherlands East Indies resident in Kupang complaining that a Chinese-owned Netherlands East Indies schooner was carrying indentured workers between Kupang and Western Australia, loaded with two passengers per ton—double the number recommended for Atlantic slave-trading ships in the days of that trade.[1]

Gafoer's immigration file indicates that he arrived for the first time in Australia on the *Centaur* in 1921, and then went home before returning to Broome in 1923 on the steamship *Gascoyne*, which had commenced working the pearling route that year. The *Gascoyne*, owned by the Western Australian Steam Navigation

Pearling luggers, Broome. Photograph by R. A. Bourne, National Library of Australia
PIC/9115/2 LOC Album 1078.

Company, travelled between Singapore, Java, and Western Australia, but added
Kupang and other ports to its route in response to the vexed issue of labor
transportation.[2] Boarding at Kupang, where there was no pier for steamships,
Gafoer and his fellow workers would have been rowed across to the *Gascoyne*
in a small boat.

But how was it that Indonesian men were still being employed in Australia in
the 1920s, at a time when the White Australia policy, which insisted on white labor, was still very much in favor? Between 1901 and 1916 there had been ongoing
debates over the importation of Asian labor for the northern Australian pearl-
shell industry, but the use of Asian labor had been upheld. Already in 1902, Prime
Minister Edmund Barton had granted the lucrative pearl-shell industry permission to import Asian indentured labor, pending further investigations.[3] This was
largely a pragmatic decision. In Broome, Resident Magistrate Warton, who had
been worried about the industry shifting to Dutch waters, noted that 1,515 "Asiatics and other colored men" who had been employed there would subsequently
need to be returned to Singapore and Kupang if restrictions on Asian labor were
imposed.[4] Despite the prevailing political and popular support for the White Australia policy, the pearling industry's political lobby was so well connected, and their
success in Dutch waters so great, that for the entire period of the Immigration

Restriction Act, the pearling masters in Western Australia, the Northern Territory, and Queensland were able to import Asian labor with only minor restrictions.

As part of the initial 1902 investigations into working conditions for pearling indents, the government asked to see copies of the indenture contract used for workers coming from Singapore. Each of these three-year contracts was signed in Singapore by the British firm Guthrie & Company on behalf of the Australian pearling master. In contrast, the Dutch contract that Gafoer would have signed in Kupang was for only two years with a mandatory return to Kupang at the end of each contract, and with at least one-sixth of his wages in his possession.[5] Of course, it is not clear how many of those being employed could actually read and write, and many indenture contracts are signed only with a mark.

The Singapore contract specified the payment of wages every six months, entitlement to thirty days of medical treatment to be covered by the employer, and a clause that allowed employers to dock wages for failure to work because of "venereal disease" or "laziness." Incoming migrants were also advised that it was illegal for them to proceed below the twenty-seventh parallel in Australia, the latitude of Brisbane. Asian workers were expected to spend most of their time out at sea and when ashore their movements were strictly curtailed.

Food provisions for indents were totally inadequate. The Singapore contract specified a daily allowance of 2 lbs. of rice, 1/2 lb. of fish or meat, 6 oz. of biscuit, 1/8 oz. of tea, 2 oz. of sugar, and 3 qts. of fresh water while at sea and vegetables when the worker was in harbor. These limited food supplies had serious consequences: When Gafoer arrived in Broome there was a large ward that cared for pearling indents suffering from the painful and lethal disease of beri-beri, caused by vitamin deficiency. The contract also specified that Malay (that is, Muslim) holidays were to be observed when in harbor, a curious clause, given that many Japanese were recruited in Singapore using this form. We are not sure if the Kupang contract included a similar clause, but with a proportion of "Koepangers" being Christian, being forced to work on Sundays was a frequently made complaint.

After this initial Singapore contract expired, workers could be re-signed in Australia. Schedule A forms were used for such seamen, and Schedule B registered the employer's payment of a £100 bond to be returned once the worker returned home. The bond was set in accordance with the Western Australian Immigration Restriction Act of 1897. The period of re-engagement was usually one year. For example, in one agreement, Ahmat Bin Mohammed consented to serve his employer from January 1 to December 31, 1903, with wages set at £2.10.0 per month, around a quarter of what tradesmen earned in major southern cities in Australia. It also specified that at the end of his period of service, the employer would provide him with the means to return to Singapore.[6] Just three years later, Justice H. B. Higgins, president of the Commonwealth Arbitration Court, determined that a (male) worker should be paid a minimum wage, based on the cost of living, in order to ensure that he could live as a "human being in a civilised community."[7] Justice Higgins, in this *Harvester Judgment,* set a wage close to four times the amount that Ahmat bin Mohammed was receiving, although it was not until the 1920s that there was a general acceptance in Australia of this principle. Indentured workers were consigned to be outside this "civilised community."

Pearling as a Special Exception

Conditions were much the same in the other pearling ports. The Commonwealth of Australia government investigation, headed by Justice Dashwood, into the pearl-shell industry in the Torres Strait and Darwin considered the possibility of moving to white labor. Ultimately, it confirmed the need for Asian labor, or at the very least white divers and Asian crew, a suggestion that could only have been about maintaining low wages.[8] In the first decade after Federation, there had been several attempts to shift to white labor under government pressure, but with almost no results. In 1908, a Queensland state government Royal Commission into the pearl-shell industry investigated whether white divers could replace Asians, with the focus being on replacing Japanese divers. There was some talk of importing Swedish fishermen but it came to nothing.[9] In 1912, the Commonwealth Labor Party government headed by Andrew Fisher announced that a ban on Asian labor was to take effect in 1913. But this ban was withdrawn before it was even implemented. Another Commonwealth Royal Commission into the industry was set up in 1912, and the question was finally resolved in 1916 in favor of continued Asian migration. Not only was Asian labor to be retained, but so too were the indentured contracts that allowed the government and individual employers almost absolute control over the workers. This decision was made with almost no regard for the international movement in this period to abolish the practice of indenture.[10]

The pearling masters had little concern that systems of indenture were being criticized in other parts of the world. For them, importing Asians was all about controlling labor costs. Historians of the industry have seen these decisions as part of a push to bring in Japanese divers, but we have also found surprising evidence that they were based on trying to bring in more Indonesian labor ahead of the Japanese, since for the pearling masters, importing Asian labor was aimed at keeping labor costs down. Their distinctly colonial attitudes toward their workforce would bring them into conflict with Australian trade unions.

At a time when both governments were attempting to cut off easy movement between Australia and the Netherlands Indies, the pearl-shell industry continued to supply thousands of Indonesians to Australia's north. Other industries that were not exempt from the White Australia policy had been encouraged to change their workforce through a system that rewarded the use of white labor.[11] Indonesians had been employed on Australian sugar plantations since the late nineteenth century, but by 1916 the largest company in Queensland, the Colonial Sugar Refinery Company—now known as CSR—employed only thirteen Javanese and four Malays.[12] That the pearling industry was granted exemption from the restrictions on importing labor demonstrates the importance of the industry and of Asian labor to its viability.

The overall movement of Indonesian labor to Australia for the pearl-shell industry during this period was in the thousands, though calculating exact figures is difficult because of the lack of centralized employment data. The labor statistics from Western Australia show that the number of Asian men employed grew substantially in the first years after 1901, although their description as "Malay" makes it difficult to know the precise origins of the indentured workers, especially since the term "Koepangers" was not in official use until the second decade of the twentieth century. The use of the ambiguous category "Malay" was not accidental. In cases where the regulations used the broad term "British subjects" to indicate those who were permitted to operate in the industry, the notion that they were employing labor from British Malaya was a useful point of ambiguity. In 1902, the employment statistics for Broome listed 326 Japanese, 787 Malays, and 294 Filipinos. Two years later the numbers for Malays peaked, with 1,235 in employment. Over the decade up to 1914, there were on average 769 Malays employed each year.[13] These are not inconsequential figures. If we include Darwin and the Torres Strait Islands in the estimates, then the pearlers were probably bringing in at least one thousand Indonesians each year to north Australia, and perhaps as many as two thousand.

In 1911, Broome's pearling masters employed some 2,275 Asian men, making it Australia's leading port for pearling. Thursday Island in the Torres Strait was next with some seven hundred men working in the industry. As described in the previous chapter, the Torres Strait fleet had been diminished when Clark left for Aru in 1905. The Australian Commonwealth government assumed control of the Northern Territory, including the port of Darwin, from the state of South Australia in the same year. Darwin was still a small player in the industry, with only 138 men on thirty-one boats of whom 120 were indentured under permit by the Minister for External Affairs.[14]

Despite the size of these estimates, scholars have, to date, overlooked Australia as a destination country for Indonesian migration labor. However, these figures

Thursday Island pearl diver in his diving gear (1899–1928). National Library of Australia PIC/8381/337 LOC Album 1054/D, Francis Birtles Motor Car Tour Collection.

are not dissimilar to those for the Dutch colony of Suriname, which is regarded as the principal destination for "Javanese" migration. Historian Rosemarijn Hoefte noted that between 1902 and 1910 a total of 5,433 Indonesians left Batavia and Semarang for Suriname.[15] In Western Australia for that same nine-year period, 7,788 Malays were employed. Similar numbers of Indonesian migrants were reported at this time in British North Borneo, where the Javanese population in 1911 reached 5,511.[16]

Nevertheless, two factors preclude a direct comparison between the migration levels to Suriname and those to Australia. The Suriname case study uses Dutch emigration figures, while the Australian statistics measure annual employment numbers, and do not take into account the fact that Indonesians were on two-year contracts. In addition it is not possible to estimate what proportion of those termed "Malays" were from Singapore or British Malaya rather than the Netherlands East

Indies, though our evidence suggests that the majority were from present-day Indonesia.

Shipping Routes and the Transportation of Labor

Counting total numbers of Indonesian immigrants to Australia is made especially difficult by the varied means of shipping that was used to bring workers to Broome, Darwin, and Thursday Island. Some companies chartered vessels when necessary, such as the steamer *Waihoi,* which sailed from Darwin to Kupang in 1908 for Burns, Philp & Company with the intention of recruiting labor for the pearl-shelling industry.[17] Many companies used their own schooners and pearling luggers to bring crews to Australia.

A number of steamship companies plied the route between Australia and the Netherlands East Indies during the first part of the twentieth century. Records from 1910 indicate that pearling crews travelled between Thursday Island and Dobo, Aru, on the Dutch steamships of the Royal Packet Navigation Company (Koninklijke Paketvaart-Maatschappij, or KPM). A KPM advertisement of the

Pearling luggers' crews, Broome, 1910. State Library of Western Australia J24323PD. Sourced from the collections of the State Library of Western Australia and reproduced with the permission of the Library Board of Western Australia.

time described its Java-Australia Line, which included two steamships, *Le Maire* and *Van Spilbergen*. These ships sailed with first- and third-class passengers from Sydney to Singapore via Thursday Island, Port Moresby, and the Indies ports of Dobo, Banda, Ambon, Makassar, Buleleng (north Bali), Surabaya, Semarang (north Java), and Batavia.[18] KPM was still sailing a similar route in 1914 with two ships, the *Houtman* and the *Tasman*, calling in at Dobo and Darwin, respectively.

The Australian-based Burns, Philp & Company sailed in competition with KPM. From 1904, Burns, Philp & Company sailed between Sydney and Singapore via Port Darwin, Surabaya, and Semarang, using the *Airlie* (replaced with *Mataram* in 1909) and the *Guthrie* (replaced with *Montoro* in 1912). Their route went via Banda, Ambon, Makassar, and Surabaya. It was not surprising that Burns Philp favored ports known for labor recruitment. The 1908 Queensland Royal Commission showed that, with thirty-six luggers, Burns, Philp & Company was the largest pearl-shell company on Thursday Island at the time. Dutch maritime historian Joseph à Campo has suggested that Burns, Philp & Company stopped visiting the ports of Banda and Ambon after a request from KPM in 1905.[19] But in 1907, the *Guthrie* was still advertising the same route as a once every six weeks service. Burns Philp did, however, change the route in 1909 at which time the *Guthrie* sailed from Thursday Island to Darwin and on to Makassar, bypassing Banda and Ambon. The Thursday Island–Makassar route was also used by the Norddeutscher Lloyd Company which serviced German New Guinea. Its *Stettin* called in at Batavia, Makassar, German New Guinea, Keppel Bay, and Brisbane.[20]

While these steamship routes help to explain the transportation of labor from the region of Maluku—that is, those workers described as "Ambonese," "Bandanese," and "Dobo Malays"—a different company serviced the Timor route. The Eastern and Australian Steamship Company, with its SS *Eastern* and the SS *Australian*, connected Port Darwin and Thursday Island to Timor, Manila, and Japan, following a route that exactly coincided with the three main sources of pearling crews at the beginning of the twentieth century.[21]

Labor migration to Broome in Western Australia came via Kupang and Singapore.[22] The voyage between Broome and Kupang was one that could easily be undertaken by a pearling lugger, as demonstrated in a report of October 1906, which described how the *Orion* was "pirated" by its Malay crew and sailed back to Kupang. The following year, when a Mr. Kirby was sent to Kupang to recover the vessel, the Dutch authorities handed over the lugger as well as its crew for prosecution.[23] While most crews were transported on luggers and schooners, it was possible that crews also came to Broome via Darwin, transferring from Eastern and Australian steamers. The *Charon*, for example, which was jointly owned by the Western Australian Steam Navigation Company and the Blue Funnel Line, sailed between Western Australian ports and Darwin.

Other historians have presumed that recruits from Singapore were all British subjects, but Singapore was a recruitment hub for migrant workers from across the region. The men recruited in Singapore were of many nationalities, including Japanese, Filipino, Chinese, British Malay, and Indonesian. Some of the early twentieth-century records of pearling indenture refer to these Indonesians as "Javanese," but the use is inconsistent. In 1903, Captain Pitts of the Western Australian Steam Navigation Company ship the *Sultan* stated that on his last voyage to Singapore, he embarked at Broome fifty-seven pearling crew members whose time had expired and who were being sent back to their places of origin. The same company also used the *Minderoo* and the *Paroo* for transporting migrant workers on the same route. Steamships bound for Singapore passed through Broome on average once a fortnight.[24]

Histories of the pearl-shelling industry often describe a shift to Japanese divers in the 1880s, which has led people to assume that Indonesians were less significant to the industry after 1900. While the majority of divers and their tenders (those who looked after the divers' lines) were Japanese, the numerically greater crew—sailors, cooks, and engineers—were mostly Indonesian. In later times Indonesians increasingly took on the role of tenders. Furthermore, one of the early outcomes of the Royal Commission investigation into the industry that had been instigated by Prime Minister Fisher was the decision to give preference to Malays rather than to Papuans or Japanese.[25] While the government favored recruitment of Malays via Singapore, the situation changed in December 1913, when they were informed that Malays were not available. Instead the pearlers turned to the Netherlands East Indies.[26] In an interview from the time, Shreinder, a resident of Broome, commented that "Koepang boys" were "growing in favour with pearlers at Broome but that the Dutch government would only allow them to sign on for two years at a time."[27] It was around this time that the term "Koepanger" started to be used in common parlance to classify this group of workers, although the term did not appear in government statistics until 1922.

World War I did not bring about dramatic changes in labor importation, particularly because the Netherlands remained neutral during the war, but it was the decline in the market for shell, caused by disruption of maritime traffic in the following years, that was to have an impact.[28] When war broke out in 1914, the pearl-shell industry in Western Australia employed 1,115 Japanese, 585 Malays, and 247 Koepangers.[29] Three months before the war started, Leon Goldstein arrived in Broome with twelve ethnic Malay divers from "the vicinity of Makassar." Goldstein, a twenty-four-year old pearler from Broome, reported that on his trip through "the pearling centres in the Dutch Indies," he had found labor to be "extremely plentiful" and that he was of the "opinion that all the men required to work the Western Australia pearling industry can be obtained from these islands."[30] The

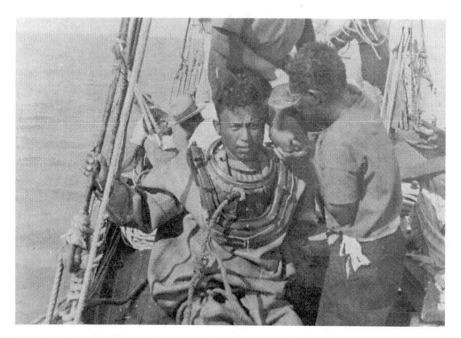

Malay diver, Darwin, 1930. Photograph by Bill Eacott. Northern Territory Library
PH0444-0010, Bill and Betty Eacott Collection.

war, however, claimed men from the industry. Leon Goldstein himself enlisted
in the army and returned from Gallipoli to Australia in 1916 gravely ill.[31]

When, in 1915, master pearler James Clark brought a portion of his pearling
fleet from the Aru Islands to Broome as part of the restructuring of the Celebes
Trading Company, he also brought 215 men from the Netherlands East Indies. The
local pearlers, who had not been consulted by the Australian government over
the decision to allow Clark to work in Broome, were fearful that Clark's arrival
would put them out of business.[32] Clark strenuously denied the allegations that he
was a monopolist, and claimed instead that he sought to improve the price of shell
to benefit all pearlers. He also denied the notion that he was an outsider, writing in
an open letter that he, like many others, had started out in Broome in the 1880s.[33]

The year 1928 marked the beginning of a decline in the Broome pearling industry, largely as a result of James Clark's nephew, Victor, and his associates shifting the focus of the trade to the Aru-Darwin axis. That year only nineteen Indonesians were recruited for Broome. Master pearler V. R. Kepert, a competitor of
Clark's, had moved eight luggers and forty men from Broome to Darwin.[34] While
the Broome figures rallied the following year, they remained low, with the Great

Depression drastically affecting world prices. Many Japanese were also moving to Darwin, and in 1932, for the first time, the number of Japanese in Broome fell below that of Indonesians with 268 Japanese and 279 Koepangers employed.[35] Toward the end of the 1930s, recruitment to Broome picked up again. A Dutch newspaper report of 1938 describes the Burns, Philp & Company ship *Gordon* on January 23, 1938, as disembarking in Kupang 110 "Timorese, Rotinese and Savunese" who had returned from their two-year contracts in Broome and embarking another 130 new recruits on February 9. The article makes it clear that, despite the hard work, the attraction of making between *fl.*3,000 and *fl.*6,000 during their service, with advances and compulsory savings paid out on return to Kupang, was a great lure for local workers. Most of the recruits were repeat hires, having done at least one term in Broome. The report also notes that seven years previously, a recruiter had been murdered by a contractor.[36]

Labor Conditions in North Australia

In 1902, the iconic Australian poet, Banjo Paterson, best known for penning Australia's national song, "Waltzing Matilda," published a poem entitled "The Pearl Diver," which tells of the death of a Japanese diver named Kanzo Makame.

> *Fearless he was beyond credence,*
> *Looking death eye to eye . . .*

The poem described the dangers of diving below twenty-five fathoms in the Darnley Deep waters in the Torres Strait. Paterson sought to remind his readers about the price of their fashion accessories, concluding:

> *Wearer of pearls in your necklace, comfort yourself if you can,*
> *These are the risks of the pearling—these are the ways of Japan,*
> *Plenty more Japanese diver, plenty more little brown man!*[37]

Public acknowledgment that this was a dangerous industry did not mean that attention was paid either to the conditions or to the remuneration of workers who faced those dangers.

The death rate for Japanese divers in the pearl-shell industry continued to rise after the publication of Paterson's poem. Seventy-two divers died in the Torres Strait between 1906 and 1911. In 1911, the death rate was 11 percent, though one company lost as many as seven of its twenty-six divers. In deep-sea diving, it was divers' paralysis that claimed the most lives, as the technique of "staging"—that is, a slow, staged, rise to the surface—was not yet developed. Apart from those who died as a result of diving accidents, an additional fifty divers and an unknown number of crew died of beri-beri during this same period.[38]

Similar data for Broome between 1905 and 1957 show that divers' paralysis was the main cause of death (158 out of 247 deaths), with heart attacks and asphyxiation, presumably related to the perils of diving, causing another 33 and 24 deaths, respectively. The Broome register of marine deaths records that 120 of those who died in this period were Japanese, with another 152 recorded as coming from Indonesia.[39]

An earlier account by adventurer Henry Taunton, filled as it is with a colorful sense of adventure, paints a very grim picture of working in the industry. Written in 1882, when he was traveling with a crew of Aborigines and "Malays," Taunton's description not only covers the danger of divers' paralysis and beri-beri, but also gives graphic accounts of divers taken by sharks, his own suffering from scurvy, and the danger for skin-divers of being dragged along by boats at speeds that might cause "shallow water blackout" and drowning.[40] While this latter fate may seem like an archaic risk, a similar death of a young Australian pearl diver occurred in Broome in April 2012, when he was dragged along underwater at high speed.[41]

Not only was the pearling industry dangerous, but it also suffered all the problems associated with the use of indentured labor. Indenture contracts set out all wages and conditions for the period of employment, binding the worker to the employer in a way that is certainly less than free for the period of employment. In 1912, the Western Australian government passed the Pearl Fisheries Bill, which set out the conditions for indentured labor, including penal provisions and specifying penalties for breach of agreement, desertion, and insubordination. Desertion, for example, could be punished with three months imprisonment or the forfeiture of all accrued wages and "lay," which was the remuneration based on the quantity of pearl shell fished.[42]

One remarkable Indonesian account of working in Western Australia was published in 1926 in the Medan newspaper, *Pewarta Deli,* by a Sumatran of Batak ethnicity, A. R. Nasoetion. He describes being sent off on a lugger with six companions, having prepared cigarettes and work equipment and been provisioned with food by his employer. Nasoetion, unlike the eastern Indonesian recruits, had no experience of the work and was reluctant to go but was instructed on what to do by the diver: "On that little boat, the Diver was king. The Tender supervised the work." After a few days sailing from Broome (he was not sure in which direction), the diver shouted out to stop, and they had to help him into his rubber diving suit. The suit had shoes of metal weighing thirty-six pounds each, with an equivalent

chest weight. Only the tender's rope slowed the dive, and that was literally the diver's "lifeline." One crew member had to guard and feed out the rubber breathing
pipe, another hold the feed-line, and two work the air pump. Then they would all
haul the diver back up to the surface using the windlass when he signaled that he
was ready. They took turns at the hard work of controlling the pump, since after
some time at that job in the hot sun, each was "bathed in sweat." Nasoetion found
the work harsher than expected, and spent much of his time trying to figure out
how to get out of his contract. As luck would have it, he was able to switch to working in a hotel when a particularly bad cyclone season made pearling impossible.[43]

Evidence presented to the 1912 Royal Commission stated that Malay divers
in Broome received a wage of £2 per month and a "lay" of £25 for four tons of
shell, and £3 per month and a "lay" of £30 for five tons of shell.[44] Wages for the
crew were far less. Monthly wages rose little over the next decade, going up only
to £5 with a £25 bonus for divers in the period 1919 to 1926; tenders received £4
between 1904 and 1922 and a raise to £5 in 1922; and ordinary crew received £1.5
to £2 and then also received a raise to £5 in 1922. The basic wage in Western Australia was £16 per month for most of this period.[45] Given that the terms of employment were set well below that of the average Australian, it is not surprising
that the final results of the Royal Commission made reference to the inadequate
working conditions.

In Darwin, the 1911 annual report of the Northern Territory recorded that divers were paid 1s per month and £23 per ton of shell. Tenders received £4 per month,
cooks £10 per month, and other types of pearling crew, £2.10 per month.[46] The
Europeans not involved in the industry were largely oblivious to the realities of
working life in the pearl-shell industry even if they did recognize the difficulties.
Elsie Masson, who later became the wife of famous anthropologist Bronislaw
Malinowski, lived briefly in Government House in Darwin and wrote:

> The life of the pearler is not an unhappy one. There is, of course, the risk
> of death, or—still more common—of paralysis, which very frequently over-
> takes the diver after some years. To make up for this, the work is not heavy
> and the wages are high. The diver is paid according to the weight of his
> catch, while each of the other men earns from £5 to £6 a month, and pro-
> visions are free. There are five men on each lugger—the diver, the tender,
> who manages the life-lines, and three others to help work the ship, one of
> whom is generally training to become a diver himself.[47]

The 1916 final report of the Royal Commission into the pearl-shell industry, which
concluded that the industry would be permitted to continue employing Asian

labor, gave a more realistic assessment. "The life is not a desirable one, and the risks are great, as proved by the abnormal death rate amongst divers and try divers. The work is arduous, the hours long, and the remuneration quite inadequate. Living space is cramped, the food wholly preserved of its different kinds, and the life incompatible with that a European worker is entitled to live."[48] The Australian government's endeavors to turn the nation into a "workers' paradise" was to be available only to white workers. Not everyone was of this opinion. During the Royal Commission, Senator Givens questioned this idea of protecting white labor:

> *Senator Givens:* If the life is so awfully bad, and the hardships so great, would it be any more Christian to subject the coloured races to it than to subject the white race?
>
> *John Mackay:* To the natives I speak of, the sea is their playground.
>
> *Givens:* But diving . . . does not suggest much of a playground?
>
> *Mackay:* [T]he Japanese is a fatalist, and does not care.[49]

It was this stereotype of the "stoic" or fatalistic Asian worker that allowed the pearling masters to argue for differential treatment.

While some of the dangers of diving were inherent to the industry, the question of low wages was clearly an area that could have been improved. But laborers under a contract of indenture were unable to negotiate for better wages. This was particularly so for the pearling crews employed from the Netherlands East Indies. In 1916, when the schooner *Muriel* arrived at Broome with twenty-eight men from Kupang, the men at first refused to sign pearling contracts that stipulated a wage of 25s per month. They were declared prohibited immigrants and put in jail. Only when they subsequently agreed to sign the contracts were they released into the custody of their employers.[50]

A Western Australian government ministerial tour was organized in June 1920 to investigate conditions in Broome. Its report made two important points to justify the continuation of the pearling industry. In the previous year a total of £230,000 had been made from pearl shell, which was selling at a price of £250 per ton. The sheer magnitude of profits was always a powerful argument. Further, it was noted that with new staging techniques, by which divers were brought up slowly to the surface, the death rate from divers' paralysis had been significantly reduced. The average death rate of thirty-three men per year had dropped to just three per year.[51]

When Victor Clark brought three luggers to Darwin from Broome in 1925, this was a sign that he was shifting the Australian base of the industry to more closely link up with Aru. At the same time, the Commonwealth government sent

the sub-collector of customs in Darwin instructions for dealing with the employment of indentured labor.[52] Pearling masters were obliged to buy permits and to
pay a bond for each indentured worker. The bond was £250 for up to ten men and
could be returned only after the indent was back in his country of origin. Each
indent was required to have a medical certificate and an identity card with two
thumbprints and two photographs. A final regulation, which was designed to prevent Japanese monopoly over the industry, was that not more than five men of
the same nationality were permitted on the one lugger.[53]

Whatever was stipulated in contracts, the reality of working conditions was
much worse. During a 1928 court case in Darwin between Clark and his competitor, Kepert, it was noted that there "was difficulty in obtaining Timor coolies
owing to wages due not being paid last year in some cases at Broome, also that
some Broome pearlers compelled coolies to work on Sundays with only a half crown
extra per month."[54]

The Role of the Unions

Victor Clark and his associates had not reckoned on the fact that in Darwin there
was greater organization of the Japanese community than in Broome, and more
importantly, that Darwin had a larger white working class and strong union activism. By the 1920s, when the pearling fleets moved to Darwin, it had a reputation as a union town, and indeed, the local newspaper, the *Northern Standard*,
was owned by the North Australian Workers' Union (NAWU).

The NAWU was ambivalent in its attitude toward the pearling crews. The union
was set up according to the rules of White Australia as promoted by the Australian Workers' Union in that the official membership rules barred "any coloured
race." This effectively excluded Asian workers, though it is doubtful that union
membership would have been permitted for indentured laborers in any case.[55]
When, in 1930, a motion was put to remove the color bar, only a minority of
communist-leaning unionists supported the change.[56] Even so, when incidents
arose involving poor working conditions for the pearling crews, it was not unusual for the NAWU to step in and mediate.

Japanese were in a better position to negotiate wages because they formed the
majority of divers, and a skilled diver could be paid well for his large hauls. In
Broome, most Japanese divers had been operating under a system known as "dum-
mying" in which divers were captains of their own luggers, but officially under a
white owner in order to satisfy Western Australian government regulations.[57]
When divers transferred to Darwin, they were ostensibly working for white pearling masters, but again they were able to demand high wages. In 1928, they were

paid £100 a ton for shell raised, on the condition that they paid for the expenses of the boat after it had been made ready at the beginning of the season. This arrangement effectively gave greater power to the Japanese diver, who gained all the control of a partner.

In order to entice men from Broome in 1929, the Darwin master pearlers offered to pay divers £130 per ton for shell. Pearling master V. R. Kepert complained that these rates would mean that very soon the Japanese would be in a position to retire, leaving the industry without divers.[58] The divers' share of the profits was very high if one considers that in 1929, the principal New York buyer, Otto Gerdau Company, was offering £185 per ton for shell.[59] An estimate of a diver's annual income would be £468 for the year, out of which he would have to pay costs associated with feeding the crew.[60] As a further incentive, the pearling masters in both towns would pay divers an advance of £100 to £150 at the start of the season. This amount was negotiated, and skilled divers could demand higher advances.[61] Darwin pearlers, however, were offering an extra £30 advance in order to attract divers.[62]

While the pearlers were busy recruiting new divers and sending the Darwin take of pearl shell to new heights, the Australian government was working to restrain the boom, prompted by the complaints of operators from other pearling ports who were afraid that the market would be swamped by Darwin pearl shell. Victor Clark, representing the Darwin Pearling Association, travelled to Canberra in February 1931 to protest against the government's decision to restrict the industry to 200 tons, one quarter of the previous year's output.[63]

A Japanese Divers' Society and a Divers' Tenders' Society was formed in Darwin in 1931. Japanese workers were necessarily vigilant as the pearling masters of Darwin were not inclined to benevolence. Kepert, who had transferred from Broome to Darwin in 1929, was unhappy with the degree of control exerted by Japanese divers. He asked the Northern Territory Commission to make pearling crews subject to the Masters & Servants Act, as was the case in Western Australia. The act's provisions would have enabled him to send employees to jail for "disobedience and refusal of orders." Kepert considered this a more appropriate system to the current one prevailing in Darwin, whereby the pearling masters could only fine an employee a day's wages for such actions.[64]

The Japanese International Development Company in Darwin, which controlled the importation of indentured labor, was obliged to intervene after an incident involving Victor Clark. At the end of the pearling season, Clark made arrangements for his Japanese indentured crews to be shipped with deck passages on the SS Mangola. However, the men insisted that they be given second-class passages instead. At that time, it was standard practice on Burns, Philp & Company steamers to place white passengers in cabins and "colored" passengers on decks. The dispute was finally resolved by force when the sub-collector of customs had the police deport the Japanese crew. In response, Japanese labor agents refused to secure further indentured labor for Clark, thus forcing him to apply to the minister for permission to employ all Malay labor.[65]

Unlike Japanese pearling crews, Indonesian crews did not have a union or club of their own. This was not because of a lack of numbers. There were 130 Japanese employed in Darwin in 1936, but the combined number of "Malays" and "Koepangers" was greater. One possible reason for a lack of unionization was that these men were from different locations in the Netherlands East Indies and British Malaya. They shared the lingua franca of Malay, although knowledge of the language would have varied considerably, with those from eastern Indonesia speaking various dialects that were not necessarily intelligible to those from the Peninsula. They were ethnically diverse, too, and in this period had no strong sense of what Benedict Anderson would term an "imagined community." Thus, worker protests were limited to smaller groups coming together to address specific cases, rather than an organized plan to achieve higher wages and better conditions.

As unemployment increased and the pearling industry expanded in Darwin after 1928, NAWU officials turned their attention to the employment of indentured pearling crews on shore. The Home and Territories Department had sent instructions on the administration of the pearling industry in 1925, which would later be formalized in the Pearling Ordinance of 1930, stating, "During the layup season the men may live ashore and engage in such work as is ordinarily connected with the boats at that period, such as overhauling, painting, repairing, refitting, etc. but they are not to be allowed to engage in other occupations on shore."[66] Nevertheless, indentured crews were employed in other jobs such as unloading, weighing, sorting, and packing shell. Over the next ten years, the NAWU noted every incident of illicit employment of indentured crew and accused the government of not taking steps to uphold the White Australia policy.

Victor Clark's shift to Indonesian labor led him into conflict with the authorities and the unions. Two Indonesians from Kupang, Mateas Lili and Martin Bela, indentured by Clark, were deported from Australia in 1929 after refusing to carry mail and stores to the Cape Don lighthouse. Such work would have constituted a contravention of the Pearling Ordinance.[67] They argued that they had signed on to engage in the pearling industry and not to carry cargo, but were prosecuted under Section 390 of the Navigation Act and sentenced to twenty-eight days imprisonment. Once released, the Indonesians went to live in the camp of Mahoney, a leading Communist in the NAWU. Having been declared "prohibited immigrants" under the Immigration Restriction Act, they were soon deported.

In January 1930, Robert Toupein, secretary of the NAWU, sent the minister a list of jobs that he argued should be reserved for white labor. He included chipping, shell-packing, box-making, loading and unloading shell, and cutting timber. He further suggested that such restrictions should be enforced by the "immediate deportation of the labourer" and a penalty upon the master pearler if the latter was the offender.[68] The NAWU may have regarded indentured crews as "cheap" competition, but the union's antagonism was directed mostly at the pearling masters who employed the labor.

The tone of union attitudes can be gauged by this 1934 letter to the *Northern Standard*. "These Darwin pearlers seem to be on a great wicket. They are allowed what no other industry is: Indentured coolie labour—in a country that boasts of its White Australia policy. If any of their coolie workers refuse work all the master pearler has to do is to inform the Customs Department and they do the rest— jail him at the taxpayers' expense."[69] The secretary of the NAWU, John Andrew McDonald, was particularly concerned that the use of indentured labor for shore work would take jobs away from local workers. He blamed the pearling masters for going against the ban on shore work, writing:

> The men used are mostly Malays, and it may be said in passing, that they are used for shore work, very much against their will. When they join a pearling lugger, their wages are fixed at 25/- per month, and they are given to understand that they have only to work on the boat. They are told that the Australian law does not allow them to work on shore, but they are soon disillusioned when the boat reaches Darwin. Under threats of being sent to Fanny Bay gaol, they are compelled to load the shell on to lorries, and unload it when they reach the sheds.

McDonald described them as "sweated alien labour" and commented that "This is taking place in a country that prides itself on its 'White Australia Policy.'"[70] McDonald was not unsympathetic to their plight, writing: "They know that they are being exploited and have no other way of seeking redress."[71] He also stated that he himself had witnessed the men being made to pack and grade shell on a Sunday. Given that a number of the men from eastern Indonesia were Christians, this was an important point.

In 1931, three Malays from Singapore approached the union asking for help. They were to be repatriated back to Singapore but had not been paid for three months and were owed £9. The NAWU secretary, Robert Toupein, took up the matter with the Customs and Fisheries Office and then approached Hubert Ulrich, the manager for Gregory and Company. Negotiations commenced, and finally

Ulrich informed Toupein that he had agreed to pay their wages of £3 per month. The money owed was for the period between the end of the season and the arrival of the next steamer. Even though a new season's crew had been signed on from March 1, those due to leave were forced to wait until April 24 for the steamer.[72] In this instance, the NAWU acted on behalf of the Malay crew as if they were union members. The only indication from the *Northern Standard* that these workers were not part of the Darwin community was the fact that the three workers remained unnamed in the lengthy newspaper report.

When Clark changed from Japanese to Indonesian divers, the annual report for the Northern Territory described their performance as "unsatisfactory," noting that "Japanese divers have maintained a higher standard of efficiency in all phases of the diving operations."[73] Nevertheless, the trend toward employing Indonesian divers continued into the late 1930s as more Japanese left to work offshore in Japanese-owned ventures. One of Clark's many concerns, the Territory Pearling Company, employed eleven divers in 1937, all Japanese apart from three Indonesians, Djadi Ratoe, Lobo Ratoe, and Kelau Serang. This company also had five Indonesian try-divers (who took shorter dives), Cornelius, Lidi Bali, Rateo Leba, Kasim, and Daniel Roemahkati.[74] Master Pearler Gregory employed Indonesian and Malays in 1938, including three divers named Amdan Bin Mahomet, Abdul Halik, and Rajap Bin Salim, and two trial divers named Jacobus Latroea and Tetoes Onewehla.[75]

As the status of Indonesian divers improved, so did their willingness to engage in unionist activism. In 1938, fourteen men recruited from Dobo went to the NAWU office complaining that their wages had been stopped for three days and that their rations had been cut. NAWU Secretary McDonald interviewed their employer, Victor Clark, who claimed that the rations were in accordance with the contract he had with the Dutch comptroller at Dobo. McDonald reported the matter to the chief pearling inspector, Karl Waldemar Nylander. Nylander, a man of Swedish descent who was from Estonia (then part of Russia), had been naturalized in Darwin in 1915.[76] He took his work as pearling inspector very seriously and was not without power, being also the acting government secretary. He wrote to Clark that

The Dutch crew from your vessels saw me. . . . There seemed to prevail a certain dissatisfaction amongst the men about rations at the camp. This would be a matter of settlement between you and the men. . . . As a matter of course I inspected the camp in the afternoon, everything was clean and tidy. . . . The crew told me they had no salt, milk, tea (there was coffee) curry or sauce. Their maintenance is a matter for the employer, and perhaps you will look into this matter, as I naturally felt restrained to discuss this phase of your camp arrangements with your crew.[77]

The reprimand was effective, and the crew wrote to the *Northern Standard* to express its appreciation of the union support. "We, the undersigned Dobo Malays, of the Dutch East Indies, . . . wish to show our appreciation to the N.A.W. Union, especially to Mr. J. A. McDonald, the Secretary, and thank him for the trouble he took in fighting on behalf of us concerning the deduction of wages, shortage of tucker, and accommodation." At the same time, they were scathing in their criticism of the government, writing: "Fancy the capitalist Government helping the slave labour industry! We do not think Hitler could do worse things in Germany than the way we are treated here." The letter was signed with six names and written with the aid of an interpreter, W. Gonzales, who was most likely from the Philippines.[78]

Their relationship to the union and their attempts to stand up for their rights demonstrate that the pearling workers were not the passive and cheap "colored" labor imagined by the pearlers. These workers struggled against the combination of harsh conditions and racial stereotyping that shaped the day-to-day realities of employment. But while indentured workers could agitate for better wages and working conditions, their living conditions and lack of contact with the communities around them were also part of the problem. As we will see in the next chapter, members of the same union that defended individual workers also argued publicly that the Indonesians should be kept away from the rest of the community. On the few occasions that governments tried to intervene, it was an attempt to create forms of segregation that they felt would control or at least manage the multi-ethnic north. Such segregation suited the pearling masters, who wanted to keep the different ethnic groups separate and to play them off against each other.

CHAPTER SIX

Challenging Social Segregation

Having permitted Asian workers to enter north Australia, the question remained as to how their presence would be regulated. One of the reasons given for the exemption of the industry was that men would be employed out at sea for the nine-month pearling season from March to November. This left only a few months a year during the north Australian monsoon for crews to be stationed ashore in Broome, Darwin, and Thursday Island. Regulations were passed in each of these locations to reassure the Commonwealth government and the supporters of White Australia that crews were being monitored and controlled. This chapter discusses the social world of the pearling ports and the implications of ethnic difference for the particular nature of the societies in those ports.

A. R. Nasoetion, a Sumatran worker who wrote an account of working in the Western Australian pearling industry, observed that once he had signed on, he was sent with other "Malays" to live in a camp where "we were given food according to our separate nationality and religion, in a way set down by the government, so that even the owners could not dispute it." Not just living conditions, but all aspects of life were meant to be segregated.[1] When Abdoel Gafoer, as a Muslim "Koepanger" was brought to Broome from Kupang in 1921, he would have been treated differently from Nasoetion, since the latter was categorized as "Malay," and was possibly a Christian.

Ion L. Idriess (1890–1979), Australia's most popular writer from the 1930s to the 1950s, published his account of the pearling industry in Broome, *Forty Fathoms Deep*, in 1937. The book went through a large number of printings over subsequent decades.[2] Idriess used his usual clipped and vivid style to depict the manly hardiness of the north, focusing mainly on the Asian pearl divers, but with the intention of arguing to Australians in the south for the importance of the industry. As he stated it, the industry was under threat from Japanese economic interests, which were undercutting the Australians and threatening to put them out of business. "The pearl-shell industry is of peculiar importance to Australia, for it holds a tiny white population at three strategic points along our immense northern coastline. Take away the cattle and three tiny pearl towns, and the north would

Luggers at work, Broome. "While B5 moves back on run with divers resting on deck, the tender on B7 has his diver at work. Each lugger carries a crew of eight or nine including two divers," 1949. National Archives of Australia A1200 L11701 11845278. Still and text from "The Pearlers," National Film and Sound Archives of Australia. http:// www.youtube.com/watch?v=K2ShP_Aoh3I.

be empty."[3] Idriess argued for expanding the existing markets for pearl and other northern exports to new markets in "an increasingly efficient, a hungry Asia," but this promise was also a threat in that his depiction of Japanese competition in the "empty north" also evoked the specter of a potential Asian invasion. Idriess was writing about national development: "We have the brains and capital and labour," he said, but as he saw it, Australia at this time lacked the markets and organization.[4] Ironically, this industry, which was supposed to maintain a white presence on the northern coast of Australia, was also responsible for bringing in Asian workers in greater numbers than the white settlers. The fear of a numerically superior Asian and Aboriginal population and the unthinkable prospect of creating a racially mixed society prompted ongoing vigilance from both Commonwealth and state governments. As historian Warwick Anderson described it, there was "an imagined struggle for existence in the north of white against black, brown and yellow."[5]

In *Drawing the Global Colour Line*, Marilyn Lake and Henry Reynolds' account of international developments in race policies, the authors examine the

Grading and sorting mother-of-pearl shell at Broome, ca. 1953. Photograph by Frank Hurley, National Library of Australia PIC FH/10863 LOC Drawer H42.

attempts by "white men" to establish themselves as separate and superior to other non-white peoples by means of a color line.[6] Idriess's evocative images of the north are certainly about the triumph of what he imagines as a "white" Australia, and his book is full of the kinds of blatantly racist expressions that make it almost unreadable to present-day audiences. Nevertheless, in tones of affection rather than fear, he described a mestizo Broome society based on the lives of "white men, Japanese, South Seamen, Torres Strait islanders, Rotumah men, Manilamen, Chingalese, Javanese, Amboinese, Koepangers, Chinese, Aboriginals, and other races." He prefaced this by saying that "the immigration restriction act had come too late," but then he even went so far as to add that "From this experiment in humanity an entirely new people was destined to arise."[7] The color line was already blurred.

Alfred Searcy, who lived in Darwin from 1882 to 1896 and worked closely with the Southeast Asians, was doubtful that immigration restriction was viable. In his memoirs, *In Australian Tropics,* he proposed shifting the color line southwards to coincide with the tropic of Capricorn, recognizing "all the country to the north of the twenty-second parallel of latitude as 'tropical country'" to be developed according to tropical conditions elsewhere.[8] The newly federated Australian government may have refused to contemplate the imagined land of "Capricornia," but they could not but be aware of its distinctive polyethnic population.[9]

Idriess certainly described a demographic reality. All across the north of Australia, the small pockets of European population were outnumbered by the Aboriginal and Asian populations, with the pearling ports being predominantly Asian. In Darwin, the resident population was small, with only 1,387 people recorded in the 1911 census data, including 442 Chinese, 374 Europeans, 247 "full-blood Aboriginals," 77 Japanese, 52 Filipinos, 49 Timorese, 21 Malays, 7 Javanese, 4 Siamese, 5 Cingalese, 5 South Sea Islanders, and a number of so-called "half-caste" peoples.[10] After visiting Broome in 1902, Senator Staniforth Smith described it as the "most heterogeneous collection of nations, creeds, languages, and race I ever saw." He described in stereotypes the "morose" Malays, the "placid" Chinese, the "sturdy" Japanese, the "ostentatious" Filipinos, and noted in the mix both Javanese and "Koepang boys."[11]

In terms of promoting the population policy of White Australia, the government's primary focus was on preventing the increase of a permanent mixed

Weighing pearl shell, Jolly's Depot, Darwin, 1910. Northern Territory Library PH0238-0181, Peter Spillet Collection.

Packing pearl shell at Darwin, 1927. State Library of Western Australia 304484PD.
Sourced from the collections of the State Library of Western Australia and reproduced
with the permission of the Library Board of Western Australia.

descent population. Most prominent was the policy of separating the Asian population from the Aboriginal population. This color line was policed at every level
of contact, from employment to socializing to sexual relations.[12] Despite the rhet-
oric of "Australia for the white man," in Darwin the separation of the white population from the non-white population was not the subject of strict regulation at
the Commonwealth government level. It was more a matter of local government
and everyday social practices enforced by those among the white population who
believed in White Australia. A third element of segregation, which arguably had
nothing to do with official regulations, came out of the rifts that occurred between
the different Asian communities.

Segregation

The early 1920s was arguably the high point in demands from the local white population for segregation. In 1923, 101 Broome residents signed a petition calling
for "the absolute segregation of all Asiatics and Aboriginal natives and/or half-
castes from the white community," citing their reasons as moral, hygienic, and
consistent with "our ideas of a pure race."[13] Accounts of the history of Broome put
the white pearling masters at the center of the town, and it is clear that they were

constantly working to maintain that centrality, with segregation being a main-stay of their power.

Sam Male, who bought out the Streeter interest in the former powerful pearl-ing partnership, Streeter & Male, also owned the major local store and large cat-tle stations, and was chairman and president of the local Roads Board and Shire, as well as a leading light of the Broome Turf Club. Male's uncle, Archie, had succeeded Sam's father, Arthur, as member for The Kimberley in the Western Aus-tralian state parliament, and Archie was also mayor of Broome for a while, as well as honorary consul of Japan.[14] Arthur Male, as a member of the Liberal Party, had resisted Asian immigration—except for diver indenture. He had also exported cattle to Java.[15] The pearlers certainly had the support of various levels of govern-ment in their endeavors, and perhaps Idriess's appeals were at work as well, since in 1938–1939 the Commonwealth and Western Australian state governments each gave £5,300 in grants to the Broome pearlers, supplementing larger loans.[16]

The local power order was reflected in Broome's famous outdoor Sun Picture Theater, where the pearling masters, along with government officials and magis-trates, sat "comfortably" in the middle of the cinema in cane chairs, with the Asians, divided into different groups in the front, and "Blacks in the back."[17] In Broome, the Knight picture show catered to a smaller Aboriginal population, and also a Japanese and Malay population of some four hundred during the wet season. This cinema also had a central section that was set aside exclusively for white patrons.[18]

Similarly, in the small town of Darwin, the cinema was a special twice-weekly event and all the residents gathered for the show. C. Price Conigrave's 1936 ac-count of Darwin commented that the Japanese divers attending the cinema, "as the most important persons in the local pearling industry[,] hold aloof, with a touch of arrogant disdain, from all save their own countrymen."[19] Conigrave omits to mention that the seating inside the cinema itself was designed to facilitate segre-gation, particularly for white people. The Star cinema, operated by Tom Harris, had an upstairs dress circle for white patrons, while downstairs was divided into a front section for Aboriginal people and a back section "mainly for Chinese, Japa-nese, Malays and half-castes." On Thursday Island, the Europeans were seated while the "natives" were described as squatting on the ground in the front.[20]

Each of the pearling areas had their own "Asiatic" quarters, but this segrega-tion worked in different ways. The pearling workers of Darwin lived in camps in Frances Bay, close to the pearling luggers. Many of the resident Chinese, "Malay," and Filipino population who had lived centrally in Chinatown up until 1913 were moved further outside of town to "Police Paddock" (now Stuart Park) when the authorities demolished some portions of Chinatown. Police Paddock soon became

An audience at the Sun Picture Gardens, Broome, ca. 1920. State Library of Western Australia 100816. Sourced from the collections of the State Library of Western Australia and reproduced with the permission of the Library Board of Western Australia.

known as the mixed area where Malay was an important lingua franca for Southeast Asians and Aboriginal people alike. Both areas were separate from Chinatown and the Kahlin Compound, which had been established in 1912 to house the local Larrakia people and as well as other Indigenous people.[21]

Both Thursday Island and Badu (Mulgrave) Island in the Torres Strait had their own "Malaytowns," and farther south, Cairns in Queensland also had one.[22] The Cairns "Malaytown," which had a population of about fifty men and five women, was destroyed in 1904 by health authorities after fears of an epidemic, but it was quickly rebuilt.[23] Australian artist Donald Friend lived there with the family of Charlie Sailor in the 1930s. Returning in 1940, Friend produced a number of paintings, including a portrait of Charlie Sailor and a vivid image of Malaytown as a series of ramshackle stilt houses, Malay style, with people in Muslim turbans and long shirts loitering in the streets. Friend was deeply impressed with the "joy of life" he found there, with the sensuous and exotic lifestyle of those who worked the luggers and lived outside the constrictions of white society.[24]

In Broome the argument for segregation come from the view that the pearling crews were a dangerous element, a sentiment inspired by a number of so-called race riots. Historian Christine Choo noted that it was Japanese attitudes of superiority toward "the Malays, Manilamen and Koepangers" that fueled antagonism, which eventually flared up in riots during 1914, 1920, and 1921.[25] According to a government report, at the beginning of 1914, some 250 men from Kupang were brought in to replace Japanese workers. It was alleged that the Japanese had treated the new Indonesian crews very badly during their time at sea. In December 1914, tensions between the eastern Indonesians and Japanese who had arrived in Broome for the lay-up period erupted in rioting. Many hundreds of men were said to have been involved in skirmishes, armed with knives and axes, and several men were hospitalized.[26]

There was also an incident between the "Malays" and the "Ambonese"—referring to men recruited from the island of Ambon in Maluku—in January 1920. At this time there were an estimated 1,500 Japanese, 400 Malays, 300 Koepangers, and 150 Ambonese in Broome.[27] Inspector Drewry of the Broome police sent a telegram to the Western Australia commissioner of police, explaining that on Saturday evening, the "differences which existed between the Malays and the Ambonese came to a head, with tragic results. A Malay, Ahmat Bin Bakar, was clubbed and stabbed to death, and another Malay was shot in the thigh, but the wound was not serious. On Sunday a crowd assembled in anticipation of further fighting, but returned soldiers and civilians disarmed them. The heads of both factions held a conference at 7 p.m. and subsequently peace was declared at the police station, in the presence of nearly all the disaffected Asiatics."[28]

For most of January 1920 Broome was in the grip of a heat wave and many blamed this extreme heat and humidity for the increase in violence. The newspaper reported one incident, stating that "a Boutonese Malay went mad, and although he was handcuffed and tied up, he threw Constable Green and Pearler Naylour out of the motor car in which he was being taken to the police station."[29]

In the hot season at the end of the same year, a fight broke out on December 21 between Japanese and Koepangers and then escalated into a riot that continued over several days. A Japanese man was arrested the next day after having allegedly advised Malays to wear a white arm-band to distinguish them from the Koepangers. He had told the Malays that the Japanese intended "cleaning up" the Koepangers that night. The authorities responded by locking up the Koepangers in a goods shed, cutting off telephone lines to Japanese stores and the Japanese Club, and sending out returned soldiers (veterans) to patrol the streets. The next day, the newspapers reported that some 500 men were to be deported on the steamship *Minderoo*, but on Christmas Day, they reported that the HMAS *Geranium* was on its way to Broome. At the end of the affair, there were two Japanese dead and several Koepangers badly wounded. Police Inspector Thomas, who had been in charge of keeping the peace in Broome, died of "apoplexy" on New Year's Eve, apparently brought on by heat and stress.[30]

The overall attitude reflected in the reporting of this incident was that the local white population was sympathetic to the eastern Indonesians, who were portrayed as victims and fearful of the numerical strength of the Japanese. Of course, not all the Japanese residents in Broome were involved in the rioting. Murakami Yasukichi, a well-educated and respected resident of Broome, was one of those who tried to quell the violence.[31]

The widespread unrest among pearling crews across northern Australia at this time indicates how strong the networks of workers were in the region. In October 1920, Reg Hockings, owner of the Wanetta Pearling Company and resident of Buton and the Torres Strait, informed police that there was "trouble brewing" between his Japanese and Malay crew laid up on Badu and Thursday Islands, and that the Japanese were refusing to work with the Southeast Asians.[32]

Ion Idriess drew on clashes between "Malays" and "Koepangers" in Broome in his description of a near riot at the Continental Hotel in 1933. On the edge of a monsoonal downpour, "seven hundred Koepangers were sullenly fashioning clubs, working up to a big fight against the Malays," but the breaking of the rains and the work of the local police, led by Sergeant Clements and Inspector Tuohy, averted the fight by ensuring that the "aggrieved" Koepangers could take their leave after two years' service.[33] Idriess makes it clear that such fights came about over claims to valuable pearls, accusations of theft, the economic squeeze of a lay-off period during the Depression when prices of pearls and pearl shell had fallen, and religious differences "amongst the Buddhists and Mohammedans."[34] The 1920 clashes also came during an economic downturn.

Given that the "Malays" and "Koepangers" were culturally very similar and that these groupings were artificial, it is likely that internal fights among the Southeast Asians were either economically motivated or went back to clan patterns of enmity and alliance at home of which the European commentators were entirely ignorant. As mentioned in the previous chapter, fights were also common on the Aru side of the frontier. As the example of a mass battle between people from Buton and Makassar in Aru in 1916 shows, such fights may sometimes have been linked to old feuds between different ethnic groups. Traditional patterns of alliance meant that other groups probably felt obliged to join in.

Idriess's description of Broome is very much one of color separation. While there was a general "Asiatic town" in which "Malays," "Koepangers" and "Amboiners" mixed in a friendly fashion, these groups were in competition with the "Manilamen," and the combined Southeast Asians groups were competing with the Japanese for the most lucrative position, that of diver. It appears that Japanese attempts to monopolize diving were at the heart of the clashes of the 1920s involving them.

Revisionist historian Keith Windschuttle, in his account of the conflicts, uncritically accepts the categories of "race" coming from the documents, while at the same time dismissing an argument by Michael Shaper that the pearling masters engineered antagonism as a means of labor price control. Yet we have seen in the previous chapters how much the pearling owners worked together to keep down labor costs.[35]

The Position of the Japanese

On Thursday Island there was also evidence that Chinese and Japanese children were treated quite differently from those of Malays and Filipinos. In their study of racial hierarchy in Thursday Island, Anna Shnukal and Guy Ramsay note that from the 1920s onwards, "Chinese and Japanese children generally attended the 'White school,' whereas the children of Malays and Filipinos who were not educated at the convent school attended the 'Coloured school' along with children of Indigenous descent."[36]

The Japanese population of Darwin fluctuated according to the relative success of the pearling industry. There had been 77 male and 4 female Japanese living in Darwin in 1911, but by 1921 there were only 33 men and 3 women.[37] When the pearling industry expanded in 1928, however, there were 96 Japanese. The male adult population increased steadily and by 1937, there were 144.[38] Almost all of these were involved in the pearling industry, although several businesses, including a photographic and a lemon-squash shop, were operated by Japanese. These were located in Cavenagh Street, the old Chinatown of central Darwin.

In 1928, the Customs Office in Darwin asked the Commonwealth Department of Home and Territories if it would be appropriate for a Japanese to rent a house and establish a home in Cavenagh Street. Sub-Collector Pierce wrote, "The question has been raised as to whether or not indentured labourers are permitted to live in the town, or whether they are restricted to the foreshore when in port. It is claimed by one master pearler that in Broome and Thursday Island, Japanese indents are permitted to live in the town whilst Koepangers and Malays are restricted to the foreshore."[39] The decision to allow the Japanese to live in the town center remained in place until World War II. In 1936, for example, a diver by the name of Saka stated that he lived in the town center behind the shop of Murakami, the photographer.[40]

The Japanese who lived in Broome were associated mainly with diving, but others had come at the beginning of the twentieth century to set up stores. For a while Broome even had its own soy sauce factory. Suzuki Tadashi was Broome's only medical doctor for much of the early twentieth-century pearling period, and entrepreneurs such as Murakami Yasukichi from Wakayama Prefecture enjoyed success during this time.[41] Broome's Japanese community created its own separate social life around the Japanese Club. Because Japanese divers had come largely from the same area of Japan, this club furthered their group solidarity, which in turn gave them a strong bargaining position with the pearlers. The pearlers' main response was to try to mix crews on luggers as much as possible,[42] but the negotiations were part of a delicate balance.

Nevertheless, in Broome, the Chinese and Japanese communities were not really apart, since the so-called quarters were side by side around Sheba Lane in what was really a very small town. The pioneers of Japanese migration to Australia and Southeast Asia had been the women who risked great danger to come over as *karayuki-san,* working in the brothels of the mining and pearling towns in northern and central Australia.[43] The Japanese brothels in Broome were situated in the same area as the Chinese shops, while the Indonesian pearling workers lived a short walk away, down by the jetty. The Asian area of Broome was quite mixed. Here also the successful Ceylonese jeweler and pearl valuer Thomas Bastian Ellies had his business and residence. The fact that Ellies had family links to other Ceylonese on Thursday Island demonstrates how the multiethnic networks operated across the whole region.[44] Only the white pearling masters in their bungalows lived away from this area. The clearest legacy of the links between the Chinese and Japanese was the famous store-keeper, John Chi, after whom a famous Broome shopping lane is now named. He married Yamamoto Yae from Amakusi Island, and their family has continued to play a significant role in Broome up until the present day. Their grandson Jimmy Chi, also of Aboriginal heritage, is the author of the widely acclaimed Australian play and movie *Bran Nue Dae.*[45]

Overriding Segregation

One of the arguments for allowing the Japanese freedom within Darwin was that divers preferred to live and socialize there and thus were less likely to work offshore with Dutch or Japanese competitors. Welsh-born pearling master, Captain Ancell Gregory, writing for the Darwin Pearler's Committee, explained that with eighty Japanese-owned boats operating near Darwin, the drain on skilled divers was keenly felt. He argued that "the only reason we have been able to keep the divers we have, is that the conditions of working out of Darwin are much easier than those on the Japanese fleet, because they come into port oftener, are able to get fresh meat and provisions and also to be ashore for a few days each month, whereas the Japanese boats stay afloat for months, being tendered by schooners and they scarcely ever get on shore."[46]

This was another period of upswing: in 1936, the pearling industry produced an estimated gross value of £88,000.[47] The power of money was evidently capable of overriding the segregationist push of White Australia. The *Northern Standard* reported, "Practically the whole of the pearling fleets cleared the harbour last week for the new patch. . . . Cavenagh Street appears deserted without the crews of coloured men that have been a feature of the town during the lay up season. Business people will miss these men for though the crews are poorly paid they were seldom without cash for amusement."[48]

The area of Chinatown in Darwin was a place of mixed socializing. In 1936, for example, when the police raided a gambling game, they found six Japanese, two Chinese, and one European playing, with one "Malay" and two "colored" men watching.[49] A Japanese man owned the gambling house. The raid does not speak well for police relationships with the Japanese, but the mixed crowd at the gambling table suggests that not all entertainment was racially segregated.[50]

The Indonesians living in Darwin also enjoyed a degree of freedom that would not have been available to them in the Netherlands East Indies. Sergeant Koop, the local police officer, complained in 1936 of the lack of control over indentured aliens:

> The Malay and Koepang divers and crews freely patronise the hotels and become very arrogant and uppish towards other members of the civilian community. It is almost certain that serious affrays will eventuate unless steps are taken to curtail the freedom of the Malay and Koepang indents and to keep them out of the town. During the last week a group of Malays came into conflict with two white men and, it is reported, an ugly clash was narrowly averted. On Friday evening last, Cavenagh Street was crowded by bands of Malays and others who were in an excited condition and who had to be forcibly pushed off the footpath and street corners, by me, to permit women and others to pass along the street. . . . I am strongly of the opinion that Compounds, for the housing of these indentured labourers, should be established and that they be only allowed in the streets by permits.[51]

At the time, there were eighty-nine Malay and Koepangers employed in the pearling industry.[52]

Jack McDonald, secretary of the NAWU, the same union that had been defending the rights of individual Indonesian workers, was scathing in his criticism of the indentured pearling crews:

> For years Darwin had been wide open for Koepangers, Malays, Maccassars, Aroe Islanders, Japanese or other races of coloured people, and no steps have ever been taken by the Customs or Fisheries Departments to

prevent them taking up their residence anywhere they care to in the town. After having strutted the streets and swaggered out and in the pub bars, they are at liberty to visit the homes of the half-castes without any hindrance by the police or any other authority. There is what can only be described as a barracks for Asiatics near the foot of Cavenagh Street, and it was well known to every resident that half caste women nightly visited this den. There is another such place at what is known as the "Stone Houses" in the same street, and every night one can see groups of men from the pearling fleets congregating there, along with the coloured girls from the town.[53]

Again in 1938, an unnamed union commentator complained that there was not sufficient segregation of "colored" workers. The columnist wrote, "There is far too much latitude allowed to coloured races in Darwin, and this does not only apply to aboriginals. There is a barracks in Cavenagh Street for indentured coloured pearlers, and they are allowed to roll about to the public gaze in an almost naked condition. There is another large crowd of Malays housed in a shell shed near the Daly Street bridge, and just what arrangements have been made for them to comply with the housing conditions which are made compulsory for whites, it is hard to say."[54] It is not altogether clear why the NAWU officials felt it their duty to protect public morals. Most were married men and strict Roman Catholics, so perhaps they disapproved of promiscuity in general, but this was a time when allegations of immorality seemed aimed at Aboriginal and Asian relationships in particular.

The Despite the apparent antagonism of unionists toward the freedom of "Malays," the NAWU was supportive of their involvement in Darwin's sporting life. In 1936, the union helped to promote an "international" soccer game in which the Singapore luggermen challenged their Aru Island equivalents. To be specific, though, it was not McDonald who supported the match, but the president of the NAWU, Bob Murray. Murray, unlike McDonald, had spent his life in Darwin and had been involved in the 1927 union protest against segregated sport. We cannot assume that all union members thought alike on matters of "race."

The game was played on Saturday afternoon on the Darwin Oval. The *Northern Standard* advised that the proceeds of the match were to be given to the hospital and invited those "interested in good clean sport" to come along.[55] The newspaper report of the match stated that attendance "was somewhat disappointing." It named Abraham and Thomas as being goal-kickers for the winning Aru Island team and Lemon for the Singaporeans. It also noted that Sale, as goalkeeper for the Aru Island team, "saved the day for his team." The teams reported that they hoped to have other matches when they returned from their season on the Aru Island pearling grounds.[56] The significance of this game goes far beyond the mere promotion of sport. The game was reported in the same fashion as the usual games in Darwin, and, as a result all of Darwin read the names of the individual luggermen. Where before they had been labeled "coolies" or "indents" and known only by their nationality and occupation, now they were named as "goal-kickers" and "goal-keepers." These were honorable positions in the eyes of local Darwin residents.

More soccer games were held the following year, and this time all the team members were listed by the *Northern Standard*. Most players gave only their Dutch Christian names, indicating the degree to which the Dutch colonial administration had encouraged assimilation. None of the players had names of obviously Muslim Malay origin, and clearly some would have been from northern Maluku where there was an established Christian community.[57] Finally a match was organized between a local Darwin team (comprised of white and "colored" locals) and the "Koepangers." Rather appropriately, well-known sporting figure "Put" Ah Mat, of Malay–Thursday Islander descent, was chosen as the referee. One of the Darwin players was policeman Fred Don, who worked alongside Sergeant Koop; Don's participation suggests that he did not share Koop's segregationist attitude.[58] The Darwin team won the match, and the newspaper commentator wrote: "The little Koepangers played pretty football, and did very well to hold the heavy Australian team to one goal."[59]

These tentative signs of inter-ethnic cooperation elicited a negative response from the Dutch colonial authorities, since in the Netherlands East Indies such interaction was regarded as subversive to their colonial rule. In February 1937, a complaint was received from a Dobo correspondent, probably the Celebes Trading Company's Charles Richard Sheldon, indicating that the Dutch administration disapproved of the freedom allowed to Aru Islanders in Darwin. It was suggested that the Australian government should take action to regulate the behavior of indents, especially to prevent them from entering hotels. The correspondent noted with approval that the Dutch at least knew how to "manage and administer their native population." Commenting on the difference between the Dutch and Australian systems, he argued that

The Dutch Government view with alarm and concern, the attitude, and the big ideas, some of the local natives (Indents) adopt when they return on completion of their term in Darwin. If the Australian Government does not feel disposed to stop the Indents from entering hotels, and take some action to regulate their behaviour in and around Darwin, the Master

Pearlers may wake up one morning and find that it is forbidden to recruit Indents from these parts.

There is one thing you must admire and take your hat off to and that is the way the Dutch Government manage and administer their native population, and in this country, it does not matter what position in life a white man holds—he is always a "Toean" and is respected as such, and it is to be hoped that those "Whitemen" of Darwin who mix and associate with the native indents, will try and uphold their prestige as a white man, and not forget that Australia is proud of her "White Australia."[60]

From the perspective of Dobo, Darwin appeared as a wayward, egalitarian society with little regard for the "proper" enforcement of "racial" hierarchy.

Broome, Darwin, and Thursday Island were like colonial Southeast Asia in their social structure, with a small white community supported by a white government attempting to separate and manage the multiplicity of ethnic groups among whom they resided. The mixed communities that became established during the early years of the twentieth century demonstrate that the ongoing legacy of the decision to allow Asian labor to be imported into the northern pearl-shell industry ran counter to the aims of the White Australia policy, but could not easily be aligned with the strict orders that colonial powers such as the Dutch were attempting to establish.

Asian-Aboriginal Relations

The most marked test of the boundaries of "race" in the northern pearling industry was the relationship between Southeast Asian indentured laborers and local Aboriginal peoples, as the story of Abdoel Gafoer's relationship with an Aboriginal woman and his integration into the Yaruwu community indicates. These were relationships that created a strong set of "creole" communities, but these communities were set up despite the aims of government officials and local white power holders. As in colonial societies such as Singapore, a government "Chief Protector" was appointed for the Aboriginal population. One of the Western Australian officials in this position stated of his role in intervening in personal relationships: "native women are not so much immoral as amoral, and therefore it must surely be our duty to protect them from themselves."[61]

When Indonesian worker A. R. Nasoetion came to Broome in the 1920s, the most obvious fact of frontier life was the lack of women. The only ones he saw were Aboriginal women and wives of the white men. He was permitted to view local Aboriginal ceremonies, and described a marriage and the ceremonial scarring that accompanied coming-of-age rites. He apologized to his readers for the description of how easy it was to obtain Aboriginal women, but then noted that "if one wants to take one of their women, that is an honor for them, as long as there is no deception involved."[62] Despite the inherent dangers of cultural misinterpretation, such connections could and did lead to permanent marriages, even if white law did not recognize them.

Indonesian-indigenous families were prominent in Thursday Island life, but throughout this period officials described such relationships as illegitimate. An official 1930 report spoke of "Malays" as "indolent and . . . , in nearly every case, . . . living clandestinely with coloured women."[63] If the relationships were viewed as illegitimate, it was because the government had denied permission for mixed marriages. Ahwang Dai, a Dayak from Borneo (but it is not clear whether from the Dutch or British side), came from Singapore to the Torres Straits in the 1880s and in 1891 married Annie, a Badu Island girl with whom he had eleven children. In 1904, Torres Strait Islanders were classified as Aboriginal and the children of Asians and Torres Strait Islanders were classed as "half-caste" if they lived with or "habitually associated with" Aborigines and Torres Strait Islanders. In order to avoid being classed as "half-caste" and subject to the restrictions imposed on Aboriginal people, Asian–Torres Strait Islander families moved to Thursday Island. There they became disconnected from their Indigenous families, who were not permitted to move to the island under new legislation aimed at segregating Asians from Indigenous people.[64] Atima, the daughter of Ahwang Dai and Annie, applied for permission to marry a Malay man in 1914, but was refused by the Protector of Aborigines, William Lee-Bryce. Instead the couple was married in "Malay fashion" with the backing of pearling master Reg Hockings. What followed was a lengthy attempt by the local protector to control Atima. The other daughters also married Indonesians, and among their descendants are the Ah Mats, a distinguished family both in Torres Strait and Darwin, whose other ancestors came from Pontianak.[65] In another case, Cissie Malay, who was "designated as a half-caste Aboriginal woman and under the age of 21" was also forbidden to marry when Drummond Sarawak (his suggesting that he came from Raja Brooke's part of Borneo and may also have been a Dayak) applied for permission in 1916.[66]

Cases from Broome give clear examples of what was happening in these relationships. The Indonesians and local Aboriginal peoples had originally worked side by side on the luggers, although the latter were displaced in the working hierarchy with the influx of Japanese divers. Nevertheless, the two groups continued to mix in the semipermanent camps along the tidal creeks. These Aboriginal camps were allowed to stay because they were convenient sources of casual labor for pastoralists.[67] In the case of Karajarri people, who were the subject of Sarah Yu's oral histories, there was a clear exchange relationship going on in these camps.

The Karajarri saw themselves as summoning up Asian trading partners through the intercession of serpent spirits. These trading partners then exchanged alcohol and other modern commodities for women.[68] From the point of view of the Indonesians, such arrangements would have been very familiar. The serpent spirits would not have been so different from their own *naga* spirits, and the exchanges of magically charged goods to create marital relationships were part of the usual structure of clan ties experienced all over the archipelago.

Anthropologist Jeremy Beckett suggests something similar for the Torres Strait: that intermarriage between Asian pearl-shell workers and indigenous women had a marked impact on Torres Strait society. The Asian men "introduced marriage payments in the form of cash and manufactured goods," which in turn forced Torres Strait Islander men to offer matching payments if they wished to have a wife.[69] This type of hybrid exchange economy was unintelligible to the white Australian authorities, who interpreted it as contrary to Christian morality, and thus repudiated the marriages that were created.

Other kinds of mixed communities besides the Indonesian-Aboriginal ones were created either by relations in the pearling industry or by connections in other working environments, such as on the cattle stations outside Broome and Darwin, and in the missions. These communities included Japanese-Aboriginal and Chinese-Aboriginal marriages.[70]

For the Aboriginal people of Broome, the community that was created from these relationships has endured. The Indonesians provided access to modern technologies and commodities that the white community wanted to deny Aboriginal people. Those who could remember the earlier form of the community, such as old Broome resident Philip Dolby, recalled the *kroncong* music of the archipelago as part of their lives, along with curries made with chilies and *blancan* (shrimp paste, also known as *terasi*), which was the staple of the luggers' rice meals. As Dolby wrote,

> We used to go for kerosene from old Yusef. He had a restaurant, curry and rice, steak and eggs, long soup. We were going to Yusef's place, opposite Tang Wei's. Used to be Japanese quarters, then Malay quarters. When we used to go past to the shop, old man Sarrip, on the verandah on top, he used to play his ukulele. The music used to be beautiful, Malay songs. Just like serenading the people as they walked into town.
>
> Every evening, you could smell the *sate* cooking and that lovely smell in the smoke from the lemon grass, which they brush the oil with.[71]

Dolby's account makes it clear that, particularly when World War II came, people moved in and out of Indonesian, Chinese, and Japanese houses, and that there was mutual respect within this creole Asian Aboriginal culture. While Yu recognizes the histories of conflict within Broome communities, she evokes a strong sense of a new society being formed and challenging the authorities' categories of racial communities and "half castes." This was a society formed in the shadow of government "protection," and which had to find ways to evade or obstruct the elaborate legal regimes that were meant to control them in the name of "welfare."

The communities also faced another challenge with the coming of World War II. Already events in China, especially the Japanese invasion of 1937, had led to a split between the Chinese and Japanese in Australia. In Darwin, for example the local newspaper *Northern Standard* reported that, "the local Chinese have evidently decided to have no dealings with Japanese and to boycott all functions they may be associated with. . . . [W]hen the Japanese endeavoured to hire four Chinese waiter boys for a reception to the Press, held at the Japanese Club House on Tuesday, they were advised not one was available."[72] Japanese were to be later interred, although some went back to Japan or moved elsewhere in Asia before the outbreak of war.[73] But the fact that Broome and Darwin were on the front line of the Japanese advance in 1942 meant that large parts of the populations there were relocated. For Indonesians, the war presented a new role as Australian allies, the chance to move south of the twenty-second parallel, and the possibility of freedom from the segregation imposed on them by their role in the pearl-shell industry.

CHAPTER SEVEN

War on the Pearl Frontier

The entry of Japan into World War II in 1941 dramatically affected the pearling world of northern Australia and eastern Indonesia. The takeover by the Japanese Navy of eastern Indonesia ended the Australian presence in Indonesian waters. In northern Australia, war caused the evacuation and a temporary halt to all pearling. More importantly, the social world of the prewar pearling communities was shattered, and the ambivalent relationship of the pearling workers to Australian government authorities was made even more complicated.

The war broke up the communities of the north, in some cases forcibly, and many of the Indonesians were relocated far to the south. After a stint back in Indonesia, long-term worker Abdoel Gafoer had only just returned to Broome the year before the war broke out. He had travelled from Kupang on the *SS Gorgon* to work as a tender for Robinson & Norman and was one of the few who stayed in Broome when the industry otherwise shut down. He lived off fishing, supplying food to servicemen stationed in the town. Some of his fellow workers found new work and new relationships in places such as Melbourne, while others were conscripted into the fight against the Japanese. This chapter looks at the effects of wartime dislocation, including the role of the pearling indents in the struggle against the Japanese.

Japanese Internment, December 1941

On December 8, 1941 (December 7 in the United States), the news was delivered to the Australian prime minister, John Curtin, that the Japanese Navy had attacked Pearl Harbor on Oahu, Hawai'i. He lost no time in making a formal declaration of war on Japan. The Japanese consul-general to Australia, Itsuo Goto, claimed to have had no warning of the planned attacks and expressed the hope that Australia and Japan would not go to war.[1] But as news came in of Japanese attacks on British Malaya, Singapore, and the Philippines, it became clear that war was unavoidable.[2]

The first element of the break-up of the old communities of the north was the removal of everyone of Japanese descent. With the Japanese declared to be enemy aliens, all Japanese civilians, including those who were naturalized and Australia-born, were rounded up and placed in internment camps for the duration of the war. Among these were the pearling indents from Broome, Darwin, and Thursday Island. In Darwin, the government patrol vessel *Larrakia* was sent out after the lugger *Donna Matilda* in order to bring back its Japanese engineer. The *Larrakia* found this boat working off Melville Island and opened fire to ensure that it stopped.[3]

In Broome, there were some five hundred Japanese divers and crew. Master pearler Sam Male recalled going down to the beach to tell the gathered Japanese the bad news. They told him that they were not involved in the war, with one remarking: "Wrong man Boss in Japan." The Japanese men were initially locked up in the Broome jail, where, according to Male, they were on friendly terms with the Volunteer Defense Corps who had been put in charge of them.[4]

One hundred and ninety-nine people classified as "Japanese" were arrested in Broome, not including children. Of the twenty-nine women and children arrested in Broome for internment, all but one had either come to Australia before 1901 or been born in Australia.[5] The personal files of Japanese civilians who were interned are held in the National Archives of Australia and reveal something of the private lives of the Japanese pearling indents. Imura Yasukichi, a thirty-seven-year-old diver from Wakayama, was taken into custody on Thursday Island on December 13, 1941. He refused to sign the papers that declared him to be an enemy alien. His contract of indenture had been signed early in 1940, and he had been away from his wife, Yoshie, for almost two years. His subsequent internment in Hay, New South Wales, meant that he would not return to Japan until 1946. We do not know what happened on his return to Japan, but his file shows that he chose to return to Australia and continued in the pearling industry until 1958.[6]

Japanese internees were held in camps across Australia, including Loveday in South Australia, Camp 4 at Tatura in Victoria, and Cowra and Hay in New South Wales.[7] Among the internees of Tatura was well-known master pearler Jiro Muramatsu, who had built up extensive holdings in Darwin and Broome, and as we have seen in chapter 4, was involved in pearling between Darwin and Aru. His internment came despite the fact that he was a naturalized Australian. In 1943, while interned, Muramatsu died of pneumonia.[8] His wife, Hatsu, from Nagasaki, survived the war, but all their assets in Darwin had been confiscated and their house destroyed by Japanese bombing raids. When Hatsu returned to claim their Western Australian home, she found it had been looted. She went to the police station to make a report but changed her mind when she noticed that her husband's desk and other effects were being used by the police.[9]

The pearling masters were quick to protest the loss of their Japanese workers. On Thursday Island in December 1941, they agreed to bring in their luggers so that Japanese crew could be interned, but the luggers were soon sent back out to sea, this time manned by Torres Strait Islander crews along with the few Indonesians and other Asians available. John B. Marco, who was involved in pearling on Thursday Island, commented at the time that they hoped to be able to import more Indonesians in the next season to take over the diving, as was happening in Broome.[10] But there was to be no 1942 season. The war put an end to pearling for the next four years.

The Bombing of Darwin and Broome

February 19, 1942, has been described as "a day that will live in Australian history as the occasion of the first Japanese attack on Darwin."[11] The bombing of Pearl Harbor had caught the Americans largely by surprise, but the bombing of Darwin was anxiously anticipated, despite Darwin later being christened "Australia's Pearl Harbor."

The bombing of Pearl Harbor brought the United States into the war on the side of Britain, Australia, and the Netherlands' government-in-exile, to which the Netherlands East Indies remained loyal after the German invasion of the mother country. These countries made up the Allied forces in Southeast Asia, with the United States bringing Filipino colonial subjects to swell the forces. They initially attempted to create a line of defense across the archipelago from Singapore to Timor, including a U.S. base at Kupang. The month before Darwin was bombed, Japanese raids on the Netherlands East Indies targeted Kalimantan and Sulawesi, and the military moved southwards toward Kupang. The bombing raids intensified, leading the Americans to relocate their flying boat base at Kupang to the other side of the island. A destroyer was sent from Darwin on January 29, and nineteen Australian soldiers landed at Timor, setting up a new base there. The men found their task made almost impossible by the harsh jungle conditions and the threat of malaria. When they were eventually rescued, they were taken to Kupang, where they survived three Japanese bombing raids. The soldiers were flown from Kupang to Darwin and taken straight to the Royal Australian Air Force (RAAF) hospital, where they were to be admitted on February 19. Fortunately, their admission process had not been completed at the time the first wave of Japanese bombers flew over Darwin and destroyed the hospital with a direct hit.[12] In the chaos that ensued, it was difficult to estimate the total number of people killed on that day, but it greatly exceeded the royal commissioner's original 1942 estimate of 250 deaths.[13]

Plans to defend Timor were abandoned, and on March 2 the newspapers reported that Tokyo claimed to have occupied Kupang with land forces and naval parachutists.[14] Portuguese Timor remained neutral, despite the presence of Japanese troops allied to the Portuguese government. These troops exacted a heavy toll on the local population when they assisted the forays of Australian commandos into the region.

Beginning in February 1942, as the Allies fought the Battle of the Java Sea, the evacuation of people from the Netherlands East Indies took place. Just over 500 Dutch and 5,416 Indonesians were evacuated directly from the Netherlands East Indies; these were a combination of military and mainly Dutch civilians, although some of the Indonesians were political prisoners relocated to Australia. Many of these nearly 7,000 people passed through Broome on their way south. The soldiers would later join up with the Allied command led by General Douglas MacArthur, based in Melbourne, and then Brisbane. After the bombing of Darwin, the Japanese bombed Broome on March 3, 1942. One writer for the Melbourne *Argus* reminded readers of the unusual predominance of Asian residents in Broome, the headline reading: "No White Australia at Broome, Raiders May Have Been Residents."[15] During the first raid, flying boats in Broome harbor were targeted. Dutch women and children were killed in these flying boats as they sat in the harbor waiting to be evacuated to the south. There had been little chance to mount a defense as the raid was over in twenty minutes. Flight Lieutenant W. Winckel stood alone in a field with a tommy gun and shot down one of the Japanese Zero fighters, killing its pilot, Osamu Kudo.[16] In all, sixteen men, twelve women and twenty-five children lost their lives. Twenty-five Allied aircraft also were destroyed.[17] During a second raid on March 22, with no defenses left in Broome, the Zero fighter planes were able to fly low over dwellings. While there was considerable damage to houses, only one civilian was killed. By April 1942, Broome was described as a virtual "ghost town" with just a small male population remaining.[18]

Pearling Operations Cease

While the evacuation of Broome meant that those remaining were supposed to support essential services only, the Broome pearling industry did not shut down immediately, and as in Torres Strait, was maintained by Indonesian workers. But disaster was piled on disaster in April 1942: The coast was hit by one of the worst cyclones in recent experience. Elias Bin Baji Amat was in charge of the *Oberon,* and he bravely chose to ride out the storm. During the night all the cargo was swept away, the ship's mainmast was blown overboard, and the keel was damaged. His ship was eventually towed to shore by other luggers. William Kada, a thirty-five-year-old Indonesian, was in charge of the *Fleetwing,* but he and his crew were forced to abandon ship after losing both the mainmast and the foremast. He headed the ship toward the shore where it grounded on a reef and was smashed up. The crew managed to make it to shore on Eighty Mile Beach between Broome and Port Hedland, where they were rescued.[19]

By May, the pearling industry had completely shut down and much of the fleet that survived the cyclone was torched for fear of Japanese invasion. The authorities decided to remove the Indonesians from Broome. They had been housing sixty-five "Koepangers and Malays" in the Broome jail alongside a number of prisoners who had been charged with looting after Broome's township had been evacuated. The authorities were suspicious of all Asians: The Indonesians had been moved to the jail "to enable them to be kept under control."[20] Before the air raids, the Volunteer Defense Corps had been in charge of setting these Indonesians to work extending the Broome airport runway.[21] When the jail was closed down, these men were sent south to Melbourne. Abdoel Gafoer managed to avoid being caught up in this evacuation south, but it is not clear how he managed to remain in Broome, perhaps by living outside the township.

Melbourne, Victoria, where the separate Netherlands East Indies colonial government-in-exile had established administrative headquarters, was to become a home away from home for those considered to belong to what was now a former colony.[22] The Broome pearling workers were sent to join evacuees from the Dutch colony, together with other Indonesians based in Australia. On their arrival in Melbourne, the Indonesian pearling indents were initially housed at the Metropole Hotel in Bourke Street, just a short block away from Dutch headquarters in Collins Street. The shift from the rugged tropical north to an urban environment in the southern autumn must have been a shock for these men, who were largely left to fend for themselves.

The National Archives of Australia contain the personal files of twenty-seven of the men who were moved from Broome to Melbourne. Thomas Kato was one, a "Koepanger" employed by Streeter & Male as part of its lugger crew. Born in 1886, he was forty-six years old at the time of evacuation. His most recent two-year contract of indenture had seen him arrive in Broome on the MV *Centaur* on February 22, 1940. In September of 1941, in accordance with the National Security (Aliens Control) Regulation, he was forced to register his residence in Australia and provide a photograph and ten fingerprints. While sitting for the photograph, the number 276 was pinned to his shirt in the fashion of someone who had just been arrested. As part of the registration process, "aliens" were asked to sign a parole undertaking to "neither directly nor indirectly take any action in any way prejudicial to the safety of the British Empire during the present war." Aliens were also obliged to register any change of address. The message of not belonging was clear enough.

There is very little information on the lives of the Indonesians in Melbourne. The archival sources only tell us that some stayed in the Metropole while others moved around the city. For example, in 1944 Kato moved to take up residence at 72 King William Street in the inner-city suburb of Fitzroy, and in 1945 he moved again to live at a different house in the same suburb, this time at 221 Brunswick Street.[23] The files indicate Noladoe Toeloe, a forty-one-year-old Indonesian who had been working for Gregory and Company in Broome, and Taba Leba, who was to apply for Australian citizenship decades later, also lived in the Hotel Metropole before they too both moved to Fitzroy.[24] They were probably kept separate from the sixty-seven Indonesian refugees who had come directly from Indonesia to Port Melbourne by boat, and who were welcomed by members of Melbourne church groups.[25] According to the *Argus,* at the same time the Indonesians arrived in Melbourne, a Dutch club was opened at the Hotel Metropole. To cater for colonial tastes, it served Indonesian food for the men of the Netherlands East Indies Forces. The Dutch minister, Baron Aersen van Beyeren Voshol, who announced the opening of the canteen, explained that the club was staffed entirely by Indonesians. At least one of the pearling indents, Biri Riwu, originally from Savu, found himself required to work in the club, and others from northern Australia joined him there.[26]

The war period saw the temporary Indonesian population in Australia increase rapidly. For the Australian government, the Indonesians from Broome were in the same category as the Japanese internees and Indonesian political prisoners whom the Dutch brought with them, potentially hostile aliens, no matter how long they had worked and lived in Australia, or whether they had married there. Even those not regarded as potentially "dangerous" were subject to harsh treatment by Australian officialdom on the basis of their racial difference.

Indonesians from Thursday Island Evacuated South

The same fears of attack and potential invasion via "alien" penetration that caused the evacuations from Broome led the Australian government to order the evacuation of Thursday Island on January 24, 1942.[27] The evacuation ships made their way south to Cairns and the SS *Ormiston* disembarked a number of Aboriginal-Indonesian families. Afterwards there were claims of an adverse public reaction to the new "colored" arrivals. The army and the deputy director of Native Affairs, Cornelius O'Leary, decided to send the next shipment of approximately two hundred Thursday Island residents, including a number of Indonesians, on the *Katoora* and the *Britha* further south to the remote Cherbourg Aboriginal Settlement located 272 kilometers northwest of Brisbane.

Once at Cherbourg, the men were signed up to work in a range of manual labor jobs, including sugar-cane cutting, cotton picking, and cattle work. O'Leary was proud to announce in May 1942 that with the help of the Indonesian and other "colored" evacuees from Thursday Island, the Kingaroy peanut crop had been harvested. The men were paid a wage of £1 per day for their labor. He added that they were subsequently to be put to work picking cotton.[28]

While the Indonesian men were sent out to work, women and children were expected to remain in Cherbourg living in bleak dormitory accommodation. They were alone, cold, and unable to leave because they were now being treated as Aboriginal "wards" of the State of Queensland under the Aboriginal Protection Act. From 1911 to 1940, nearly six thousand Aboriginal people from across Queensland had been removed to settlements such as Cherbourg as part of an attempt to segregate the Aboriginal population. Their first experience of this regime was shocking to the families from Thursday Island.[29]

The Indonesian men did not take this incarceration without protest. Willem Dewis (also known as Olie Daybees) went to Cherbourg to try to get the Indonesians and their families released so that they could move to Brisbane. Dewis was born in Tepa, on Babar, in southern Maluku in 1893. His wife, Noressa, was born on Boigu Island in the Torres Strait.[30] They had seven children; another was to be born in 1945. Initially, Dewis did not understand the extent of O'Leary's power over them. O'Leary believed in racial segregation to an extent that was largely unfamiliar to Thursday Islanders. He condemned Dewis' attempt to "get every Malay to Brisbane" where, O'Leary argued, "they would become a menace to health and objectionable residents of any suburb."[31]

Dewis sought help from Police Sergeant Holly at Thursday Island. Living in Red Hill, Brisbane, Dewis wrote that they had been forced to go to Cherbourg, which he described as "not a nice place" and one "not for us because you know for yourself Sir how we lived up T.I. [Thursday Island]." He complained about the quality of the food, being given bread and jam but no butter. They were given meat every second day but no vegetables. He said he had complained to O'Leary but had been ignored. Dewis wrote that he did not wish the Department of Native Affairs to be in charge of them. To demonstrate the extent of their lack of personal freedom, he wrote that the families at Cherbourg had been split up, with husbands and wives sleeping apart in dormitories, and brothers and sisters also sleeping apart. He wrote that they "are like prisoners because they are not allowed to sit with their family and have their meals."[32] Historical accounts of the treatment of Aboriginal families in prewar Cherbourg confirm this inhumane system of family separation.[33]

But O'Leary was determined that the Thursday Island evacuees were not to leave Cherbourg. He wrote to the superintendent of Cherbourg stating that "Under no circumstances must any evacuee leave your Settlement without my permission." He expressed concern that the superintendent had given permission to Paolos Annidlah, stepfather of Sammy Lewin, to leave. Sammy Lewin had come to Brisbane and had been admitted to Wattlebrae Hospital suffering from typhoid fever, which he was presumed to have contracted at Cherbourg Settlement. The superintendent was ordered to arrange for inoculations immediately.[34] Typhoid fever is usually contracted from contaminated food or water and in this case was no doubt caused by the lack of proper sewerage facilities in Cherbourg Settlement.

Bora Bin Juda, originally from Makassar, was living at the Cherbourg Settlement with his wife, Mareja, and their four children. He worked there until he fractured his arm while breaking in a horse. In January 1943, Bin Juda left to look for work, but his wife remained at Cherbourg. He was subsequently employed in a range of short-term jobs: as a builder's laborer for £4 per week, as a sugar-cane cutter; and then in the Farleigh Sugar Mill for £5 per week. Later in 1943, Bin Juda went to Red Hill, Brisbane, and was employed by the Civil Construction Corps (CCC) on the New Dock at Bulimba for £15 per fortnight. He paid £1 per week to rent a house that he shared with his son, Saul Juda, who was then fifteen years old.[35]

While the men were able to leave Cherbourg to seek employment, it was another matter to get their wives and children out. The director of Native Affairs charged a fee for accommodation at Cherbourg of one shilling per person per day, payable by the husband. In the period from March to October 1942, the accommodation of one wife and six children was calculated as £64.1, or several months' wages. The men were sent letters demanding payment before their wives and children would be released. A poignant record of this troubled time was a telegram from Doseena Bin Garape to her husband, Assan Bin Garape, another Makassarese, stating: "Can't leave here unless you pay settlement, love Dos." In December 1942, Bin Garape, who was employed at the Mackay aerodrome, sent money for fares to Mackay and agreed to pay the rest of the money in installments. Dorseena was finally given approval to join her husband in Mackay that same month.[36]

Even for those Indonesian pearling workers who managed to avoid internment, the war years were very difficult, especially for those with large families. Hassan Bin Awel (or Awal), who was born in Ambon in 1893 (or 1896), was married to Saia Ah Wang, born on Badu Island in 1909. They were married in 1926 and had seven children. Before the war, Hassan was working on shore in a job connected with the pearling industry. During the war years, Hassan was moved around Queensland from Mackay to Chermside in February 1943 to work in the CCC camp. After one month, he was transferred to Tamborine for another five months. After that, he went on to Meeandah for a few months and then to the Banyo CCC to work for the Main Roads Commission. In January 1944, he was living with his wife and children in Kelvin Grove, Brisbane, adjacent to Red Hill. By the end of the year he had moved to Paddington, although he was still employed by the Banyo CCC. The government files that so carefully tracked his whereabouts have very little to say about the difficulties that his wife and children, two of them just babies, must have experienced during these years of constant moving. Hassan moved again to live in Red Hill in February 1947, where he was employed by the city council. The government then requested that he return to Thursday Island, where he worked until his retirement in 1956.[37] His story is typical for the Indonesians who were evacuated from Thursday Island.

Indonesian Internment

Escaping from Cherbourg did not mean that Indonesians were free from the surveillance of government, Australian and otherwise. Their status was ambiguous since the Allied government-in-exile of the Netherlands East Indies claimed sovereignty in relation to its subjects in Australia. It was able to exercise its powers over the Indonesians who had come down with Dutch forces, as well as the refugees who had escaped from Indonesia to Australia. The pearling workers and their families, however, were an uncertain category.[38] The case of Anima Ahmat, Saia's sister, illustrates this problematic status. On February 8, 1943, she had been released from Cherbourg, but was then "captured" in Mackay and interned at Gaythorne in Brisbane. There was nothing in the file to suggest that she could be regarded as a threat to national security. Her internment papers listed her place of birth as Badu Island in the Torres Strait. She was fifty years old, of Church of England religion, and her occupation was shown as "housewife." Her next of kin, her son Ali Ahmat, was also living in Mackay. She was subsequently released nearly six weeks later, on March 22, 1943.

The officers who processed her internment papers were well aware that she was Australian-born. They noted that she had grown up on Thursday Island, had been evacuated to Cherbourg Settlement, and had remained there for seven months. She had then moved to Brisbane and then Mackay for one month each before being detained.[39] Anima was not the only Thursday Island "Malay" woman to go from Cherbourg to internment. Leah Barba was only twenty-six in 1943 when she was captured, also in Mackay. May Woodhead was captured in Bundaberg after leaving Cherbourg.[40] Also captured at Bundaberg was Jena (Jean) Shibasaki, classified as "Malay," daughter of Seden and Hassan and wife of Kyukichi Shibasaki, who was interned in New South Wales. Jean had six children with Shibasaki; they were also interned in the Gaythorne Camp. Jean and her family were released on April 27, 1943.[41]

Indonesians were subject to a variety of regimes of incarceration, and the refugees from the Japanese invasion of the Netherlands East Indies were in some cases interned, while in others they were put to work in the same way as evacuees. The majority of the Indonesians who had come with the Dutch were merchant seamen and other sailors who were granted permission to remain in Australia given that their home was now under Japanese occupation. Some two thousand of these Indonesian seamen were not prepared to work under orders, and from April 1942, they began a series of strike actions. For these they were first fined and then jailed, before the Australian government, under pressure from the Dutch, had them rounded up and sent to internment camps. Some eight hundred were detained at the Prisoner of War Camp No. 12 at Cowra in New South Wales.[42]

In November 1942, the Dutch military authorities decreed that men refusing to rejoin their ships would be sent to Queensland to work in labor camps under military law. Two months later, men were released from Cowra and sent to camps at Blackbutt, Toowoomba, Helidon, and Wallangarra in Queensland as the Thirty-Sixth Australian Employment Company. These men were paid a wage of 6 shillings and 6 pence a day for their labor. Many continued to engage in strikes and other industrial action against their harsh conditions and low pay. In 1943, a large Dutch camp was established at Casino in New South Wales, where this time the residents were "loyal" Indonesian troops. The local people got to know the Indonesian forced workers and those in the Casino camp as "Javos," Javanese.[43] Despite the Indonesians introducing a fascinated local population to the beauties of *gamelan* music and traditional costumes, the New South Wales government was particularly worried about Indonesians mixing with Aboriginal people. There was also social rejection of this "alien" presence: The local Casino men resented the liaisons that developed between Indonesian soldiers and white women, and this sometimes led to brawls.[44]

Also interred in Cowra were Indonesian political prisoners, who were members of the nationalist movement, and their families. These prisoners were moved in 1943 from concentration camps in Boven Digul, Papua, where many of them had been incarcerated since their participation in abortive Communist uprisings of 1926–1927. Despite their being fervent anti-Fascists, the Dutch initially had the Indonesians detained in Cowra, along with Japanese prisoners of war, convincing the Australian government that the political radicals posed a threat. Eventually, pressure from Australian trade unions and civil rights groups led to their release, although it took until March 1945 for the "hard liners" to be freed.[45]

Military Service

Not all civilians were evacuated from the northern towns at the start of the war, and despite their treatment, many Indonesians demonstrated their loyalty to the Allied cause, if not to Australia. Some of these Indonesians were recruited into military operations both in Australia and overseas.

On Thursday Island, the Torres Strait Light Infantry Battalion included 830 Torres Strait Island men and forty Torres Strait "Malays," as well as mainland Aboriginal people. Initially, when the Battalion was formed in 1941, it was restricted to men of European ancestry. It was only later that Indigenous and Indonesian men were recruited. The 2nd Australian Water Transport Company was formed in 1943, with 108 personnel including Torres Strait Islanders, Aboriginals and Malays. This generic use of the term "Malays" encompassed Filipinos, Chinese, and people from the Malay Peninsula as well as Indonesians. Their roles were to guide RAAF water-craft and cargo boats through the dangerous waters of the Torres Strait, to rescue downed airmen, to gain advanced intelligence, and at times to directly attack the Japanese. One of these men, Walter Nona, recalled guiding American PT boats from Thursday Island to the Netherlands East Indies side of Papua in order to drop depth-charges onto Japanese submarines.[46]

The different classifications of northerners had a variety of implications. Indonesians in the Torres Strait Light Infantry Battalion were paid the same as non-Indigenous soldiers, but Aboriginal and Torres Strait Islander men were paid far less. In 1944, a military interdepartmental conference was held in Melbourne to address the question of wages, where Indonesian and Indigenous men were employed in the same area on different rates of pay. The outcome of the conference was that Torres Strait Islander soldiers' wages were increased, going up to 66 percent of white wages. The War Cabinet approved this raise on March 20, 1944. Simultaneously, the Indonesians in the battalion were transferred to other units.[47]

Some of the Indonesian pearling crews who were discharged from the Torres Strait Battalion later joined the Small Ships section of the United States Army Transport Service (USATS). One of them was forty-eight-year-old Torrikie Bin Hassan, originally from Ambon. Bin Hassan worked as part of Small Ships operations between Queensland and New Guinea for eighteen months before he was discharged in Townsville.[48] Another Indonesian to join Small Ships was fifty-six-year-old Tamsie Cassine from Timor.[49] However, not everyone was supportive of Indonesians having a role in USATS. The Brisbane collector of customs, James Fox, expressed concern that so many "colored" aliens had been allowed to join USATS and that without proper surveillance of them, he anticipated future difficulty in rounding them up in the postwar period.[50]

Behind Enemy Lines—Z Force

Torres Strait was only one of the front lines of the war in which those who had been involved in the pearling industry served. The Allied Intelligence Bureau was established by General MacArthur to coordinate intelligence-gathering in the

South West Pacific Area during the war. One of its sections was the Services Reconnaissance Department (SRD). The Netherlands East Indies military maintained a separate Netherlands East Indies Forces Intelligence Service (NEFIS), which was responsible for many dangerous operations in Indonesia, including one led by the Australian-based Ambonese Sergeant Julius Tahija, who was later to marry an Australian woman and become a leading businessman in independent Indonesia.[51]

The combined SRD and NEFIS activities attempted to bring in "those in professions from the Far East," which included a number of the Australians from eastern Indonesia. The managers for the Celebes Trading Company in Aru had already been providing reports on the area for the Australian public, particularly former World War I officer Charles Sheldon. As a consular agent in the late 1930s, Sheldon was sending reports back on Japanese activities.[52] His family moved to Dobo from their plantation on the small island of Babi, and from there, on February 13, 1942, Elizabeth Sheldon (Chum Jardine's sister) and her daughter, Pamela, were evacuated to Darwin, whence they were flown south. Charles Sheldon, Danish Australian Carl Monsted, and the Sheldon's Javanese employee, Wongso, hid all the valuables, killed the seven dogs, and evacuated to Merauke, Papua, and thence to Thursday Island.

Sheldon trained with the SRD and was promoted to captain, then major. He led two missions to Aru, Operation Walnut I and II. Walnut I included Carl Monsted's nephew, Niels, who had grown up with the Sheldons in Aru. However, Sheldon was betrayed by Aruese on Jambual Island, captured and interrogated, and then taken to Kei. From there he was brought to Ambon, where he was beheaded in August 1943 on the orders of Lieutenant-Colonel Sumizu Junichiro, along with two RAAF personnel and thirty Indonesians. Their executioner was volunteer chief prison guard, Wagatsuma Junzaburo. Others from Walnut II were executed a few days later. Niels Monsted subsequently led Walnut III, but was later killed in action.[53]

Sheldon's eighteen-year-old son, Chum Junior, had been working with the Dutch navy and was also captured in Ambon. With his mixed Samoan heritage and his fluency in Malay, he was able to pass as an Indonesian. In this guise, he managed to organize the escape of Australian prisoners and local resistance, but he too was captured by the Japanese and also beheaded.[54]

A similar fate was suffered by Robin Hilliard, who was taken prisoner by the Japanese on Flores when they invaded in 1942. In a story eerily similar to the Sheldon's story of the dog killing, Robin's son, George, not yet five years old, remembered the Japanese killing all the dogs in the family compound. George and his siblings fled to the hills, but Robin was suspected of having a radio, which was quite likely, and therefore of spying for the Allies. Thus, he was taken prisoner to

Makassar, where the Japanese later executed him. Robin's wife, Sara, was left with five small children to survive on the estate. The fact that George was granted Australian citizenship in 1948 was most likely in belated recognition by the Australian government of his father's role in providing intelligence.[55] Other siblings remained Indonesians.

The SRD became known as "Z Force," and was the forerunner of Australia's elite commando units, in particular the Special Air Service Regiment (SAS). One of the main Z Force training bases was Fraser Island, located along the southern coast of Queensland. Many of the Indonesians who were part of Z Force had been on the staff of the training camp.[56] White Z Force member Rowan Waddy says of his training at Fraser Island: "We learnt to speak Malay, we had Malays there and everywhere we went you had to be able to speak Malay."[57] Others were trained in jungle warfare on a property called "Fairview" (known as "the House on the Hill") in Cairns.[58]

In October 1942, the head of SRD, Lieutenant-Colonel G. E. Mott, asked to set up a base in Darwin. He established a top secret "Z" special base at the old quarantine station outside the city, where the unit maintained the small craft used for operations into occupied Netherlands East Indies. This unit included Dutch, Australian, and Indonesian soldiers who were to be deployed in dangerous operations behind enemy lines.[59] Personnel for the new base sent up from Melbourne included six Indonesians to work as crew on the luggers that would be used to navigate from Darwin to Timor. These were men, chosen from those "Koepangers" evacuated from Broome, went by the cover name of "Lugger Maintenance Station" While Indonesian workers were expected to join the war effort and to risk their lives, there remained the notion that as Dutch colonial subjects and as Australian indentured laborers, they were in a different category from European soldiers. Lieutenant Meynderts, who accompanied them from Melbourne, complained that the Indonesians had been "spoilt" by the easy life in Melbourne.[60]

Jack Wong Sue was one of the few non-European members of Z Force to have left an extensive document of his experiences. His loosely structured memoir offers a very different picture from many popular narratives, which give the impression that only white people joined Z Force. His story also challenges the official histories that maintain that "no distinction of race was permitted or ever crept in."[61] Sue, from a family of Chinese migrants to Perth, spent time behind the lines in Sabah (North Borneo). In particular, he was one of those sent behind enemy lines, where he observed Japanese atrocities, particularly the horrific Sandakan Death Marches. These were the forced movement of prisoners of war hundreds of kilometers from the coast to the rugged jungle interior, where nearly all were worked to death or were killed by the guards when unable to work. Sue's unit helped rescue the six survivors out of the 2,500 Allied prisoners who perished in the interior.[62]

The picture of Z Force that emerges from Sue's account is of a multiethnic group, and he knew well the young men from Broome and other pearling ports who were his comrades. He mentions Sargent Ma'aruf Bin Said, who had been recruited to Broome from Kupang and had trained with Sue at Fraser Island.[63] Bin Said took part in Agas I and II operations with Sue, as well as Operation Stallion on Sarawak. During a subsequent operation, Platypus VII, an insertion made in preparation for the Allied invasion of North Borneo, Bin Said's team was parachuted into the wrong area, he and two others were seen by the Japanese, and they were killed.[64]

Jack Wong Sue also refers to "one of the very popular Malays from Fraser Island, Ali Bin Salleh," as a participant in operations in Palawan.[65] Bin Salleh took part in Operation Squirrel involving a dangerous landing at Tarakan, Kalimantan, in a prelude to capturing the island from the Japanese. He and five others went into an area where there were 2,100 Japanese troops in order to gain intelligence, but the operation failed when their radio did not work.[66] He survived, and also took part in the Stallion and Platypus Operations in the first half of 1945.

The Indonesians were referred to at the time and in subsequent accounts as "Malays." Thus, in some of the popular accounts of Z Force activity, they are confused with the local indigenous Malay and Chinese groups with whom Z Force also worked.[67] One of the leaders of Z Force even boasted of not having lost any Europeans in Borneo operations, with only "light" loss of "native" life, despite the death of Ma'aruf bin Said and Corporal Mohammad Salim.[68] Salim, who was born in 1914 and was from Singapore, was captured and executed at Balikpapan during Operation Platypus XI.[69]

Other people from Indonesia and Malaysia who were field operatives were Corporal Abdul Samat Haji Omar; Ali Bin Amen, who took part in operations at Balikpapan, Kalimantan; Sargent Bahrom Bin Ali; and Samsudin Bin Katib, who had been backup in the Semut operations in the interior of Sabah and Sarawak. Sergeant The (or Teh) Soen Hin from Rote had been part of Semut II, along with Corporal Abu Kassim, originally from Beraung Ulu, now Malaysia.[70] The Soen Hin, originally a Broome pearling indent, had enlisted in Western Australia and from there had been sent to Fraser Island for training. He served a total of 250 days outside Australia.[71] According to one unverified source, The Soen Hin later won the Military Medal, but it is not recorded as part of his Australian service record.[72]

It was quite clear why the Indonesians and Sue were recruited: "By virtue of our oriental appearance, combined with our ability to speak the necessary languages that enabled us to act in a clandestine capacity, and masquerade as 'locals'

The Soen Hin in military uniform, 1939. National Archives of Australia B883 WX36793 5281593.

in Far Eastern countries, we were guaranteed rewards by our Australian Government 'if we survived the ordeal.'" As Sue goes on to say, however, "A number of Australian born orientals plus the loveable Malay Pearl divers, and those in professions from the Far East, did not survive. Captured by the Japanese, they were tortured to death while others survived torture, only to lose heads later to Japanese Samurai swordsmen."[73] Sue, no doubt traumatized by what he had witnessed in Sabah, was very bitter about the treatment of the Indonesians: "All were promised a home after the war, not one received one. Is it little wonder we feel cheated? A few of the Malay boys have since died almost poverty stricken, some unable to secure a pension."[74] The Soen Hin indeed later claimed that when he signed up, he had been promised naturalization and a house.[75]

By categorizing the "Malays" as foreigners helping Z Force, subsequent writers of historical accounts of their activities have been unwittingly complicit in their exclusion from being "Australian," thus perpetuating a White Australia view of the world. This exclusion was not helped by the fact that the secret nature of Z Force service meant that all soldiers were not publicly acknowledged until many years later. Worse still, not only was the service of the Broome Indonesian Z Force members not honored, but a number of them, including The Soen Hin, were threatened with deportation under White Australia regulations, as we will see in chapter 9.

At our 2010 public meeting in Broome, we met with the children of some of these war heroes. Abu Kassim's daughter, Georgia Dobson, drove all the way from Halls Creek, over seven hours away, to hear what we had to say and to ask for recognition for her father. With her was the daughter of Ali Bin Salleh, comrade-in-arms of Abu Kassim and "Tom The." Georgia Dobson told us that Abu Kassim had been a diver for Streeter & Male, and was buried at the Karakatta cemetery in Perth.[76] He died in the Repatriation Hospital in Perth in 1949 under threat of deportation.[77] These families were concerned that because the official records often involved false versions to cover up the intelligence work of their family members, there had been no real recognition of their service. It still remains for Australian government authorities to rectify this injustice.

By March 1945, the Japanese troops began to withdraw from the pearl frontier. Australian Brigadier Lewis Dyke accepted the official Japanese surrender in eastern Indonesia from Colonel Tatsuichi on September 11, 1945, on board the HMAS *Moresby* in the harbor of Kupang.[78] Not long after, the Dutch reasserted control over their part of the island; however, the process of returning troops to their respective homes took some time.[79] The calls for the pearling industry to be restarted began in that very month but it would take some time before recruitment of Asian labor resumed.

For some of the Indonesian pearling workers, it was a dangerous and difficult few years. For others, it was an opportunity to leave the confines of the pearling luggers and to venture out from the pearling ports. The war was a period when new friendships were made between Indonesians and Australians. In some cases these friendships went far beyond the limited range of association that was permitted by the restrictive indentured labor code. But at the end of the war, these freedoms were withdrawn and the pearling indents were recalled once more to the northern ports of Australia where their search for recognition within the Australian community was frustrated.

CHAPTER EIGHT

Disputed Borders on the Pearl Frontier

The period after World War II saw the northern part of Australia returned to its state of polyethnic diversity, albeit in a very changed political and social context. Australia had established its own foreign relations independent of Britain but was ambivalent about the new era of decolonization that gripped its region. Decolonization was to change both the shape of the pearl frontier and labor relations within the pearling industry.

Indonesians waged a revolution for independence from Dutch colonial rule beginning with Sukarno's proclamation of independence on August 17, 1945, just after the Japanese surrender. The Indonesians succeeded, and sovereignty was gained on December 27, 1949. During the course of that struggle, the Dutch had resumed control in eastern Indonesia, proclaiming in 1946 the Federal State of East Indonesia under the government of Balinese president, Tjokorde Raka Sukawati. It was not until August 17, 1950, that this State of East Indonesia was incorporated into the Indonesian Republic. Even then, the Dutch maintained authority over Dutch West New Guinea. The continued colonial presence chagrined the Indonesians, who argued that this part of Papua, designated by them as "Irian," should be part of their new republic. The pearl frontier was caught up in this political struggle, particularly when some in Maluku declared that they preferred to remain under the Dutch monarch. The Australian government had supported Indonesian independence, but also expressed a preference for the stability of the Dutch colonial order particularly in this case where Irian shared a land border with the Australian territory of Papua New Guinea.

In the Cold War context of new international relations, maritime boundaries were up for negotiation, as were fishing rights over the lucrative pearl beds. The Australian pearling industry realized that the old days of easy access to the pearling fields of eastern Indonesia were at an end as their access to Aru was cut off and Indonesians began to negotiate with Japanese pearlers. There were still hopes that the Australian pearling industry could continue to rely on imported labor from Kupang, but the pearling masters found that it was more difficult to operate on an indenture system in an era of decolonization. Men who were already working in Australia, such as Abdoel Gafoer, continued on their previous contracts. Nevertheless, they were still liable to deportation. Abdoel Gafoer moved from Broome to Darwin when the war finished to work for a smaller pearler, Ah Dep, but moved back to Broome in 1948, mainly to avoid being sent back to Kupang when Ah Dep went out of business. Gafoer was not affected directly by the larger political changes, but he was subject to the local effects of instability, manifested in changing economic circumstances and the fluctuations of the pearling industry.

Australia, which in the 1950s claimed to be a leader in international labor reform, continued to import indentured Asian labor for the pearl-shell industry until the early 1970s. In this chapter, we examine the complex relationship between Australia and independent Indonesia, which provided a new context for the last phase of indenture of pearling workers.

Australia Supporting Indonesian Independence

On a government-to-government level, Australia and the new Indonesia got off to a very good start. Australians campaigned for Indonesian independence, leading the government to give official recognition to the new Republic ahead of many other Western countries. Despite later ups and downs in the relationship, this stood Australia in good stead during the initial years of the Republic.

It was the internment of Indonesians in Australia that, ironically, helped to foster this positive relationship. Australian progressive groups were horrified by the presence in Australian territory of Dutch colonialism, in the form of the Netherlands Indies Civil Administration (NICA). NICA had been formed out of the wartime government-in-exile. Left-wing unions linked up with formerly interned Indonesians to put pressure on the Australian Labor government. Even conservative groups started to express support for the idea of Indonesian self-determination, encouraged by church groups in Melbourne and Sydney, which had provided social support for the Indonesians in exile.

The initial campaigns of support were on behalf of Indonesian nationalists interned at Cowra, New South Wales. These campaigns were supported by the Communist Party of Australia, especially through stories published in its newspaper, *Tribune.* They were joined by the Civil Rights League and the Australian Council for Civil Liberties, both of which lobbied in the first instance to the Commonwealth attorney general, Dr. H. V. Evatt.[1] Once freed, the Indonesians were then able to organize their own groups and political parties and to link up with the Indonesian Seamen's Union, which had been formed out of the dispute with the Dutch.[2] The alliance was furthered by the creation of new bodies, especially the Australian

Indonesian Association (AIA), formed in July 1945, a month before Indonesia's proclamation of independence.[3]

The AIA in Sydney included members of the Anglican Church and ordinary Australians who had gotten to know Indonesians socially, such as Charlotte Read, a young woman who fell in love with Anton Maramis, an organizer of the Seamen's Union. The first president of the AIA was the professor of anthropology at the University of Sydney and an Anglican clergyman, A. P. Elkin. Left-wing membership included Molly Warner, who married Mohamad Bondan, one of the Indonesian leaders. Popular sentiment against the Dutch was magnified by events at the internment camp in Casino, New South Wales. There, clashes between the Dutch authorities and rebellious Indonesian troops under their command led to the deaths of three Indonesians and the deportation of thirteen others to Kupang against the express views of the Australian government.[4] Such souring relations with the Dutch spilled over into other aspects of the relationship.

Action to support Indonesian independence expanded in the latter months of 1945. The Dutch authorities attempted to ship military and other supplies to reestablish their colonial control. The Waterside Workers Federation, a communist union, worked with Indonesian nationalist groups, public bodies such as the AIA, Chinese community groups, and Indian seamen's unions in a series of public campaigns to boycott these ships. Although only partly successful in stopping military supplies, these efforts placed further pressure on the Australian government and roused popular support against the Dutch NICA.[5]

The Australian Labor government under Prime Minister Chifley, which had initially claimed to be neutral in its view of Indonesian independence, established consular representation to the Republic, which had moved its capital to Yogyakarta when the Dutch recaptured Batavia. By early 1948, the Australian government, through the United Nations, where Dr. Evatt was beginning to play a significant role, threw its support firmly behind the Indonesians. The United Nations set up a Good Offices Committee to adjudicate the dispute, and the Australian representatives on that committee, Justice Richard Kirby and Tom Critchley from the newly established Commonwealth Department of External Affairs, played important advocacy roles on Indonesia's behalf.[6]

The political settlement involved significant movement of peoples. Not only were there Australian prisoners of war to be repatriated from Indonesia, but throughout the Revolution the Dutch attempted to repatriate their Indonesian subjects from Australia. The Labor government acceded to these Dutch demands under the Immigration Restriction Act, and were also keen to send back the Indonesian political organizers. Despite having married Australians, men like Bondan and Maramis were sent back to Indonesia. Their new wives, Molly Bondan and Charlotte Maramis, accompanied them to the young Republic.

Tensions over Eastern Indonesia

When the state of East Indonesia was merged into the Indonesian Republic in 1950, there remained a number of disputed regions along the pearl frontier. Important for the pearling industry on the Aru Islands in Maluku was the establishment of the Republic of the South Moluccas (RMS, Republik Maluku Selatan), formed on April 25, 1950, by pro-Dutch elements opposed to incorporation into the Indonesian Republic. The movement consisted of Christians, mainly Ambonese, many of who had been in the Dutch military. The Indonesian Republic fought back strongly against the RMS with a naval blockade, and most of the RMS leadership was forced to flee to the Netherlands. A newspaper report from 1950 shows that Australian pearlers were anxiously monitoring the Indonesian takeover of the eastern Indonesian islands:

> Darwin, Aug. 16—The Indonesian military occupation of the Aru Island, 300 miles north of Australia has been completed and Tenimber Island, only 180 miles north of Australia may now be under Indonesian control.
>
> This was stated in letters received to-day by Mr. H. S. Cross, a master pearler, who reached here recently from Aru.
>
> The Aru and Tenimber islands were formerly under Ambonese control. One letter from his partner, Mr. Carl Monsted, of whom he had heard nothing for some months, warned him obliquely that his return to Dobo, the Aru capital, would not be wise at present.[7]

Cross, as we saw in chapter 4, had been operating a pearling fleet out of Dobo and other parts of Indonesia for twenty-five years, and Carl Monsted, a Danish-Australian, owned a half-share in the Combined Trading Company, the successor to his former employer, the Celebes Trading Company. The other half of the company was owned by the "Ambonese" government.[8] This newspaper report is one of the only glimpses available into the pearlers' attempts to restore the prewar industry, and it seems that their businesses faded away in the political struggles after 1950, when Indonesians were pursuing a strongly nationalist economic agenda that rejected the white presence.

Another Australian ex-pearler, Bill Edwards, was also allegedly involved in supporting the RMS. On February 7, 1952, Edwards, who was the proprietor of the Coastal and Island Trader, was arrested by the Royal Dutch Navy while captaining the *Tiki*.[9] The Dutch returned the *Tiki* to Darwin, where the local authorities charged Edwards with customs offenses. The subsequent trial threatened diplomatic relations with the Indonesian government, for Edwards and his passengers were alleged to be running guns and providing support to the separatist RMS.[10] Also on board the *Tiki* was Pieter Willem Lokollo, a member of the RMS leadership, who had been seeking to gain support in the United States; a Dutch adventurer and probable spy for Dutch intelligence, Johannes Thijssen; and a Russian who Edwards later claimed was also a spy.[11]

The trial received much newspaper coverage because of Edwards' claims that the Australian intelligence agencies, particularly Naval Intelligence, were also behind the mission. This claim is probable since the agencies would have wanted to get information about the situation in eastern Indonesia, but the Department of External Relations, which had no prior knowledge of the events, was furious. It managed to convince the Indonesian ambassador, Dr. Oetoyo, that there was no official support for the venture. It appears that the RMS was lobbying the Australian and U.S. governments to support its republic as a Southeast Asian version of Taiwan, drawing on fears that Indonesia was increasingly leaning toward communism. Lokollo had received funding from unnamed American backers.[12] The Australian government was embarrassed when Edwards was declared innocent. Edwards himself claimed later to have made a second trip in which he succeeded in bringing weapons to the Moluccan rebels; "old Sukarno go[t] onto me and he chased me around for two years, and couldn't find me."[13]

There were indeed others in Australia who were antipathetic to Sukarno, who was increasingly seen as a communist. After 1950, when Australia elected a conservative government led by Liberal Party Prime Minster Robert Menzies, the government increasingly took a Cold War view of the region. By the end of the decade, it was concerned enough about the specter of communism in Indonesia to set up departments in Australian universities for the study of the Indonesian language. Of particular concern was the campaign for Indonesian control over West Papua or Irian, which had assumed a more aggressive form after Sukarno instituted the authoritarian system of Guided Democracy in 1957. Indonesia finally gained control of what is now called West Papua, but that was not confirmed by the United Nations' recognition until 1969, four years after Sukarno lost power to the military-dominated regime of General Suharto, which lasted until 1998.

The *Tiki* trial gives a glimpse of Australia's strategic and economic interest in the waters to its north. This was the same area that was the subject of an ongoing dispute with Japan over access to pearling beds along the pearl frontier. Japanese companies, particularly Mitsui, had been able to swiftly reestablish a hold on the pearling industry in Indonesia and wanted to expand further south. In January

1953, the Japanese government banned its citizens from working as divers in Australia as a protest over Australian attempts to exclude Japanese pearling operations from northern Australian waters.[14] In September of that year, Australia proclaimed sovereign rights over the continental shelf. Because this declaration was based on the one-hundred-fathom line, it effectively extended control over the pearling beds northwards toward the Aru Islands. The rights were determined to include the seabed and the subsoil, even if that control could not be enforced.[15] This declaration coincided with the enactment of the Australian Pearl Fisheries Act of 1952–1953, which was designed to restrict Japanese nationals from pearling in Australian waters. However, the diplomatic wrangles with Japan led to the concession that a small area was excluded from the act. This concession allowed the Australian government to grant Japanese pearlers permission to operate. It was not until the 1980s that maritime boundaries between Australia and Indonesia were settled via the creation of a joint zone of exploitation in the Arafura Sea, and even then the settlement was disputed because it gave recognition to the 1975 Indonesian invasion of East Timor.

Restricting Labor Migration across the Pearl Frontier

The pearling masters had hoped that they could reestablish their industry on the same kind of footing that had allowed them to reap huge profits in the prewar years. Some of the big names, notably Victor Clark who died in 1946, had disappeared from the industry, while others such as Streeter & Male remained. The new industry context was quite different, especially because international prices remained unstable. Initially, pearl shell prices were good, and by the 1948 season, average prices had risen to £450–£475 per ton. These were not to last, for in June 1949, a meeting was held in Darwin between the Australian pearlers and Allan Gerdau, president of Otto Gerdau Company of New York, the world's largest shell-buying company at the time. Allan, who had taken over from his father, attempted to renew Otto's control over Broome's output. Gerdau offered to buy the pearlers' entire season for the reduced price of £325 per ton for sound shell. Gerdau argued that during the war, when pearl shell had been unavailable, there had been a rise in the use of plastic alternatives and now there was less demand for shell.[16] Gerdau himself was trying to push prices down and corner the market, since by 1952, he was offering Australian pearlers from £635 to £703 per ton for their pearl shell.[17] The Western Australian figures show a total value of just £109,136 for pearl shell in 1949, whereas by 1953, it had risen to £284,503, and then peaked in 1957 at £604,801 for an annual harvest of nearly one thousand tons.[18] During this decade, the Japanese pioneered the new technique of cultivating pearls, but this did not affect the Australian industry on a large scale until the subsequent decade.

Another element that created difficulties for those reestablishing the pearling industry was a particularly bad cyclone season in 1948. The lugger *La Grange,* under the command of Boyce Benobi, was one of that year's casualties. *La Grange* was one of three luggers owned by Male & Company and had been on its way back to Darwin. These luggers had a larger complement of crew in comparison to the prewar practice. An air search finally found the wreckage of the missing lugger off Melville Island, but a search of the site failed to locate the missing men: eight Kupang men, two Aboriginal men, and the captain had been on board.[19]

For the master pearlers, access to cheap labor was essential. They wanted a return to the old indenture system. The Australian Labor government had initially resisted the reintroduction of indentured workers in the post-war period, but not because of concerns about relations with Indonesia. The Department of Immigration, whose minister was Arthur Calwell, maintained its allegiance to the White Australia policy and was even more reluctant to grant the pearling industry exemptions to import Asian workers.[20] While many Australians were beginning to view Asia in a more sympathetic light, others insisted on immigration restrictions and on segregating those who came to work in pearling. But up against the pearling masters were a range of protesters including Australian unionists, humanitarians and politicians, the Indonesian government, and, perhaps, most importantly, Indonesian and Malaysian workers themselves.

The statistical evidence shows that there had been a significant change in the ethnic composition of the northern labor force over the period from 1949 to 1957. In 1949, there were 230 men employed in pearling in Western Australia, including 105 "Koepangers," 41 "Malays," 39 Aboriginal Australians, and 25 Chinese. By 1957, this had increased to 482 men employed, including 119 Malays, 117 Japanese, 110 Chinese, 80 Aboriginal, but just 31 Koepangers. These compiled figures were based on old ethnic categories and made no mention of the term "Indonesian."[21] There is some question as to how long Indonesians continued to be recruited, given that a 1956 request from the Broome sub-collector of customs spoke of the arrival of "pearling specialists from Japan, Hong Kong, Singapore, or Indonesia."[22]

The thirty-one Koepangers listed were presumably men like Abdoel Gafoer, who were long-term residents. One such person was Lamadoe Salawatoes, who had been born in Endeh, Flores, in 1917 and had remained in Australia during World War II. He was still diving on October 11, 1957, for Male & Company when, at age forty, he died from divers' paralysis, leaving a widow, Una Rahman, and two small children. He had already been advised by the Commonwealth migration officer that he had permission to leave the pearling industry and engage in an occupation of his own choice, but had chosen to remain on as a diver.[23]

While the Australian use of indentured labor in the nineteenth and early twentieth centuries had been established along the lines of other colonial labor systems in Southeast Asia and the Pacific, by the 1940s the idea of indenture was regarded as an anachronistic relic of the colonial era.[24] The struggle to end labor indenture had already been well under way before the war—as early as the 1930s, the International Labor Organization (ILO) had sought to abolish all forms of unfree labor, with the Netherlands Indies as a chief target.[25] Ordinances permitting the infliction of penal sanctions against indentured workers in breach of their contracts had been gradually repealed in British Malaya from 1932 onwards. While these and other harsher aspects of indenture were eased, the use of contract labor continued with only slight modifications, leaving the effectiveness of abolition open to question into the postwar period.[26] Elsewhere, there was also evidence of ongoing indenture. In the Pacific, Indonesian men and women were still being brought in as contract laborers to French New Caledonia as late as 1949, and in 1955, the French negotiated a new contract agreement with the independent Indonesian government.[27]

Darwin's being a highly unionized town meant that it was the site where the question of indenture and working conditions of Indonesians was a matter for public debate. While the unions were prepared to take on the issue of wages, they did not directly confront the indenture system. Wages during this time, being fixed by indenture contracts, could vary according to the price of shell. In 1948, divers were making £10 a month in addition to their keep, with a bonus payable on the amount of shell raised. Diving was done in pairs, with the bonus shared between the two divers. For low-grade shell, the bonus was £40 a ton; for other grades, £70 per ton for up to fifteen tons, with a sliding scale that went as high as £120 per ton for amounts over thirty tons. Tenders were paid £28 per month, engineers £27 per month, and crew from £15 to £20, according to experience. While divers could potentially make a small fortune, the unions advocated a fixed rate of pay in preference to the bonus system. They argued that a change in the wage system could make the industry safer because it was the desire to gain the maximum amount of pearl shell that gave divers the incentive to take great risks. The unions also argued that if boats employed more than two men, divers would be able to take shifts and so make it possible for each individual diver to work an eight-hour day. This was a time when the eight-hour working day was something that most Australian workers took for granted, but divers worked from sun up to sun down to gain the maximum harvest.[28]

Part of the reason that indenture was able to gain a foothold in the reconstructed industry was that it was first reintroduced in Broome, where unions and government were less influential. It was the Broome pearlers' lobby that was able to persuade Labor Prime Minister Chifley to relent in 1947 and allow Streeter & Male to import fifty-seven indents from Kupang, still part of the Dutch-sponsored East Indonesian State until 1950.[29]

Nevertheless, even Broome was experiencing a new spirit of unionism among pearling workers. Experienced pearling worker Abu Bin Jacob persuaded nine of these new arrivals not to sign on at the prewar rate of £4 per month. Pearling master Sam Male responded by having Jacob jailed on a flimsy pretext, but Male was forced to ask the police to release him when Sumatran-born former Z Force member Samsudin Bin Katib called a workers' strike the day after Jacob's arrest.[30] Male refused to make any concessions on pay, arguing that he could easily import new workers at even cheaper prices. On February 9, 1948, when Samsudin and the rest of the men refused to sign on at reduced rates, Male asked the Commonwealth migration officer, R. W. Gratwick, to have Bin Katib deported for "spreading disruption and unrest" and "inculcating what appears to be ideas of a Communistic order."[31] Since he had been recruited in Singapore as a "Malay," he was to be returned to there, rather than to Indonesia.

This case became a national issue, especially in light of Samsudin's status as a war hero. The activist Elizabeth Marshall, living in Melbourne, contacted the federal secretary of the Seamen's Union of Australia, Eliot V. Elliott, for assistance. Bin Katib was sent to Fremantle into the care of the Seamen's Union while he awaited deportation.[32] Pressure was put on Arthur Calwell to prevent the repatriation, leading Calwell to deliver a speech in the House of Representatives that asserted: "We have not reached the state in Australia at which people who agitate for better conditions must be deported merely because of their colour." Calwell also made mention of Samsudin's military service.[33] But in Broome, the pearlers were determined to have Samsudin removed. Mary Dakas (née Paspaley), the first woman to own a lugger, had offered Samsudin employment, and perhaps her own Greek family background made her sympathetic to his plight. However, the widowed Dakas was pressured by Broome pearlers to withdraw the offer in a campaign that included her being slandered with accusations of inappropriately "fraternising with her Asiatic crews."[34] Finally, on May 12, Calwell gave permission for Samsudin to be deported along with the new secretary of the Indonesia-Malay Association, Johnnie Pattiasina from Ambon. Because both men were no longer employed in the pearling industry, they were outside the scope of their indenture contracts.[35]

This case was the beginning of further activism. Eric and Elizabeth Marshall published a pamphlet in 1949 which had a list of demands for pearling industry workers, including the right to organize, compensation for death and injury, decent camps, supervision of gear and luggers, fixed hours and wages by law, the right to leave "districts" where they were employed, the right to permanent residency after ten years of service, radios on luggers, and supervision of the methods by which workers were engaged.[36]

During these years, the dangers facing Indonesian divers in Australian waters were made public in order to emphasize the problems in the industry. Some deaths were due to the relative inexperience of many of the Indonesian and Malaysian recruits. The local newspaper, the *Northern Standard,* reported two deaths in 1948. One, a Kupang man, Willem Djawa, who was only twenty-eight years old, died after diving to twenty-eight fathoms. His lugger, the *Plover D70,* was owned by Broome's Male & Company. During the inquest, the first diver, Malay Bin Hussein, stated that he had never worked below twenty-one fathoms.[37] The following year another young Kupang man, Poeloe Wila, who was working for Mary Dakas' brother, Nicholas Paspaley, on the *Pam,* died from divers' paralysis. The same newspaper had reported this death, and added that Wila had no relatives in Darwin.[38] However, at this time it was common knowledge among the public at large that many of these men who risked their lives had wives and children in Darwin. Relationships with Aboriginal women were still not recognized by the government.

Indonesians were under considerable pressure to prove themselves to the pearling masters, and the price of failure was deportation from Australia. The Australian unionists in Darwin, knowing of this fraught situation, took steps to expose the problem in the *Northern Standard.* One contributor argued that "the constant threat of deportation acts as an effective check on militant action for better conditions." But the situation was made worse by the fact there were always other men from eastern Indonesia from which the pearling masters could choose. The writer continued: "These men, who are in the main unorganised and backward, are being used as a potential means of weakening whatever fight the more advanced workers in the industry may make for better wages and conditions."[39]

When Streeter & Male applied in July 1949 to repatriate, mid-season, seventy-five of its Malayan and Timorese workers for showing widespread resistance, the Commonwealth Chifley Labor government set about investigating the conditions of indenture. The final report concluded that the treatment of workers was in breach of the Draft Covenant of the International Commission on Human Rights, which Australia had helped to draft. This report might have signaled the end of indenture but for the fact that Labor lost government soon after the report was submitted.[40] The incoming conservative Menzies Liberal–Country Coalition government was prepared to continue the practice of indenture.

The year after the new government's election, there was still no decision from the Australian Department of Immigration regarding allowing more recruits from Kupang to be brought to Australia. There were approximately one hundred men working in Darwin at this stage. As part of the policy of segregation, new regulations insisted that indentured laborers were not permitted to live within thirty miles of Darwin, meaning that a pearling base would need to be established on an island. Truant Island was suggested, but there were no buildings or material with which to build and no facilities for servicing the motors of the luggers. In Broome, however, indentured workers were permitted to live in town.[41] The Darwin industry was barely surviving by 1951. At that time, just twenty-two men were employed, including a diver, five divers' tenders, twelve crew, and three engineers. There were signs that the Australian government was willing to find ways to support the industry, and in 1952, it gave permission to import Japanese pearling workers. By the following year, conditions were improving slowly in Darwin, with thirty-four men employed, including nine divers, eighteen tenders, and seven crew.[42]

Indonesian Responses

The government of the Republic of Indonesia was particularly sensitive to the continued practice of colonial-style recruitment. In August 1950, when eastern Indonesia was absorbed into the republic, the Indonesian embassy contacted the Australian Department of the Interior to express concern that Indonesian nationals in Darwin were being paid less than the official basic wage. By denying Indonesians the basic wage the pearling industry was effectively maintaining their exclusion from the "civilized" community defined by the 1906 Harvester Judgment which used the term to explain its justification for setting a basic living wage. The Indonesians themselves were introducing new labor legislation for their republic, with principles of equal rights and a basic wage, so were sensitive to the Australian situation.

The Australian government took no action to address Indonesian concerns. Frank Anderson in the Fisheries Division argued that an increase in wages was not advisable and that there was no need for any official regulation of wages. In January 1952, the Indonesian government appointed Oh Sien Hong (a.k.a. M. A. Husino), a UNESCO fellow conducting research into industrial arbitration in Melbourne, to investigate working conditions in Broome and Darwin. His report concluded that conditions were "shameful," that indents were living in over-crowded camps, and that they were the virtual prisoners of their employers. Public reporting in Indonesia emphasized the discrimination and victimization of indents in Australia, particularly criticizing the restrictions placed on the movements of workers.[43]

By March of that year, the Indonesian government was considering banning Indonesian indents from working in Australia. They were also reluctant to permit the resumption of indenture to New Caledonia until a more humane code of labor was established there. The Indonesian government suspected that Australians were attempting to recruit workers from Ambon without permission, under the cover of the Republic of the South Moluccas rebellion.[44]

In its continued efforts to improve conditions of indenture, the Indonesian embassy in Canberra contacted the Australian Department of Immigration in 1952 to request that indents be permitted a short period away from pearling bases during the lay-up season. There was cautious approval from the Department of External Affairs and most of the pearling masters, but opposition from local officials in Darwin and Broome. The Commonwealth migration officer in Darwin argued against holiday leave, describing the indents as "persons of low mentality" who would be unable to comprehend that they must abide by the set conditions of leave. The same official also argued that if some indents were granted permission while others were rejected, this would only "add to the already existing discontent and difficulty of control and administration of the industry."[45] The master pearlers and the sub-collector of customs in Broome argued that indents could not be trusted to return and that their services were required for the painting and careening of pearling luggers. The Australian Immigration Department finally agreed that leave would be approved on the basis of individual merit, and only with the approval of the local immigration official. The resulting decision was sufficiently vague as to make it unlikely that pearling indents would be granted leave. As a result of the Australian government's response, the Indonesian government imposed a ban on the importation of indents from Indonesia to Australia.

A confidential report to cabinet in 1954 indicated that the Menzies Liberal–Country Party government still hoped to facilitate access to Indonesian indents, particularly as other source countries, such as Japan, were also reluctant to provide labor.[46] The first secretary of the Indonesian embassy, I. Hamzah, visited Darwin, Broome, Onslow, and Port Hedland in January 1954 to examine conditions for Indonesians working in the pearl-shell industry. Hamzah's concerns related to the standard of lodging, the freedom of movement, and the "failure of many Indonesians to save any of their wages and the desirability of making some provision against their returning to Indonesia destitute."[47] Under the pre-1950 Kupang agreement with the Dutch, the men were expected to return with 25 percent of their earnings at the end of their two-year contracts. Responding to this report, F. E. Wells, the chief pearling inspector in Darwin, argued that the men themselves did not want to return to Kupang with 25 percent of their earnings and would resent any retention of their money. He also noted that there was a problem of "currency manipulation" on money brought into Indonesia whereby the men were likely to lose some of their earnings.[48] Following Hamzah's report, the Indonesian embassy informed the Australian Department of Commerce and Agriculture that the existing ban would be amended, thereby allowing Indonesians to work in Australia.[49]

Still unwilling to allow resumption of the previous modes of indenture, the Indonesian government requested in February 1955 that Australia and Indonesia enter into a formal agreement. This was to be modeled on an earlier agreement Indonesia had made with France, which pertained to Indonesians working in New Caledonia. But the Australian government protested that the New Caledonia agreement had a range of provisions that were "not applicable to Australian conditions." In particular, those for family migration and permanent settlement went against the White Australia policy.[50] The opinion of the administrator of the Northern Territory was that if Indonesians were to be engaged, it would be as crew members, and that it would be "unreasonable to expect the Master Pearler to guarantee them salary and bonuses . . . equal to the local basic wage."[51]

In 1955 the Northern Australian Workers Union was successful in bringing into force the Northern Territory Pearl Fishing Award. This determination directly contradicted the views of the master pearlers and guaranteed the crews of pearling luggers the basic wage. The victory was limited, however, as the award applied only to the Northern Territory, leaving Thursday Island and Broome unaffected. In addition, the award did not address rights to citizenship or restrictions on the movement of indents.[52]

Insofar as the award was victory of sorts, it became something of a moot point. With the two governments unable to reconcile their differences and reach an agreement, the direct Indonesian indenture to Australia was formally ended in the 1950s. Independent Indonesia would not tolerate the continuation of colonial-style indenture, while Australia remained bound by the White Australia policy and its assumptions of racial difference.

New Contracts in the 1960s and 1970s

The pearling industry itself underwent significant changes in the 1970s. Of particular importance was the shift to cultured pearls, which began with Japanese expansion of the technique in the 1950s. The cultivation process resulted in the need for fewer divers and less dangerous diving practices, although there were still deaths and injuries in the industry.

In 1960, there was some back-tracking on the Indonesian government's principled stand against inequitable labor contracts. Despite a change in regime from a constitutional democracy to Sukarno's revolutionary-style Guided Democracy in 1959, the Indonesians expressed an interest in reopening labor migration to north Australia. They had received word from its employment office in Timor that a number of divers had asked to go to Broome. It was this direct request from the workers themselves that prompted the Indonesian government to approach the Australian embassy in Jakarta.

The continued poverty of the eastern islands was the main reason that workers wanted to leave, but when they got to Australia, they found that problems with human rights were still rife in the pearling industry. In 1961, the Australian Immigration Department attempted to deport three Darwin divers who wanted to stay in Australia: Daru Bin Saris, Jaffa Madunne, and Zainul Bin Hashim. These men were "Malays," who had been in Darwin between seven and thirteen years. Their plight drew local support in the form of strikes, protests, and a petition signed by 1,100 residents. Those lobbying on their behalf included the newly formed Student Action, an anti–White Australia policy group. The workers went into hiding during the protests, and their deportation was challenged in the High Court of Australia, with lawyer Frank Galbally, later famous as the "father" of Australia's future policy of multiculturalism, representing them.[53] But before the case had even been heard, Immigration Minister Alexander Downer (Senior) announced in May 1962 that the deportation order had been dropped.[54]

A review of the immigration regulations relating to the engagement of indentured labor at the end of 1969 dealt a final blow to the remaining pearling masters. The new regulations made important changes. It was recommended that all indents who could satisfy new criteria should be granted resident status. The chief criteria were that indentured workers had to have been living in Australia for five years and could demonstrate proof of good character. Many experienced pearling indents were able to gain residency and, importantly, were no longer obliged to remain in the industry. But at the same time, the Department of Immigration took steps to ensure that future indents could not become eligible for resident status. The new regulations limited the term of contracts and renewals to four years, after which indents were to be repatriated and not reengaged until four years had lapsed.

The general immigration policy regarding Asians in 1969 was that migrants should be "well qualified and readily integrated." Manual workers were regarded as unsuitable, supposedly being less likely to assimilate into the Australian way of life. According to the government, pearling indents were not "the type of persons who would come within the revised non-European policy."[55]

In protesting in April 1970 against the new policy, pearling manager P. A. Haynes of A. C. Morgan Proprietary Limited in Broome argued that the Malays he recruited were without training, meaning that it took a minimum of three years for them to become efficient divers. Regarding the offer of permanent residency, Haynes noted that life at sea was rigorous and that with job opportunities ashore "almost boundless in Australia," why would they not take the chance to leave?[56]

The Immigration Department report concluded that "what the pearlers really want is a stable, docile, and obedient work force."[57]

In response to the protests from pearling masters, the Department of Immigration held an interdepartmental meeting in July 1970. It concluded that the industry in Broome warranted special consideration because the town was economically dependent on pearling for its existence. The industry, now focused on cultured pearls, was worth up to AUD$10 million per annum and depended upon traditional pearl-shell diving for its live shell for pearl cultivation. But while acknowledging these economic benefits, the meeting was unable to agree to the resumption of the previous system in view of the "outdated" nature of indenture whereby some indents were still receiving rates below the minimum adult wage. The Western Australian port of Broome was regarded as the worst offender, but in the Northern Territory, where indents were supposedly covered by the 1955 Northern Territory Pearl Fishing Award, employers were also failing to pay award wages. An arbitration inspector sent to investigate reported that the award was being applied to crew members only in the narrowest sense, and not to other indents such as divers. The report concluded that "employment contracts under which overseas workers are introduced are well out of date and include a number of restrictions on the freedom of the individual which would attract criticism in the light of present day attitudes."[58] Extensive investigations were recommended.

While the Indonesian government had banned recruitment of indentured workers from Indonesia, it was unable to prevent Indonesians from being signed on in Singapore, as occurred into the early 1970s. In December 1970, the Australian government noted that "Malays" were the main source of labor for Broome. In a recent round of hiring, the pearling company, A. S. Male & Company was reported to have employed fifteen Japanese and forty-five Malays.[59] These men were probably recruited in Singapore, but many were Indonesian. Ahmat Bin Fadal was still a very fit and lively man when the authors met him in Broome in 2010. At that time the senior leader of the local Indonesian community, he and some of his friends who had been in the group of forty-five were from Bawean, near Java, an island with a long history of connection to Singapore.

By 1970, the total number of Asians employed under indenture was very small, with just 101 indents working in pearl-fishing by December of that year.[60] Immigration officer B. H. Barrenger wrote in the following year that he had no doubt "that Europeans would not accept the employment conditions even with a substantial increase in pay rate." He acknowledged that the new immigration rules would mark "the finish of the previous era" in which overseas workers provided "relatively cheap labour, completely subservient to the employer."[61]

Ahmat Bin Fadal. Photograph by Adrian Vickers.

Of the prewar pearling masters, one family in particular became synonymous with pearls in the postwar period, the Paspaleys. In 1962, Nicholas Paspaley, who operated in postwar Darwin, started his first cultured pearl farm, following the example of the Otto Gerdau Company. The following year Paspaley set up a £200,000 pearling company together with the Arafura Pearl Company of Japan to realize an ambition for producing cultured pearls.[62] In 1986, after the death of Allan Gerdau, Paspaley's son and now head of the business, Nicholas Junior, took over the Otto Gerdau Company interests in Australia. Two years later, he subsumed Streeter & Male, and in the next decades gradually incorporated all of the major Australian competitors, the last of which was the Kailis family company.[63] In 1999, Nicholas Paspaley Junior was recognized for his role in creating a AUD$200 million export industry in quality cultured pearls and was awarded the Companion of the Order of Australia. By 2012, Paspaley Pearls, a company with international connections to the United States and Hong Kong, accounted for 70 percent of Australia's pearl production.[64] Today divers are more likely to be Australians. But they still gather pearl shell from the sea floor, and modern diving technology has solved most of the problems associated with diving.[65]

The major threat to the future of the Paspaley-dominated Australian industry is now cheaper pearls, not just those produced in large quantities in China, but Indonesian competition from companies such as the Nusantara Pearl Group, which can produce on a scale far larger than the Australians.[66] With the severing of the pearl frontier, one side can now out-compete the other.

The postwar period saw a gradual decline in the migration of Indonesian workers across the pearl frontier from eastern Indonesia to northern Australia. The labor migration finally came to an end almost one hundred years after the indenture of workers for the pearling industry had commenced. While immigration had been permitted to continue for several years under an independent Indonesian government, there was no question that the Dutch colonial policy of indentured labor could not persist in its original form. However, for the workers of eastern Indonesia for whom employment opportunities were limited, the end of this colonial recruitment was not necessarily a welcome change. The loss of shipping and later air connections, particularly between the previous hubs of Kupang, Broome, and Darwin, left a blank space on the map that stands out as an anomaly in an otherwise interconnected region.

CHAPTER NINE

Marriage and Australian Citizenship

A combination of changes in the international scene and in Australian society saw a gradual weakening of the White Australia policy between the late 1950s and 1972. A significant step was taken in 1958 when the Immigration Restriction Act of 1901 was replaced with the Migration Act which ended the notorious Dictation Test, though non-white immigration was not specifically permitted until the act was amended in 1966. The Australian Labor Party removed mention of the White Australia policy from its party platform in 1965, and when the Whitlam Labor government came to power in 1972, it put the final nail in the coffin of a race-based immigration policy.

The changes that had been going on in the pearling industry in the postwar period played an important role in challenging the White Australia policy. In 1957, the Menzies Liberal government had introduced policies that allowed pearling indents to acquire citizenship.[1] In the period up to 1966, some 142 Indonesians were granted citizenship.[2] The troubled process of gaining acknowledgment of the right to stay in Australia reveals how closely these indentured workers had been integrated into the communities of the north, and how much they had helped to form a new kind of Australia.

The legislative changes and political pressures that we outlined in the previous chapter do not give a full picture of what it meant for these former indents to be able to satisfy the 1957 legislation's provision of living a "normal Australian life." It is the stories of individual families that give a sense of the human cost of the industry, and of the new society that was created in Australia around the work of pearling, as the cases in this chapter show.

Abdoel Gafoer was just one of the pearling workers whose many years of living in the north finally resulted in his being granted Australian citizenship under the 1957 legislation. He was the father of Susan Edgar who had welcomed us to country at our 2010 Broome seminar. Gafoer, born in Alor in the Netherlands East Indies in 1897, had come to Australia in 1921. He had worked for four different employers, including Broome's powerful pearling master and former mayor of Broome Hugh Norman, from 1932 to 1939. Gafoer had returned briefly to Indonesia

Abdoel Gafoer in his application for registration, 1949. National Archives of Australia, Perth 3504995.

and was re-employed by the firm of Robinson & Norman in Broome between 1940 and 1941. A photograph of him taken as part of his 1949 application for registration, when he signed on as a diver's tender, shows him as a man worn out by the hard life of pearling.[3]

As we have seen in previous chapters, Gafoer remained in Broome during the war working as a fisherman to provide food for members of the Allied army and navy based there. After the war, he moved to Darwin to work for local pearler Ah Dep. When Ah Dep went out of business, Gafoer was told he was liable to deportation despite having worked in Australia for twenty-seven years.[4] He returned to Broome as a diver's tender for the smaller pearling concern of McDaniel. In 1955, Gafoer was deemed by the authorities to be permanently incapacitated due to health problems and was permitted to work ashore in other jobs associated with the pearling industry. At the age of sixty-two, he was granted permission to work in an employment of his own choosing.

In 1961, Abdoel Gafoer applied for permanent residency and was interviewed by the sub-collector of customs at Broome, R. K. Moon. Now retired, Gafoer lived five miles from Broome with his de-facto Aboriginal wife and Susan, their seven-year-old daughter. Gafoer was successful in his application because despite his rather solitary life in retirement, Moon determined that Gafoer was a "respected member of the community" who spoke good English. Moon noted that Gafoer enjoyed going to films as his main form of recreation—perhaps this was the sign of a "normal Australian life" that was one of the government criteria for natural-ization. Moon also noted that unlike Thursday Island, Broome had no social clubs for Indonesians, despite the long-standing nature and size of the community. Prob-ably this was because the Indonesians were so well integrated into the local mul-tiethnic society.[5]

There had been few advocates for men like Abdoel Gafoer, even though men of Moon's standing, knowing the communities of the north, sympathized with the plight of the Indonesians. The Indonesian government was not concerned about people who had left the country before independence and who wanted to remain permanently in Australia. The master pearlers showed little interest in those men as they got old since the heavy physical toll that pearling took made it difficult for men over fifty years old to sustain employment on pearling luggers. Even after the infamous Dictation Test was abolished by the Migration Act of 1958, the White Australia policy remained the guiding principal of the Department of Immigra-tion, which was keen to deport workers when their contracts expired. There was no formal recognition that Indonesian pearling indents might have a moral right to seek citizenship on the Australian side of the pearl frontier, and pearling in-dents were forced to lobby for their rights on a case-by-case basis.

Deportation under the War-Time Refugees Removal Act of 1949

The slow process of dismantling the White Australia policy began in the 1940s with the widely-publicized citizenship case of an Indonesian woman, Annie O'Keefe. She had arrived in Australia on September 18, 1942, as Annie Maas Jacob with her seven children, having been evacuated from the Aru Islands on the HMAS *Warrnambool*.[6] After the wartime death of her husband, Samuel Jacob, she remar-ried to an Australian man, John O'Keefe. According to the Nationality Act 1920, Annie was now entitled to British nationality.[7] But according to the Minister for Immigration, Arthur Calwell, she remained a prohibited migrant under the Im-migration Restriction Act and was liable to deportation. Calwell was afraid that her case would set a precedent. There were many thousands of Chinese Austra-lian men who wanted permission to bring their Chinese wives to Australia, and Calwell was afraid that one exception would lead to a flood of applications.

At a time when independent Asian nations were intent on removing the ra-cial discrimination imposed by European colonial rule, Calwell was widely criti-cized for his undiplomatic handling of the O'Keefe case. Calwell's critics came from both sides of Australian politics, including the Left of his own Labor Party, and Liberal Party members such as future Prime Minister Harold Holt. They described

Calwell's approach as inhumane on a personal level and undiplomatic at a regional level. Commentators from Asia saw the O'Keefe case as proof—if further proof were needed—that the White Australia policy was a race-based policy. The major justification for White Australia adduced by its supporters in the Labor Party was to preserve economic standards by excluding supposedly "cheap" Asian labor. The other rationale was that cultural homogeneity needed to be safeguarded to avoid social and political disruption. Neither of these arguments could be applied in the O'Keefe case. In a statement to Singapore newspapers at the time, Malay Nationalist Party leader Tahu Kalu said his party was drafting an appeal to the United Nations Human Rights Committee on the matter and told newspapers that "The action against Mrs O'Keefe had laid bare to the peoples of Asia, if not the world, what lay at the core of the 'White Australia' policy. It had 'thrown overboard' the face-saving Australian contention that the policy was based on purely economic consideration."[8]

Historian Sean Brawley argues that Calwell's claim to be concerned about cultural assimilation was nonsense, given that Annie's children spoke perfect English, lived with an Australian stepfather, and just as Calwell had himself, attended a local Catholic school in Melbourne. Even as Calwell continued to deny the racial basis for the White Australia policy, claiming, improbably, that this term was never officially sanctioned, he confirmed his own race-based beliefs by speaking out in parliament about the fear of a "Mongrel Australia."[9]

Annie O'Keefe took her case to the High Court of Australia in February 1949, seeking to avoid deportation. The High Court ruled in her favor based on a legal technicality. To be a prohibited migrant under the Immigration Restriction Act, she should have been given the Dictation Test. The test, administered in any European language, was designed to ensure that the person failed. But the test could be given only within the first five years of the person's arriving in Australia, and Annie had been in Australia since 1942. Thus the High Court ruled that she was not and could not be declared a prohibited migrant.[10]

In response, on July 12, 1949, Arthur Calwell passed the War-Time Refugees Removal Act. This act, he announced, was intended "to remedy defects revealed by the High Court judgment" in the case of Annie O'Keefe.[11] It was designed to enable the government to deport any "alien" who had entered Australia during "the period of hostilities," which was defined as September 3, 1939, to September 2, 1945. Section 10 of the act also made it illegal to "(a) conceal, receive or harbour a person whom he knows to be a deportee; (b) aid or assist a person whom he knows to be a deportee in concealing himself; or (c) assist a person whom he knows to be a deportee to evade deportation under this Act." The penalty for such aid was a fine of £100 or six months imprisonment.[12] Under this act the Indonesian political activists mentioned in the previous chapter were deported, regardless of the fact that a number of them were married to Australian women.

While exemptions were noted for diplomatic representatives or those born or domiciled in Australia, there was no mention of pearling indents as a separate exempted category. Even though many of the indents had been working in Australia for twenty years, as contract laborers, they were not legally "domiciled" in Australia. And because the pearling masters had continued to import indentured labor during the first years of World War II, it was easy for the government to confuse them with seamen whose ships had been allowed to remain in Australia because of the Japanese occupation of Southeast Asia. The fact that the Indonesians had been recruited before the Japanese occupation of the Netherlands East Indies did not stop the authorities from declaring Indonesian pearling indents to be war refugees under this new act.

Indonesian Pearling Indents Lobby for Citizenship

In 1951, the authorities recorded a population of some twenty-two Indonesians and their fifty Australia-born dependents on Thursday Island in the Torres Strait.[13] The list included ten men recruited from Timor who had arrived in Australia between 1908 and 1934, four men from Makassar, six from Ambon, and three others. The men were members of the Thursday Island Indonesian Social Club, which proved to be helpful in supporting their lobby for citizenship. A letter was sent to Labor Senator Benjamin Courtice, previously Minister for Trade and Customs, on behalf of H. Joseph, secretary of the Indonesian Social Club. Joseph protested that while the Thursday Island Indonesians had been in Australia from fourteen to thirty-four years, they were not naturalized "although a considerable amount of money has been spent on legal costs in order to achieve naturalisation."[14] Not only were the men denied citizenship, but under the terms of their contracts, they were obliged to remain on Thursday Island and continue working in the pearling industry.

C. W. Kirk, sub-collector of customs, who had been in contact with Joseph, wrote in June 1950 to support a request by the Thursday Island Indonesians to go on holidays to the Australian mainland, stating:

> I might point out these people all have pretty large families all born on Thursday Is, they had sons overseas on active service in World War 2, and themselves worked on Allied small ships or on defence on the Island. The visits to the mainland for holiday purposes is requested that all should be permitted to go at different times, and it was also suggested at the meeting that the person going on a months holiday with his family should put

up a bond. The attached list shows 23 Men and 16 Wives, including one De-facto, the number of Children would average five per family.[15]

After failing to gain the attention of the Australian government, these men turned to the Indonesian government. The Indonesian embassy in Australia made representations in 1952 on behalf of these workers regarding their freedom of movement, which led to permission being granted for them to take holidays on mainland Australia.[16]

The war period in Australia had provided many opportunities for Indonesians to socialize with the broader Australian community, and it was not surprising, therefore, that by the end of the war, many Indonesians had married Australian women. This was to prove awkward for Arthur Calwell who was intent on deporting Indonesians. The newspapers made the most of public sympathy for the plight of Australian women who faced the difficult choice of losing the father of their children or going to live in Indonesia. One Indonesian pearling indent who was a friend and coworker of Abdoel Gafoer, Theios Poeling-Oer, was married to Katherine Marshall from New South Wales. Poeling-Oer was faced with deportation in 1948 after his and Abdoel Gafoer's employer in Darwin, Ah Dep, shut down his pearling operations. Katherine was quoted in the newspaper, as stating, "Naturally I want to stay in my own country but I will go with my husband wherever he is sent. If we are sent back to Koepang, we will have no house there but that won't make any difference to me and the five children. If my husband has to camp under a tree my place will be there beside him."[17] However, their deportation was delayed when the government was unable to secure passage to Kupang for Katherine and the children, transport being available only to Dili in East Timor. In the meantime, the Poeling-Oer family's quest to stay in Australia was warmly supported by the Darwin Indonesian community.

The Malayan-Indonesian Association in Darwin had roots in the community going back before the war. A celebration was held for the Poeling-Oer family at the home of Herman Pon in February 1949. The Pon family were old Darwin residents.[18] Herman and his brother, Jacob, had gone to school in Darwin in the 1910s. Their father, Carl Pon, was a "well-known known Darwin identity" who had come to Australia from Kupang in the 1880s and had worked for pearling Jolly & Company. Their mother, Kitty Pon, an Aboriginal woman from the Macarthur River district, had been raised by a respected white family, the Strettons, and taught Sunday School.[19] There were more than two hundred guests of the Malayan-Indonesian Association gathered at the Pon residence to celebrate the birthdays of two of the Poeling-Oer children, Patrice and Peter.[20] Fortunately, the family was never deported, and much later Theios Poeling-Oer was naturalized.[21]

Despite the obvious public support for Indonesian men with Australian families, Arthur Calwell was not sympathetic toward the families. In a speech to foreign diplomats in 1949, he suggested that two cases in particular, that of Annie O'Keefe and of a Filipino man married to an Australian woman, Sergeant Gamboa, had been used by newspapers to attack the government. He accused the press of exploiting the "sentimental aspects" of these cases.[22] The *Free Press* had even published a plea from General MacArthur regarding the Gamboa case.[23] The position of Gamboa, being a man, was quite different from that of Annie O'Keefe. Under Australian law, women were supposed to take their nationality from their husbands. Speaking in parliament, Calwell dismissed Gamboa's claim to Australian residence, commenting in derisive tones: "There was a time when a wife went with her Husband to her husband's domicile. We have reached a new order, apparently, in this age of sex equality, when a wife determines or has equal right in determining where the husband shall reside."[24] For those Indonesian pearling indents who had married Australian women, gender- and race-based discrimination were equally at issue.

After the federal elections, the change from a Labor to a Liberal–Country Party government did not immediately remedy this situation. Speaking in Jakarta, the new Minister for External Affairs, Percy Spender, claimed that the Menzies government would administer the White Australia policy more humanely.[25] But despite these assurances, the government made no attempt to revoke the War-Time Refugees Removal Act.

Married men continued to be subjected to deportation during the 1950s. In 1951, the authorities were informed that pearling indent and Z Force war hero, Rote-born The Soen Hin, had married Philomena Howard, a Broome woman of Aboriginal Filipino descent. This information did not prompt the cancellation of his deportation orders. The migration officer wrote that "if the terms of the Bond furnished by The Soen Hin's last employer, L. Placanica, are not enforced a precedent which will be hard to overcome will be established."[26] The Soen Hin was thirty-two years old at the time. He was due to be repatriated to Kupang on December 1951, and the authorities had already organized a new photograph for his passport.

The Soen Hin was determined to fight the deportation. He provided the information that his wife already had five children by another man and had had a sixth child with him. L. H. Townsend, the sub-collector of customs wrote: "he thinks he will not be sent away from Australia now that he has a wife and family to support. It is possible that other Indents married in Australia have thought the same."[27] He was saved from deportation only because he was able to sign on to a new pearling contract with McDaniel & Son.

The Soen Hin was eventually granted permission to leave the pearling industry and work in an employment of his choosing on September 22, 1955, and he subsequently found work as a yardsman at the Continental Hotel in Broome. The permission letter was signed in person by the Minister for Immigration, Harold Holt, after a special request passed on from the Minister for External Affairs, R. G. Casey. These ministers had received representations sent by H. V. Sykes, secretary of the Returned Sailors', Soldiers' and Airmen's Imperial League of Australia (RSS and AILA) in Melbourne. The Soen Hin clearly had acquired some powerful allies. Sykes informed the government of The Soen Hin's remarkable war record as a member of Z Force, and noted that he had trained as a parachutist before being dropped into Borneo to fight behind enemy lines. Not only was he allowed to remain in Australia, but in 1956 he was sent three war medals via Sykes. The Soen Hin wrote again to Central Army Records in 1958 asking about becoming naturalized and claiming that he had been told he would qualify for citizenship when he signed up for Z Force. Eventually his lobby was successful, and he was granted permission to become an Australian citizen.[28]

Another Indonesian who was saved by his war record was Jeskial (or Jack) Mesak, an ethnic Rotenese from Oebello, Timor, who had arrived in Broome in 1940 and was married to an English woman, Gladys Dunn. He was naturalized in 1961 and at the time was living in Parap, Darwin, working as a carpenter for the railways.[29] In 1954, when many of the pearling indents faced deportation, Mesak was granted an exemption on the basis of his Australian war service record. He was a member of the Darwin Returned Soldiers' League, and A. Brewster, the branch president, declared he was working to gain exemptions for both Mesak and another returned serviceman, Ben Ali Guya Kanon. Brewster told the newspapers: "Both served their country and have as much right as any Australian to stay here."[30] The Returned Services League in Darwin helped support Indonesian ex-servicemen with housing, education, and gaining citizenship.[31]

Biri Riwu, born on Savu Island in 1901, was another Indonesian who obtained permission to leave the pearling industry in the mid-1950s, but only after several years of negotiations.[32] His wife, Mavis E. Wright, had written to Harold Holt, minister for immigration, in June 1951 asking permission for her husband to work outside the pearling industry: "He has supported myself and three children for approximately three years and we are a very happy family. He has a very good record and has never been in trouble of any kind."[33] But in November, she received a reply stating that he would not be permitted to leave pearling. Official records showed that Riwu had arrived in 1940 though in fact he had first come to Australia in 1918.

It was not until 1954 that C. F. Brown, sub-collector of customs in Broome, provided the Immigration Department with an impressively long list of Riwu's previous employers in Australia, going back to 1920. He had worked for A. Ward from 1920 to 1926, and for five other master pearlers up until April 1942. During the war, he had been evacuated to Melbourne, where he worked in the Dutch Club in the Metropole Hotel and later at the James Seymour Wool Store. Returning to Broome in 1947, he had worked for four pearlers, namely Daniel McDaniel, Mary Dakas, M & W Scott—M being liberal Senator Malcolm Scott—and Male & Company, until 1954. Brown concluded: "It is submitted that, as this man has worked in the Industry for such a long time and only staying in his Home country 1935–36, his application be approved."[34]

In Broome, the issue of freedom of movement was also a problem. Bernardus Senge, born in Kupang in 1914, had come to Darwin in 1937 and been employed by Gregory as a diver. During the war, he had been evacuated to Adelaide, where he worked for one year carting firewood for the Australian military forces. In 1943, he moved to Melbourne, where he met Violet Anthony. After the war, he was forced to return to Broome, and was employed as a diver with Male & Company and M & W Scott.[35]

Violet, his de-facto wife, was interviewed in 1951 by the sub-collector of customs in Broome. She was seeking permission for her husband to accompany her on a trip to Darwin. The authorities expressed concern that if permitted to go, Senge might not return to Broome, but it was noted that since he owned his own home there, "he would more than likely return without any trouble."[36] Senge, Violet, and their son, John, who was born around 1946, were able to take holidays regularly but each time Violet was required to put a case to the sub-collector.[37] The Department of Immigration took the precaution of taking Senge's thumb-print before he left for one of these trips, and noted that he would be staying at the Salvation Army People's Palace in Perth en route to Melbourne.[38] Senge became a citizen in 1960. At that time he was staying with an Indonesian, Barak Sambono, in Stuart Park in Darwin and working for the Municipal Council as a laborer.[39]

The wages paid to pearling indents did not take into account whether or not they had wives. This was unusual in Australia where the basic or living wage was intended to support a family. Hari Bin Adam, born in Solor in 1923, was married to an Australian woman, Marjorie, and worked for pearling master Nicholas Paspaley (Senior). Bin Adam was granted permission to work outside the pearling industry in 1953 after he complained that he was unable to support his wife. Under the conditions of the pearling contract, Paspaley was not obliged to provide Bin Adam's wife with food, nor was he expected to provide Bin Adam with a wage during the three-month lay-up period. Bin Adam wrote that he was ashamed that his only other option was to have his wife work to support them. Bin Adam remained in Darwin with his wife and son, Paul, working as a laborer for the Darwin City Council. He was naturalized in 1963.[40]

Spouse of an Australian Citizen

The Menzies government set up the Commonwealth Immigration Advisory Council to review the policy regarding non-Europeans in Australia, in response both to cases in Australia and to pressure from overseas. The council voted in 1954 to grant Australian citizenship "to Asians who have permission to remain in Australia without any restrictions under the Immigration Act," a criterion that unfortunately did not apply to pearling indents.[41] A commitment was made to grant permanent residence to Asians with professional qualifications or distinguished government or humanitarian service, but admission of "lower class" Asians was to be prevented. When Harold Holt, Minister for Immigration, presented his recommendations to Cabinet in July 1956, they included an additional proposal to adopt "a more 'liberal attitude' towards non-Europeans already in Australia who had breached their entry conditions, especially in relation to restrictions on their occupation."[42]

It was not until 1956 that a new rule was passed that could be applied to Indonesian pearling indents. This rule allowed the "spouse" of an Australian to apply for citizenship. It was the case of a Japanese woman, Cherry Parker, that had inspired this decision. Cherry Parker was the wife of Australian Gordon Parker, who had served with the British Commonwealth Occupation Force in Japan. She entered Australia in 1952, as the first Japanese bride permitted to do so. Her story, splashed across the newspapers of the time, prompted a rethinking of the stringent restrictions of the White Australia policy. The media emphasized the romance of their love story and made much of her personal beauty.[43] The front page of the *Argus* carried a photograph of their two young daughters and their Australian grandmother with the caption: "The happiest grandmother in Melbourne."[44] Cherry was naturalized in January 1957.[45] As historian Keiko Tamura observes, "Their experience presented a case in which faithful love could conquer all barriers: racial, cultural, linguistic and of international relations."[46] The term "spouse of an Australian citizen" was soon applied to Indonesian men married to Australian women, including white Australian and Indigenous women. Since the passing of the 1948 Nationality and Citizenship Act, Aboriginal peoples had been formally recognized as Australian nationals. While this act did not confer all the rights held by white citizens, it did allow for legal recognition of the Indonesian spouses of Aboriginal women.

This new ruling proved to be useful for a number of Indonesians. For example, Esek Anaktotote, born in Tepa on Babar Island in 1910, had married in 1946 while living in Brisbane. His wife was a Badu Island woman, Possa née Usope, the widow of Paolos Annidlah. Possa had four children from her previous marriage to Timorese pearling indent, Henry Lewin, who had died in 1935.[47] The Department of Immigration decreed in 1948 that if Anaktotote were not prepared to return to work in the pearling industry, he would be given one month's notice to leave the country. The Hockings' Wanetta Pearling Company had offered to sign him on, but since they had no pearling boats operating that year, the government was not satisfied with this arrangement.[48] By good fortune, in 1957 his status was changed from "pearling indent" to "spouse of an Australian Citizen." The sub-collector of customs, H. J. McMahon, reported in 1957 that he "supports his wife, working on the waterfront as a casual labourer, when available. He receives very good pay. He owns and works a small vegetable farm on one of the neighbouring Islands."[49] At a time when the category of "spouse of an Australian Citizen" could apply equally to a husband as to a wife, there was still the notion that Anaktotote's financial support for his wife was a necessary factor in his qualifying for this category.

Citizenship through Assimilation—"Normal" Australian Life

The most important change for Indonesian pearling indents came in June 1957 with the recommendation to extend citizenship rights to all non-Europeans who had lived in Australia for fifteen years and who were otherwise still classed as temporary residents.[50] The Minister for Immigration, Athol Townley, on the advice of his distinguished head of department, Sir Tasman Heyes, imposed further conditions: that the applicants were "of good character; had not wilfully disregarded the conditions of their admission; had an adequate knowledge of English; and had taken part in normal Australian life."[51]

This new cultural test left it up to individual officials to determine if an applicant was taking part in "normal" Australian life. The case of Alexander Batfini, for example, challenged the government about the morality of making such judgments against Indonesians who were advancing in age. Batfini was born in the Tanimbar Islands in 1900 and had been in Broome before World War II.[52] During the war, he worked in a cotton-spinning mill in Melbourne. In 1954, Batfini was working for pearler Nicholas Paspaley (Senior) when he applied to be released from indenture as pearl-shell industry work had become too arduous for him. Because he had lost all contact with home, it was recommended that he be permitted to remain in Australia and to engage in an occupation of his own choosing.[53]

The Department of Immigration reported in December 1959 that Batfini had lost his job working for the Municipal Council and was in receipt of Commonwealth Social Service benefits.[54] His application for permanent residency was initially rejected because he failed to satisfy two of the main criteria: being competent in English and taking part in Australian life. Les Liveris, the Commonwealth migration officer in Darwin, wrote in June 1960 that Batfini was unable to speak or understand English and that he was almost completely deaf. He wrote, "I am satisfied that Alexander Batfini takes no part at all in normal Australian life."[55]

Batfini's case came at a time when attention was turning to the predicament of indents. During the debate over the 1958 Migration Bill in the House of Representatives, the left-wing Labor member for Yarra, Jim Cairns, spoke specifically about the men who worked in the pearling industry. "I believe that after they have been here for some years—in the pearling industry some have remained for thirty—and their employment has finished, they should be given the opportunity to become naturalised. They may be too old to work and, failing naturalisation, must return to their own country. Such people surely have very strong claims for naturalisation."[56] Following the refusal to grant permanent residence to Batfini, the acting secretary of the Department of Immigration, A. L. Nutt, wrote a letter attempting to justify the decision to Jim Cairns:

> In certain circumstances, non-Europeans who have resided in Australia on a temporary basis for a minimum period of fifteen years may be permitted to remain here permanently. This applies only to those non-Europeans who, inter alia, have acquired an adequate knowledge of the English language and who have made some attempt to adopt the Australian way of life. . . . However, even allowing for this relaxed criteria inquiries which have been made indicate that Messrs. Noladoe Toeloe, Gee Sir Sar, Ali Bin Lakey and Alexander Batfini cannot meet our requirements and their applications therefore cannot be approved. . . . Mr. Barak Sambono has married an Australian citizen and provided that our enquiries show that he is supporting his wife according to reasonable Australian standards he will be allowed to remain here permanently.[57]

Noladoe Toeloe, listed here as one of those not qualifying for Australian citizenship, did not let the matter rest. Toeloe was Rotenese, born in Oebelo in 1901, and had come to Broome in 1924 to work for H. Kennedy.[58] During the war he had been assigned to factory work in Melbourne. By 1952, he had moved to Darwin to work, like Batfini, for Nick Paspaley in the pearling industry. When his application for citizenship was refused, Toeloe wrote to Elizabeth Marshall in Melbourne, who had been involved in agitating for workers' rights, seeking support from her "For Friendship with Asia" organization, which had been founded in 1945. Marshall wrote to Les Liveris in 1960, stating, "These men were in Melbourne during the war, and I knew them well. They are quite good fellows, and did a good job during the war in factories here. All 'my boys' in Melbourne have had their applications granted without any trouble. They are very happy, and have a sense of security. Before this they were always nervous that deportation might overtake them. All those whom you permitted to come to Melbourne are in constant work. They come to see me every two or three weeks."[59] Noladoe was successful and became an Australian citizen in September 1962. At the time, he was single and living in the Railway Cottages in Darwin working for the Commonwealth Railways.[60]

Elizabeth Marshall also wrote to the Department of Immigration to support Batfini's application. She explained that she had known him very well for about four years when he was in Melbourne, at which time she placed him in a job "which he performed very satisfactorily." She confirmed that he spoke English and had no difficulty making himself understood. She noted that it was his deafness that now made it difficult for him to understand English, pointing out that "it would be a shocking thing to refuse permanent residence to a man who has grown old doing arduous and valuable work in this country for so many years. What his lot would be if he were returned to his own country I should not like to contemplate." She noted too that Nutt had stated that "in determining applications for permanent residence in the north and north-west of Australia a relaxed criteria is applied because opportunities for real assimilation may be limited." She finished with "an earnest plea" that his case be reconsidered.[61] Her request was successful, and in October 1961 Batfini was given formal permission to reside permanently in Australia. This time Liveris wrote a far more supportive letter regarding Batfini, stating, "Batfini is very well liked by the people with whom he associates, and, I am of the opinion that he would never have very much difficulty in finding a home with one of his many friends. In consideration of all the circumstances, and with due regard to BATFINI's contribution to the then under-manned pearling industry, I strongly recommend that approval be given for him to reside permanently in Australia."[62] Batfini was naturalized in May 1962, and became an Australian citizen.[63]

When applying for residence on Thursday Island, Albertos Herwawa was also supported by the sub-collector of customs, but was very nearly refused because of a letter from the local police sergeant. Herwawa came from Babar to Australia in 1926, aged twenty.[64] During the war, he had enlisted in the Australian army. His army file notes his religion as Church of England.[65] He returned to Thursday Island after the war and married a Torres Strait Islander woman, Ruth Ketchell. Following his application for naturalization in 1961, the sub-collector of customs sent the Immigration Department a favorable report. Herwawa was found to qualify for the criterion of "mixing with Australians," given that as a wharf laborer his coworkers were Australians. The sub-collector also noted that his home, which was very tidy, was among those of Australians, and that he was able to converse freely in English. He also mentioned that Herwawa was a member of the Malay Club, and that his main hobby was fishing.[66]

A second report, however, was sent from the Thursday Island Police Station raising questions about Ruth Ketchell because she "is many years younger than he."[67] This police report prompted the Commonwealth migration officer, T. M. Nulty, to write to the director of Native Affairs seeking his view as to whether or not Herwawa should be granted citizenship. Nulty wrote, "Asian pearling operatives, or former operatives, are only normally eligible to apply for citizenship by virtue of their marriage to Australian citizens but this in itself does not entitle them to naturalization, and each case is considered individually. As the majority of these pearlers . . . qualify to apply for naturalization only by reason of their marriage to native women, it is considered desirable to obtain the views of your Department on their suitability to acquire citizenship of this country before proceeding with the grant of naturalization to them."[68] This request questioning the marriage criterion reveals that the days of Indigenous and Torres Strait Islander women requiring permission to marry were not over. In fact the Church of England marriage register for Herwawa's marriage in 1960 stated that permission for an Islander to marry another Islander had been granted by the deputy director, Patrick James Killoran.[69] The director in this instance did not comment, but simply pointed out that the sub-collector was responsible for reports on permanent residency applications. Herwawa was granted citizenship in 1962 on the evidence of his participation in "Australian" life.

A number of the Indonesians on Thursday Island had had their applications accepted, and to celebrate there was a large gathering on August 11, 1960 to watch nine Indonesians, all former pearling indents, become naturalized. The town clerk reported that some 250 people attended the ceremony. The speakers were alderman and previous mayor of Cairns, W. J. Fulton; the Queensland member for the electorate of Cook, H. A. Adair, Member of the Legislative Assembly or MLA; and the member for Tablelands (west of Cairns), Tom Gilmore, MLA, who had a special message of congratulations from Dr. Noble, the Commonwealth Minister for Health and Home Affairs.[70] One of those being naturalized was Bora Bin Juda, whose war service was mentioned in chapter 7. Bin Juda had returned to Thursday Island in 1947 and engaged in pearling until advanced years forced him to retire from the industry. He was still employed casually on the wharf in 1952 and had lodged his application for citizenship in 1958.[71]

The Price of Delayed Citizenship

For some men, the process of gaining naturalization took too long. In the years officials mulled over reports and decisions, these men suffered unnecessary anxiety and financial hardship. Some even died before their naturalization was finalized.

The issue of financial security in retirement was a serious problem for those waiting for citizenship, as is shown in the case of Karel Kaprisi. Kaprisi came from Babar to Thursday Island in 1926, aged just nineteen, and in 1948 married Sophia Takai (née Barba), a local Thursday Island widow of Malay descent. Sophia's sister, Leah Barba, had been in the Cherbourg Settlement during the war. At that time she was already widowed with three Malay Japanese children. She and Karel had four children together, and when she died, it was left to Karel to care for the large family. In 1955, divers' paralysis left him crippled with arthritis, and he received workers' compensation. In 1960, just months before his naturalization, he received a letter from the Department of Social Services advising him that his benefits were to be terminated as he was not an Australian citizen. The sub-collector of customs on Thursday Island wrote to the Commonwealth migration officer in April advising that Karel was distressed because he was supporting a family. Karel's naturalization in August that year came none too soon.[72]

Other men did not survive to enjoy the security of citizenship. Danggi Hanoe, born on Rote in 1910, was granted permanent residency in 1961 and in August 1965 applied to be naturalized. But Hanoe died in December before the naturalization interview could take place. Similarly, Bagu Bin Amat (Bargo Bin Ahmat), born in Pontianak, Kalimantan in 1891 (or 1887), was married to Badu Island woman Raima Ah Wang and had six children.[73] The government finally approved his naturalization application on January 27, 1959, but he died on February 12 the following year, before he could take up Australian citizenship.[74] So too went the story of Taba Leba, born in Savu in 1902. He had arrived in Broome first in 1924 on board the *Centaur*. He returned to Savu between 1934 and 1940, but on return to Australia spent the war in Melbourne before going back to Broome in 1947. He was granted permanent residency in 1963, but he too died in 1964 before being able to take up citizenship.[75]

Perhaps most tragic were the men who faced the prospect of being denied citizenship by both the Indonesian and Australian governments. The case of Hati Oel, who was born in Timor in 1900, demonstrates the sad plight of statelessness. Hati applied in 1956 to be released from his contract of indenture, but was denied, so in 1958 he asked to be repatriated to Timor. Under the indenture contract, his employer, Clark, was liable for the cost of repatriation. Clark advised the Immigration Department in April 1959 that Oel desired to return home but could do so

Karel Kaprisi in his application for registration, 1948. National Archives of Australia, Brisbane J25 1959/156 1050504.

only if he could obtain an Indonesian passport. The Indonesian embassy, however, required a date, a place of birth, and a place of domicile in Timor from before Oel went to Australia, and the name and address of a near relative in Timor. Oel and his brother, Saoe, were interviewed in July 1959, together with several other Indonesian indents. Neither Hati nor Saoe could remember their parents, having been orphaned at a young age. They had another brother, Ban Oel, but did not know where he was. Their applications for Indonesian passports were refused. The Australian Department of Immigration finally advised Hati on March 16, 1960, that he would be permitted to remain in Australia and work in an employment of his choice. Three days later, he was hit by a truck while crossing the road and killed.[76]

The stories of men who fought over many long years for the privilege of Australian citizenship reveal some of the real-life consequences of a restrictive immigration bureaucracy. At times the system seemed impossibly inhumane: doubting the validity of marriages; questioning the rights of fathers; denying years of hard labor. On the other hand, there were many generous people who supported the Indonesians over the years: customs officers who argued for flexible notions of what should constitute an Australian lifestyle; politicians who reminded immigration officials of the debt owed to those men who had served during the war. Most importantly, we acknowledge the women who sustained years of patient lobbying, using the weight of their moral and legal citizenship to persuade officials that their families should be protected.

Conclusion

Historians of migration often seek to measure the strength of diasporic communities by demonstrating the extent to which they retain personal ties to their homeland. Having rejected the notion of cultural assimilation that was so favored in the 1950s, we now celebrate the maintenance of cultural heritage. But given the difficult political atmosphere in eastern Indonesia of the 1950s, not all Indonesians in the pearling industry were eager or able to maintain connections with their homeland. In practical terms, we need to acknowledge that any return to Indonesia would have been financially beyond the means of most migrant families. Despite the fact that their island homes were just a few hundred kilometers away, the disappearance of regular shipping or flight services between northern Australia and eastern Indonesia made such travel prohibitively expensive. Furthermore, many of the men had lost contact with their homes long before they settled and raised families in Australia.

For those men who would have welcomed a visit home, there was the added problem that any "unauthorized" travel outside of Australia might have jeopardized their right to return. By the time the naturalization process was completed, most men were already too old to consider the trip. Of the naturalization files examined, only two contained applications for Australian passports. One was for Salem Bodah, son of Bodah Bin Nassia, born in Flores in 1913, who first came to Broome in 1931. A series of two-year contracts meant that Salem had short returns to Kupang between contracts, and his 1942 application for registration stated that he had a wife in Kupang. Bodah, aged fifty, was naturalized in Darwin on December 7, 1963, and obtained his Australian passport in 1968. He wrote on his passport application that he would travel to Singapore and Malaya.[1] It is not known if he returned to Australia afterwards. The only other Indonesian known to have obtained a passport was The Soen Hin. He applied for an Australian passport in 1972, aged fifty-one.[2] Unlike Bodah, The Soen Hin had family in Broome.

Today in the pearling ports of Broome, Darwin, and Thursday Island, many locals proudly acknowledge their mixed Indigenous and Asian heritage. When historian Regina Ganter made a trip across Australia's north, she found cultural echoes of Indonesia in food, music, and family stories.[3] Even without regular contact with Indonesia, the families themselves still remember their origins, and even today some continue to find ways to make trips there possible.

The award-winning singer-actor Jessica Mauboy is a "Darwin girl" and one of the younger descendants of Indonesian Aboriginal heritage. In an interview, when asked about her mixed heritage, she said: "I'm Australian. You know, I'm Aboriginal, Indonesian, Timorese. But I'm a full Aussie."[4] Mauboy's mother is Aboriginal and her father, Ferdy Mauboy, was born in West Timor. Already a public figure after starring in *Australian Idol,* in 2008 she arranged a trip to Indonesia, including a trip to Timor and a visit to a school in Kupang. Her grandfather, Sammy Mauboy, came to Darwin to work in the pearling industry and ended up working as a gardener in the Botanic Gardens. He was granted Australian citizenship in 1976 and brought his wife and children over from Timor. According to the family story, the authorities had to grant him citizenship because they had lost all his records during Cyclone Tracy, which wiped out the city in 1974. With her family, Jessica sings songs in Indonesian, keeping alive her Indonesian heritage.[5]

Indigenous writer Samantha Faulkner reflects on the Indigenous Malay heritage of her grandfather. She published his story to explain both their Malay heritage and the strong Aboriginal and Torres Strait identification that he demonstrated as a cultural ambassador in "educating non-Aboriginal and Torres Strait Islander peoples about Aboriginal and Torres Strait Islander culture."[6] Her story also highlights the blending of Muslim and Christian faiths among the Indonesians. She explained that members of the "Malay Club" "would assist one another with family and community obligations" and that this help was open to all the pearling indents and their children.[7] Her grandfather, Mohammed Ali Drummond, who was born in 1917 on Thursday Island, went to the "Malay Club" in 1952 for assistance to build a new house. Ali was the son of Drummond Sarawak from Sarawak and Cissie Malay. Cissie was the child of Nara Para, an Aboriginal woman of the Yadhaigana people, from Red Island, and a Javanese man, Jimmy Malay. Both Ali's parents were practicing Muslims but Ali was not taught their religion as his parents had died in 1931 when Ali was just fourteen.[8] Ali married a Catholic woman, Carmen Villaflor, in 1936 in a Catholic ceremony.[9]

Faulkner celebrates both her Indonesian and Indigenous heritage, and their family history demonstrates the rich cultural diversity found in the north Australian ports along the pearl frontier. For all the years that it took for Indonesians to break down the White Australia policy and to have their relationships with Indigenous women recognized, their families are now acknowledged and held dear in the heart of northern communities.

Sally Bin Demin, a Broome woman, published the story of her family and friends in a joyful tribute to multicultural life in Broome. As with so many Broome people, religious and ethnic diversity was part of her life. She was baptized in the Sacred Heart Church in Beagle Bay near Broome in front of a luminous pearl-shell altar. Her mother, a Jaru-speaking Aboriginal woman from the eastern part of The Kimberley, had been raised in the Beagle Bay Mission and had been educated in a Broome convent.[10]

Bin Demin recalled that, as a child, social hierarchy was determined by "race," but that women who married into the pearling industry also acquired higher status if their husbands were divers. Her mother lived with Simeon Bin Said, a Muslim Malay from Singapore. He was a diver and served during the war in the Australian Special Forces in New Guinea. Her mother did not marry Bin Said, as her de jure husband, Cass Drummond, had been sent to the Derby leprosarium soon after they had married.[11]

Bin Demin's parents lived in Broome in a shared house with Con Gill, the Hindu landlord; Indonesian Ahmat Mustafa—known as Ahmat Jawa—and his family; a Filipino Aboriginal woman, Esther; and the Japanese Matsumoto family. She recalls eating Irish stews and Malay food—*nasi bubor* [*bubur,* rice porridge] for breakfast and hot fish curries. Many languages were heard in their home including "a Broome-style Malay" with "a lot of Indonesian mixed in," English and Aboriginal languages such as Bardi, Nyul Nyul, Yawuru, Jaru, and Karijarri.[12] Her story vividly documents the harmonious blending of Aboriginal, Asian, and European people that was Broome society.

We have mapped the history of the pearl frontier, but recognize that many of its stories are yet to be described. As we rediscover the connections between Australia and the islands of eastern Indonesia, we can only hope that both academics and families will be inspired to fill in the gaps so that we can understand fully the legacy of the pearl-shell industry. When Abdoel Gafoer left Alor in 1921, what became of those who stayed behind? Do local communities in Indonesia remember the men who left for Australia? We know that the Dutch insisted that the men return with a portion of their wages in hand, and that much of the money was spent in Kupang, but was there some flow on to their island homes? These are important questions that could be taken up by local historians in Indonesia. And perhaps the many pearling families who are able to trace their heritage to Indonesia will find some benefit from our research as they themselves take part in the important endeavor of preserving the cultural legacy of the pearl frontier.

When we look back over the century of mobility in the pearl-shell industry, we can see how the Indonesian presence in northern Australia helped to shape a unique multiethnic society. It was the influence of British and Dutch colonialism in Southeast Asia that encouraged Australians to import Indonesians as indentured labor, but over the years their lives came to represent a subaltern challenge to that colonial system. They challenged colonial expectations by seeking a place of equality within Australian society. They were aided in this challenge by a remarkable range of people who recognized the justice of their cause. Their attempts to earn equal wages were supported by Australian labor organizers; their attempts to gain citizenship by Australian activists and politicians, from communists to liberals. Finally, in their personal lives, they were welcomed into, and helped to create, the vibrant Indigenous Asian communities of Australia's north.

Abdoel Gafoer, the Alorese man who left his Muslim community in the Netherlands East Indies to become a respected member of the Yaruwu people of Broome in Australia, was a typical man of the pearl frontier. His life was one of rupture, as he challenged the harsh labor laws of Australia and overcame the restrictions of the White Australia policy. But there was also a sense of continuity in his moving from Alor to Broome in that both locations share a strong community connection to the sea. It is that maritime culture that underpins the deep relationship between Australia and Indonesia and indeed the wider region.

For one hundred years the harvesting of pearl shell provided the catalyst for social, cultural, economic, and political interactions between Australia and eastern Indonesia. Pearl shell as a commodity helped shape the region. The historical pearl frontier was and is challenging because it undermines the notion of sharply defined borders that are deemed to be so important to present day nation-states. At a time when individual mobility is often posited as needing to be controlled and restrained by the state, we can learn from these examples of maritime mobility. Rather than viewing border crossings with suspicion, we find that they produce stronger and more meaningful ties between nations.

Appendix

Lists of "Koepanger" Pearling Workers in Broome

Name	Occupation	Location during World War II
Nataniel Rupadara	diver	Merchant Navy, NEI
Eli Nafoe	diver	Merchant Navy, NEI
Bois Benobe	diver	Merchant Navy, NEI
Johannis Dengoe	diver	Broome
Adam Sini	diver	Broome
Moedo Bolo	diver	Melbourne
Lomi Hadjoe	diver	Water Transport
Bernadoes Laga	diver	Died
Markoes Sir	diver	Died
Muyama Ra	diver	Died
Felix Manaha	diver	Died
Lazoroes Bengoe	tender	Merchant Navy, NEI
Toelang Garoe	tender	Merchant Navy, NEI
Lani Foes	tender	Broome
Adoe Delas	tender	Melbourne
Soleman Nale	tender	Melbourne
Molo Nome	tender	Melbourne
Nanoe Natoen	tender	Melbourne
Besing Seo	tender	Melbourne
Martinoes Lodo	tender	Melbourne
Poeling Weng	tender	Melbourne
Seko Floei	tender	Melbourne
Lusi Bois	tender	Melbourne
Poelina Oer	tender	Melbourne
Taoe Suloes	tender	Melbourne
Rani Riki	tender	Melbourne
Sunoen Poelina	tender	Melbourne
Ali Laki	tender	Melbourne
Willem Toeka	tender	Melbourne

(continued)

Lists of "Koepanger" Pearling Workers in Broome (*continued*)

Name	Occupation	Location during World War II
Dupong	tender	Melbourne
Djaman Samoen	tender	Melbourne
Mano Melo	tender	Melbourne
Hassan Likoer	tender	Melbourne
B. Sofue	tender	Melbourne
Kassim Kadir	tender	Melbourne
Mousala	tender	Melbourne
Djara Wila	tender	Melbourne
Lisi Lasi	tender	Melbourne
K. Seba	tender	Melbourne
Soeiji Hana	tender	Melbourne
Abdul Rhaman	tender	Melbourne
Benjiman Bangoe	tender	Melbourne
Kolan Tino	tender	Melbourne
Arnolos Giri	tender	Melbourne
Mangoe Iwa	tender	Melbourne
Doela Ali Daku	tender	Melbourne
Modo Sabah	tender	Melbourne
Laoe Baoen	tender	Melbourne
Deni Mojo	tender	Melbourne
Izak Salankey	tender	Melbourne
Moesak Soei	tender	Melbourne
Paulus Pingga	tender	Melbourne
Thomas Willem	tender	Melbourne
Wini Goma	tender	Melbourne
Doloe Bitang	tender	Melbourne
Sekatasi	tender	Melbourne
Beri Rewi	tender	Melbourne
Lay Behi	tender	Melbourne
Johanese Bangoe	tender	Melbourne
Jacob Bengoe	tender	Died
Fesak Feh	tender	Died
Tjian Nomi	tender	Died
Martin Louter	trial diver	Merchant Navy, NEI
?olo Wela	trial diver	Melbourne
Manas Neto	trial diver	Melbourne
Jeskai Mesak	trial diver	Melbourne
Koto Izak	trial diver	Died

Source: Pearling—Post War Re-establishment of industry in W.A., 1945/0040, Acc 477, SROWA.

Indentured Men at H. Kennedy's Station. Tuckered Account, Navy Department, 1941–1942*

Ahmat Bin Hassan	Lobo Pela
Radja Toloe	Kiroe Iye
Elias Laimeherewa	Marcus Damoe
Hanok Adoe	Doaed Kore
Loeang Serang	Pierer Bam
Frans Manaha	Johannes Kadja
Mesak Soei	Letoe Kehi
Ley Behi	Hendrix Papitoe
Gilbert Mahoori	Patti
Frederick Rupidara	Pakio Radjab
N'doloe Bintang	Johan Lano
Ibrahim Lay	Jermias Ratoe
Roebin Radja	Willem Kada

Note: *Names not included in the previous list.
Source: Lois Anderson, B.A. Honors Thesis, 1978, appendix.

NOTES

Introduction

1. For more details, see Ben Collins, "The History of Indonesians in Broome," ABC Kimberley recording of the event, and accompanying interview with Susan Edgar, http://www.abc.net.au/local/stories/2010/07/08/2947883.htm?site=kimberley.

2. The term "pearling industry" was commonly used during this period to refer to what was technically speaking the "pearl shell industry" in that it was the shell rather than the pearls that provided the main source of income.

Chapter 1. Border-Crossing on the Pearl Frontier

1. C. C. Macknight, *The Voyage to Marege': Macassan Trepangers in Northern Australia* (Melbourne: Melbourne University Press, 1976); Pamela Swadling, *Plumes from Paradise: Trade Cycles in Outer Southeast Asia and Their Impact on New Guinea and Nearby Islands until 1920* (Boroko: Papua New Guinea National Museum in association with Robert Brown and Associates, Qld., 1996).

2. Adrian Vickers, "'Malay Identity': Modernity, Invented Tradition, and Forms of Knowledge," *RIMA* 31, no. 1 (1997). "Southeast Asia" (or more strictly, South East Asia) is an even more recent term, coined to identify the World War II military command led by Lord Mountbatten.

3. Although it was Earl's colleague James Logan who put forward the argument for the term, see Robert E. Elson, *The Idea of Indonesia: A History* (Cambridge: Cambridge University Press, 2008), 1–2.

4. Ewen McPhee, "Archaeology of the Pearl Shelling Industry in Torres Strait," *Memoirs of the Queensland Museum, Cultural Heritage Series* 3, no. 1 (2004); J. D. F. Hardenberg, "De Parelmoervisscherij in het Oosten van den Indischen Archipel," *Indische Gids* 2 (1939); P.N. van Kampen, "De Paarl- en Parelmoervisscherij langs de Kusten der Aroe-Ielanden," *Mededeelingen van het Visscherij-Station te Batavia* 2 (1908). Kampen, who may be using an older terminology, says however that the local pearls of Aru are of the variety *Margaritifera maxima* (*meleagrina margaritifera*), of the gold-lipped variety, while the related beds of Tanimbar and the islands of West Papua (New Guinea) are of the silver-lip form. Shells caught weighed around 3 kg, though one was as much as 4.5 kg.

5. Steve Mullins, "To Break 'the Trinity' or 'Wipe Out the Smaller Fry': The Australian Pearl Shell Convention of 1913," *Journal for Maritime Research* 7, no. 1 (2005): 226, where he also mentions the black-lip "Tahitian," "Green snail," and "Japan ear shells." See also "Commercial Pearl Shell Sales," *Northern Miner*, September 15, 1913. "Characters of Broome, Episode 1: Donnelly McKenzie," aired August 7, 2013, 21:30, on NITV (National Indigenous Television), http://www.nitv.org.au/fx-program.cfm?pid=6185D122-A8DE-482B-38CDEFD7429165A7&pgid=61AF0DB6-0A5F-9010-AF7519DC0E1E9607, accessed May 18, 2014.

6. Triono Widodo et al., "Report on National Survey of Remittance Patterns of Indonesian Migrant Workers, 2008" (Jakarta: Bank Indonesia, Directorate of Economic and Monetary Statistics, 2009).

7. Michele Ford and Lenore Lyons, "Travelling the Aspal Route: Grey Labour Migration through an Indonesian Border Town," in *The State and Illegality in Indonesia,* ed. E. Aspinall and G. van Klinken (Leiden: KITLV, 2011).

8. Sidney Jones, *Making Money off Migrants: The Indonesian Exodous to Malaysia* (Hong Kong and Wollongong: ASIA 2000 and the Centre for Asia Pacific Social Transformation Studies, University of Wollongong, 2000).

9. Ann Loveband, "Positioning the Product: Indonesian Migrant Women Workers in Taiwan," *Journal of Contemporary Asia* 34, no. 3 (2004).

10. Catharina Purwanti Williams, *Maiden Voyages: Eastern Indonesian Women on the Move* (Singapore: ISEAS, 2007).

11. Craig A. Lockard, "The Javanese as Emigrant," *Indonesia* 11 (1971).

12. Rupert Lockwood, *Black Armada* (Sydney South: Australasia Book Society, 1975).

13. Jan Lingard, *Refugees and Rebels: Indonesians in Wartime Australia* (North Melbourne, VIC: Australian Scholarly Publishing, 2008). In 2010, a special issue of the *Review of Indonesian and Malaysian Affairs* was the first significant contribution to the wider study of political refugees and exiles from Indonesia, including those escaping from the anti-Communist killings of 1965–1966. This group included students whose overseas study left them stranded in a category of political unacceptability. The authors have edited a special issue of *Indonesia and the Malay World* 40 (2012) intended as a step toward a long-term set of studies that will bring together understandings of Indonesians in different parts of the world.

14. Adrian Vickers, "A Paradise Bombed," *Griffith Review* 1 (Spring 2003).

15. Julia Martínez, "The 'Malay' Community in Pre-War Darwin," in *Queensland Review: Asians in Australian History,* ed. Regina Ganter, 6, no. 2 (November 1999): 45–58.

16. Epeli Hau'ofa, "Our Sea of Islands," in *A New Oceania: Rediscovering Our Sea of Islands* (Suva: University of the South Pacific, 1993); C. C. Macknight, "Outback to Outback: The Indonesian Archipelago and Northern Australia," in *Indonesia: Australian Perspectives,* ed. R. G. Garnaut, J. J. Fox, P. T. McCawley, and J. A. C. Mackie (Canberra: Research School of Pacific and Asian Studies, Australian National University, 1980).

17. Ruth Balint, *Troubled Waters: Border, Boundaries and Possession in the Timor Sea* (Crows Nest, NSW: Allen & Unwin, 2005). Another relatively undocumented aspect of maritime mobility currently being explored by Pam Nilan is the contemporary crewing of cruise ships by Indonesians.

18. Eric Tagliacozzo, "Navigating Communities: Race, Place, and Travel in the History of Maritime Southeast Asia," *Asian Ethnicity* 10, no. 2 (2009).

19. Both the Labor and Liberal parties have drawn on this contention, most famously by former Prime Minister John Howard, "Australia in the World," in *Address by the Prime Minister, the Hon. John Howard MP, to the Lowy Institute for International Policy* (Sydney: The Lowy Institute, 2005).

20. David Walker, *Anxious Nation: Australia and the Rise of Asia 1850–1939* (St. Lucia: University of Queensland Press, 1999).

21. A. M. Jones, *Africa and Indonesia: The Evidence of the Xylophone and Other Musical and Cultural Factors* (Leiden: E. J. Brill, 1964).

22. Anthony J. S. Reid, *Southeast Asia in the Age of Commerce 1450–1680,* 2 vols. (New Haven, CT: Yale University Press, 1987, 1993).

23. Engseng Ho, *The Graves of Tarim: Genealogy and Mobility across the Indian Ocean* (Berkeley: University of California Press, 2006).

24. Adrian Vickers, "The Country and the Cities," *Journal of Contemporary Asia* 34, no. 3 (April 2004).

25. David Sissons, "*Karayuki-San:* Japanese Prostitutes in Australia, 1887–1916," *Historical Studies* 17 (1977); David Sissons, "The Japanese in the Australian Pearling Industry," *Queensland Heritage* 3, no. 10 (1979).

26. Regina Ganter, with contributions from Julia Martínez and Gary Lee, *Mixed Relations: Asian-Aboriginal Contact in North Australia* (Crawley: University of Western Australian Press, 2006); Julia Martínez, "Plural Australia: Aboriginal and Asian Labour in Tropical White Australia, Darwin, 1911–1940" (PhD diss., University of Wollongong, 1999); Regina Ganter, *The Pearl-Shellers of Torres Strait* (Melbourne: Melbourne University Press, 1994); see also Peta Stephenson, *The Outsiders Within. Telling Australia's Indigenous-Asian Story* (Sydney: University of New South Wales Press, 2007).

27. See Ganter, *The Pearl-Shellers,* and Timothy G. Jones, *The Chinese in the Northern Territory* (Darwin: Northern Territory University Press, 1990).

28. Macknight, *The Voyage to Marege'.*

29. James Urry and Michael Walsh, "The Lost 'Macassar' Language and Culture of Northern Australia," *Aboriginal History* 5, no. 2 (1981); Athol Chase, "'All Kind of Nation': Aborigines and Asians in the Cape York Peninsula," *Aboriginal History* 5 (1981); Jeremy Beckett, "The Torres Strait Islanders and the Pearling Industry: A Case of Internal Colonialism," *Aboriginal History* 1, no. 1 (1977).

30. Macknight, "Outback to Outback."

31. R. H. Barnes, *Sea Hunters of Indonesia: Fishers and Weavers of Lamalera* (Oxford: Clarendon Press, 1996), 13–15.

32. Anthony J. S. Reid, Introduction to *Slavery, Bondage and Dependency in Southeast Asia,* ed. Anthony J. S. Reid (St. Lucia: University of Queensland Press, 1983).

33. B. A. Hussainmiya, *Orang Rejimen: The Malays of the Ceylon Rifle Regiment* (Kuala Lumpur: Universiti Kebangsaan Malaysia, 1990).

34. Barnes, *Sea Hunters,* 15.

35. Eric Tagliacozzo, *Secret Trades, Porous Borders: Smuggling and States along a Southeast Asian Frontier, 1865–1915* (New Haven, CT: Yale University Press, 2005).

36. P. C. Emmer and R. Shlomowitz, "Mortality and Javanese Labour in Surinam (1890–1936) and Malaya (1912–1933)," in *Working Papers in Economic History* (Adelaide: Flinders University, 1995).

37. Ernst Spaan, "Taikongs and Calos: The Role of Middlemen and Brokers in Javanese International Migration," *International Migration Review* 28, no. 1 (1994): 94.

38. Spaan, "Taikongs and Calos."

39. Maureen De Silva, "Javanese Indentured Labourers in British North Borneo, 1914–1932" (PhD diss., School of Oriental and African Studies, University of London, 2009), 58.

40. De Silva, "Javanese Indentured Labourers"; Thio Termorshuizen, "Indentured Labour in the Dutch Colonial Empire 1800–1940," in *Dutch Colonialism, Migration and Cultural Heritage,* ed. Gert Oostindie (Leiden: KITLV Press, 2008).

41. Jean Luc Maurer, in collaboration with Marcel Magi, and with a contribution by Marie-Jo Siban, *Les Javanais du Caillou: Des affres de l'exil aux aléas de l'intégration* (Paris: Association Archipel, 2006).

42. Emmer and Shlomowitz, "Mortality and Javanese Labour"; Rosemarijn Hoefte, "A Passage to Suriname? The Migration of Modes of Resistance by Asian Contract Laborers," *International Labor and Working Class History* 54 (1998): 61.

43. Hoefte, "A Passage to Suriname?," 20. This is also the subject of new research by Pam Allen.

44. Report to Governor-General of Indochina on Javanese Contract Labour, 1909, 11, GGI 42591, ANOM, Aix-en-Provence.

45. Telegram from Monguillot, March 1, 1928, GGI 42596, ANOM.

46. Maurer, Magi, and Siban, *Les Javanais du Caillou.*

47. Fidayanti Muljono-Larue, *Histoire de l'immigration des Javanais sous contrat en Nouvelle-Calédonie, 1896–1950* (Noumea: Centre territorial de recherche et de documentation pedagogiques, 1996), 28.

48. Dorothy Shineberg, *The People Trade: Pacific Island Laborers and New Caledonia, 1865–1930* (Honolulu: University of Hawai'i Press, 1999), 141–143.

49. Muljono-Larue, *Histoire de l'immigration des Javanais,* 26.

50. R. S. Roosman, "A Shadow over a Silent New Caledonia Community," *Pacific Islands Monthly* (March 1978).

51. Maurer, Magi, and Siban, *Les Javanais du Caillou.*

52. Muljono-Larue, *Histoire de l'immigration des Javanais.*

53. Maurer, Magi, and Siban, *Les Javanais du Caillou.*

54. Lockard, "The Javanese as Emigrant."

55. "Javanese for Queensland," *Brisbane Courier,* September 24, 1886, 6.

56. *Brisbane Courier,* October 26, 1885, 4.

57. V. J. H. Houben, "Javanese Labour Migration into Southeast Asia, the Pacific and Australia," in *Proceedings of the University of Queensland History Research Group, No. 5,* ed. Paul Crook (Brisbane: University of Queensland, 1994).

58. "Aliens at Queensland Mills, 1916," Colonial Sugar Refining Company Papers, CSR 142/1479, Noel Butlin Archive Centre, Canberra.

59. Houben, "Javanese Labour Migration," 19.

Chapter 2. The Birth of the Pearling Zone, 1860–1890

1. William Eisler and Bernard Smith, *Terra Australis: The Furthest Shore* (Sydney: Art Gallery of New South Wales, 1988).

2. Diana Preston and Michael Preston, *A Pirate of Exquisite Mind: The Life of William Dampier, Explorer, Naturalist and Buccaneer* (London: Doubleday, 2004).

3. Hans Hägerdal kindly pointed out from his own research that Dampier's claims about French pirates are not substantiated by VOC reports, and "may be due to a misunderstanding," although the Dutch reported other pirates in the region (pers. comm., April 17, 2013). See also Hans Hägerdal, *Lords of the Land, Lords of the Sea: Conflict and Adaptation in Early Colonial Timor, 1600–1800* (Leiden: KITLV Press, 2012), 314.

4. Eisler and Smith, *Terra Australis;* C. C. Macknight, *The Voyage to Marege': Macassan Trepangers in Northern Australia* (Melbourne: Melbourne University Press, 1976).

5. George Windsor Earl, *The Eastern Seas, Voyages and Adventures in the Indian Archipelago, in 1832–33–34, Comprising a Tour of the Island of Java—Visits to Borneo, the Malay Peninsula, Siam* (London: W.H. Allen, 1837), 433.

6. Earl, *Eastern Seas,* 435.

7. Earl, *Eastern Seas,* 440.

8. "Port Essington," Extracts from Mr. Earl's Report, August 30, 1841, *Sydney Morning Herald,* September 4, 1843, 4.

9. P. Drabbe, *Het Leven van den Tamembarees: Ethnografische Studie over het Tamembaree-sche Volk* (Leiden: Brill, 1940).

10. James Francis Warren, *The Sulu Zone, 1768–1898: Dynamics of External Trade, Slavery, and Ethnicity in the Transformation of a Southeast Asian Maritime State* (Singapore: Singapore University Press, 1981).

11. Russel Braddon, *Thomas Baines and the North Australian Expedition* (Sydney: Collins, 1986).

12. Alfred Russel Wallace, "On the Arru Islands" (Charles H. Smith, "The Alfred Russel Wallace Page," archival materials, Unpublished Diaries S41: 1858), http://people.wku.edu/charles .smith/index1.htm, accessed August 13, 2012.

13. Penny van Oosterzee, *Where Worlds Collide: The Wallace Line* (Kew, Victoria: Reed, 1997).

14. Oosterzee, *Where Worlds Collide.*

15. Johan Gerard Friedrich Riedel, *De Sluik- en Kroesharige Rassen tusschen Selebes en Papua* ('s-Gravenhage: Martinus Nijhoff, 1886).

16. Macleay's collection became the basis of the University of Sydney's Macleay Museum. Adrian Vickers' great-grandfather, James Clarence Wilcox, was a member of the main D'Albertis expedition, following in the footsteps of his father, James Fowler Wilcox, who had been a naturalist on the *Rattlesnake.* Thanks to Iain McCalman for discussion of these voyages.

17. L. M. D'Albertis, *New Guinea: What I Did and What I Saw* (London: Sampson Low, Marston, Searle, & Rivington, 1880).

18. Pamela Swadling, *Plumes from Paradise: Trade Cycles in Outer Southeast Asia and Their Impact on New Guinea and Nearby Islands until 1920* (Boroko: Papua New Guinea National Museum in association with Robert Brown and Associates, Qld., 1996).

19. H. J. Gibbney, "D'Albertis, Luigi Maria (1841–1901)," in *Australian Dictionary of Biography,* National Centre of Biography, Australian National University, http://adb.anu.edu.au /biography/dalbertis-luigi-maria-3351/text5045, published first in hardcopy 1972.

20. D'Albertis, *New Guinea,* vol. 1, 163.

21. D'Albertis, *New Guinea,* 167.

22. Wallace, "On the Arru Islands."

23. Paul Battersby, *To the Islands: White Australians and the Malay Archipelago since 1788* (Lanham, MD: Lexington Books, 2007), 36.

24. Alan Kerr, *A Federation in These Seas: An Account of the Acquisition by Australia of Its External Territories* (Barton, ACT: Attorney General's Department, Commonwealth of Australia, 2009), 196.

25. "The Whaler Costa Rica Packet," *Sydney Morning Herald,* August 23, 1888, reports him as whaling in "the Banda Straits, the Arafura and Flores Seas." Steve Mullins, "The Costa Rica Packet Affair: Colonial Entanglements and Tests of Empire in Pre-Federation New South Wales," *Journal of the Royal Australian Historical Society* 87, no. 2 (2001): 270, notes that he was originally a partner in Ross and Carpenter; presumably this is Clunies-Ross.

26. Mullins, "The Costa Rica Packet Affair"; Battersby, *To the Islands,* 35.

27. Mullins, "The Costa Rica Packet Affair"; see also "Country News," *Queenslander,* January 16, 1892.

28. "The Costa Rica Packet Case," *Sydney Morning Herald,* November 16, 1893.

29. Mullins, "The Costa Rica Packet Affair."

30. Mullins, "The Costa Rica Packet Affair," esp. 283.

31. John Bolton Carpenter, as a mercantile marine master, was made an assessor under the Navigation Act 1900, and is reported as an assessor sitting on Marine Courts in Sydney in the early twentieth century. See "Assessors under the Navigation Act," *Brisbane Courier,* June 20, 1900; "Court of Marine Inquiry," *Sydney Morning Herald,* November 25, 1910.

32. Kerr, *A Federation in These Seas.*

33. R. H. Barnes, "Lamalerap: A Whaling Village in Eastern Indonesia," *Indonesia* 17 (April 1974): 152.

34. R. H. Barnes, *Sea Hunters of Indonesia: Fishers and Weavers of Lamalera* (Oxford: Clarendon Press, 1996), 323–331.

35. Alfred Russel Wallace, *The Malay Archipelago. The Land of the Orang-utan and the Bird of Paradise: A Narrative of Travel, with Studies of Man and Nature* (London: Macmillan & Co., 1869). Text available at http://people.wku.edu/charles.smith/index1.htm, accessed March 14, 2012.

36. Kerr, *A Federation in These Seas,* 324–328.

37. Edwin W. Streeter, *Pearls and Pearling Life* (London: George Bell and Sons, 1886; repr. Hesperian Press, Carlisle, WA, and Matching Press, Harlow, 2006), 169–170.

38. Streeter, *Pearls and Pearling Life.*

39. Battersby, *To the Islands,* 35; "The Mergui Pearl Fisheries," *Northern Territory Times and Gazette,* May 31, 1895, reporting on Frank Jardine's trip to Burma.

40. Steve Mullins, "To Break 'the Trinity' or 'Wipe Out the Smaller Fry': The Australian Pearl Shell Convention of 1913," *Journal for Maritime Research* 7, no. 1 (2005): 225.

41. Mullins, "To Break 'the Trinity,'" quoting a letter from Jardine.

42. J. N. A. "A Valuable Pearl," *West Australian,* August 25, 1898.

43. "News and Notes," *West Australian,* June 15, 1888; "Our Pearl Shell Fisheries," *West Australian,* June 16, 1888; Steve Mullins, "Australian Pearl-Shellers in the Moluccas: Confrontations and Compromise on a Maritime Frontier," *Great Circle* 23, no. 2 (2001): 12.

44. Hugh Edwards, *Port of Pearls: Broome's First 100 Years* (Swanbourne: Hugh Edwards, 1984).

45. Carl Edmonds, "Pearl Diving: The Australian Story," *Supplement to SPUMS* [South Pacific Underwater Medicine Society] *Journal* 26, no. 1 (1996).

46. An excerpt from Earl's *Handbook* titled "Labour for North Australia" was published in the *Northern Territory Times and Gazette,* November 21, 1873, 3, the same year when Australian pearlers begin to engage labor from Kupang on a large scale. Warren, *The Sulu Zone,* 167.

47. Henry Taunton, *Australind: Wanderings in Western Australia and the Malay East* (London: Edward Arnold, 1903), 211.

48. "Honour to Whom Honour Is Due and Captain Francis Cadell," *Argus,* June 6, 1874.

49. "Treatment of Natives in North Australia" (letter to the editor by Samuel Tomkinson), *South Australian Register,* November 19, 1878.

50. J. H. M. Honniball, "E. H. Laurence, Stipendiary Magistrate," *Early Days: Journal of the Royal Western Australian Historical Society* 7, no. 7 (1975): 23.

51. Mullins, "Australian Pearl-Shellers in the Moluccas," 11.

52. Cadell is reported to have left Sydney in 1877, then to have sailed to Somerset, thence to Singapore and back via "Tientein, Macella, Bardo"; "A Peculiar Case," *Morning Bulletin,* September 12, 1879; "The Missing Schooner Gem," *South Australian Register,* September 2,

1879. Ian Mudie, "Cadell, Francis (1822–1879)," *Australian Dictionary of Biography,* National Centre of Biography, Australian National University, http://adb.anu.edu.au/biography/cadell -francis-3136/text4675, published first in hardcopy 1969.

53. Mailrapport 1873: 566 (July 31, 1873) Vormalig Residenten van Kupang, De Wit, NAN. Our thanks to Hans Hägerdal, via Emile Wellfelt, for this quotation.

54. Kamerstuk Tweede Kamer 1876–1877, kamerstuknummer 5 ondernummer 2, *Koloniaal Verslag* van 1876 [Nederlandsch (Oost-) Indië]: 31. http://www.statengeneraaldigitaal.nl/ accessed July 8, 2012.

55. Hans Hägerdal, pers. comm., April 24, 2013.

56. "Mutiny and Murder on Board the Schooner Gift," *Brisbane Courier,* February 18, 1873, 2; Mullins, "Australian Pearl-Shellers in the Molluccas," 11, mentions that "George Roel" owned the *Onward,* while B. Mayne was master of the *Gift* in 1878.

57. "Tragedy at Sea," *West Australian,* December 14, 1899.

58. "The Ethel Murders," *Inquirer & Commercial News,* May 18, 1900.

59. Staatsblad 1835 No. 29, amended in 1862, Staatsblad No. 93; Staatsblad 1875 No. 49; amended and declared in Staatsblad of 1876 No. 289, van 1881 no. 171, van 1887 no. 31 and 1903 no. 203. Staatsblad van Nederlandsch-Indië over het Jaar 1816. These regulations were later extended to include other recruitment ports. See Resident Timor to Resident Ambon, September 26, 1935, Mailrapporten 525, Ministerie van Koloniën, Nationaal Archief, Den Haag. Staatsblad available online at http://babel.hathitrust.org/cgi/pt?id=mdp.35112105251930;seq=744;view=1up., accessed April 20, 2013.

60. Edwards, *Port of Pearls,* 46–47; Ronald Moore, "The Management of the Western Australian Pearling Industry, 1860 to the 1930s," *Great Circle* 16, no. 2 (1994): 127.

61. Lois P. Anderson, "The Role of Aboriginal and Asian Labour in the Origin and Development of the Pearling Industry, Broome, Western Australia, 1862–1940" (B.A. honors thesis, Murdoch University, 1978), 62.

62. Mike McCarthy, "Before Broome," *Great Circle* 16, no. 2 (1994): 85; "Coupang," *Inquirer & Commercial News,* August 25, 1875, 3.

63. Edwards, *Port of Pearls,* 1.

64. Edwards, *Port of Pearls,* 47; Moore, "The Management of the Western Australian Pearling Industry," 129–130.

65. "News from the North-West," *Inquirer & Commercial News,* August 22, 1889, 5.

66. "The Pearlers and Responsible Government," *West Australian,* November 11, 1887, 3.

67. "Local," *West Australian,* May 31, 1886, 3.

68. Mullins, "Australian Pearl-Shellers in the Molucas," 12.

69. Alan Powell, *Far Country: A Short History of the Northern Territory,* 5th ed. (Darwin: Charles Darwin University Press, 2009), 37–38.

70. "Pearling near the Australian coast," *Queenslander,* April 5, 1873, 7.

71. M. Stanley, Inspector of Fisheries and Chief Pearling Inspector, Report on the Administration of the Northern Territory for the Year Ended 30th of July 1932, *Commonwealth Parliamentary Papers* (Canberra, 1932).

72. "Fate of the Lugger Minnie," *South Australian Register,* May 31, 1886.

73. Powell, *Far Country,* 88–89; Douglas Lockwood, *The Front Door: Darwin, 1869–1969* (London: Angus & Robertson, 1969), 126.

74. Anna Shnukal and Guy Ramsay, "Tidal Flows: An Overview of Torres Strait Islander–Asian Contact," in *Navigating Boundaries: the Asian Diaspora in Torres Strait,* ed. Anna Shnukal, Guy Ramsay, and Yuriko Nagata (Canberra: Pandanus Books, 2004).

75. J. W. Tyas, "Loose Notes," in "Pearling near the Australian Coast," *Perth Gazette and West Australian Times,* June 19, 1874.

76. Regina Ganter, with contributions from Julia Martinez and Gary Lee, *Mixed Relations: Asian-Aboriginal Contact in North Australia* (Crawley: University of Western Australian Press, 2006).

77. "Pearling near the Australian Coast," *Queenslander,* April 5, 1873, 7.

78. *Brisbane Courier,* October 26, 1885, 4.

79. "Javanese for Queensland," *Brisbane Courier,* September 24, 1886, 6.

80. Battersby, *To the Islands,* 32–33.

81. Jacqui Donegan and Raymond Evans, "Running Amok: The Normanton Race Riots of 1888 and the Genesis of White Australia," *Journal of Australian Studies* 25 (2001).

82. Shnukal and Ramsay, "Tidal Flows," 37–38; Jeremy Beckett, "The Torres Strait Islanders and the Pearling Industry: A Case of Internal Colonialism," *Aboriginal History* 1, no. 1 (1977): 82.

83. Shnukal and Ramsay, "Tidal Flows," 37–38.

84. J. P. S. Bach, "The Pearling Industry of Australia. An Account of Its Social and Economic Development," 1955, A8985/1, Barcode 1184708, NAA.

85. "Latest News from the Pearling Grounds," *Daily News,* August 1, 1887, 3.

86. Shnukal and Ramsay, "Tidal Flows," 31.

87. "Pearlshell and Beche-de-Mer," *Brisbane Courier,* November 24, 1897, 5.

88. C. J. Dashwood, *Pearl-shelling Industry in Port Darwin and Northern Territory* (Melbourne: Government Printer, 1902), 4.

89. "The Japanese Question," *Brisbane Courier,* May 12, 1897, 4.

90. Fred Hodel, "The Japanese Question, To the Editor," *Brisbane Courier,* July 23, 1898, 9.

Chapter 3. Maritime Mobility in Eastern Indonesia

1. Ministry of Trade of the Republic of Indonesia, *Indonesian South Sea Pearls* (n.d., n.p.), citing 2005 data.

2. Adrian Vickers, "From Bali to Lampung by Way of the Pasisir," *Archipel* 45 (1993); Adrian Vickers, "'Malay Identity': Modernity, Invented Tradition, and Forms of Knowledge," *RIMA* 31, no. 1 (1997); Leonard Y. Andaya, *Leaves of the Same Tree: Trade and Ethnicity in the Straits of Melaka* (Honolulu: University of Hawai'i Press, 2008).

3. Syarifuddin R. Gomang, "The People of Alor and Their Alliances in Eastern Indonesia: A Study in Political Sociology" (M.A. thesis, University of Wollongong, 1993); Syarifuddin R. Gomang, "Muslim and Christian Alliances: 'Familial Relationships' between Inland and Coastal Peoples of the Belagar Community in Eastern Indonesia," *Bijdragen tot de Taal-, Land- en Volkenkunde* 162, no. 4 (2006); Emilie Wellfelt, "Diversity and Shared Identity: A Case Study of Interreligious Relations in Alor, Eastern Indonesia" (M.A. thesis, Göteborg University, 2007); Hans Hägerdal, "Cannibals and Pedlars," *Indonesia and the Malay World* 38, no. 111 (2010). In earlier outside accounts, the islands were also known as the Malua and Ombai, since Alor was the name of one of the dominant domains or kingdoms.

4. C. DuBois, *The People of Alor: A Social-Psychological Study of an East Indian Island,* 2 vols. (New York: Harper, 1944).

5. Johan Gerard Friedrich Riedel, *De Sluik- en Kroesharige Rassen tusschen Selebes en Papua* ('s- Gravenhage: Martinus Nijhoff, 1886); Hägerdal, "Cannibals and Pedlars."

6. Gomang, "Muslim and Christian Alliances."

7. Martha M. Nicolspeyer, "De Sociale Structuur van een Aloreesche Bevolkingsgroep" (PhD diss., Leiden University, 1940).

8. Additional information from Hans Hägerdal, pers. comm., April 24, 2013, who notes that this language is also spoken on the coastal area of the Kabola Peninsula, in the old kingdom of Alor.

9. Gomang, "The People of Alor"; Hans Hägerdal, *Lords of the Land, Lords of the Sea: Conflict and Adaptation in Early Colonial Timor, 1600–1800* (Leiden: KITLV Press, 2012).

10. Hägerdal, "Cannibals and Pedlars," 221.

11. The latter term is regarded as derogatory.

12. Gomang, "The People of Alor."

13. Hans Hägerdal, pers. comm., April 24, 2013; and Hägerdal, *Lords of the Land, Lords of the Sea*, 37.

14. R. H. Barnes, *Sea Hunters of Indonesia: Fishers and Weavers of Lamalera* (Oxford: Clarendon Press, 1996), 323–331; Shepard Forman, "East Timor: Exchange and Political Hierarchy at the Time of the European Discoveries," in *Economic Exchange and Social Interaction in Southeast Asia: Perspectives from Prehistory, History, and Ethnography,* ed. Karl L. Hutterer (Ann Arbor: Center for South and Southeast Asian Studies, University of Michigan, 1977), 97–111.

15. Arend de Roever, *De Jacht op Sandelhout: De VOC en de Tweedeling van Timor in de Zeventiende Eeuw* (Zutphen: Alberg Pers, 2002).

16. Hägerdal, "Cannibals and Pedlars," 241; Hans Hägerdal, trans., "Memorie van Overgave van den Fundgeerend Controleur van Alor G. A. M. Galen, dated 15 December 1946," *HumaNetten* part 1, 25 (2010), and part 2, 27 (2011), part 1: 23–24; Steven Farram, "From 'Timor Koepang' to 'Timor NTT': A Political History of West Timor, 1901–1967" (PhD diss., Charles Darwin University, 2003), 109.

17. Farram, "From 'Timor Koepang' to 'Timor NTT,'" 132–137.

18. James J. Fox, *Harvest of the Palm: Ecological Change in Eastern Indonesia* (Cambridge, MA: Harvard University Press, 1977).

19. Ruth Balint, *Troubled Waters: Border, Boundaries and Possession in the Timor Sea* (Crows Nest, NSW: Allen & Unwin, 2005).

20. J. H. Moor, *Notices of the Indian Archipelago and Adjacent Countries* (London: Frank Cass & Co., 1837; repr. 1968), 10.

21. Natasha Stacey, *Boats to Burn: Bajo Fishing Activity in the Australian Fishing Zone* (Canberra: ANU E Press, 2007).

22. Stacey, *Boats to Burn*, 8–22; James J. Fox, "Notes on the Southern Voyages and Settlements of the Sama-Bajau," *Bijdragen tot de Taal-, Land- en Volkenkunde* 133, no. 4 (1977): 459–465.

23. Robyn Maxwell, *Textiles of Southeast Asia: Tradition, Trade and Transformation* (Melbourne: Oxford University Press, 1990), 397.

24. Ruth Barnes, "The Bridewealth Cloth of Lamalera, Lembata," in *To Speak with Cloth: Studies in Indonesian Textiles,* ed. Mattiebelle Gittinger (Los Angeles: Museum of Cultural History, University of California–Los Angeles, 1989), 48–49.

25. Susan McKinnon, *From a Shattered Sun: Hierarchy, Gender, and Alliance in the Tanimbar Islands* (Madison: University of Wisconsin Press, 1991); Nico de Jonge and Toos van Dijk, *Forgotten Islands of Indonesia: The Art and Culture of the Southeast Moluccas* (Singapore: Periplus, 1995), 33.

26. Hägerdal, "Memorie van Overgave van G.A.M. Galen," part 2, 59.

27. De Jonge and van Dijk, *Forgotten Islands,* 76–85; Cécile Barraud, *Tanebar-Evav: Une société de maisons tournée vers le large* (Cambridge: Cambridge University Press, 1979).

28. Vickers, "From Bali to Lampung."

29. Vickers, "From Bali to Lampung"; Vickers, "'Malay Identity.'"

30. Sandra Pannell, "Of Gods and Monsters: Indigenous Sea Cosmologies, Promiscuous Geographies and the Depths of Local Sovereignty," in *A World of Water: Rain, Rivers and Seas in Southeast Asian Histories,* ed. Peter Boomgard (Leiden: KITLV Press, 2007).

31. Pannell, "Of Gods and Monsters," 84–85.

32. Nico L. Kana, *Dunia Orang Sawu* (Jakarta: Sinar Harapan, 1983); McKinnon, *From a Shattered Sun.*

33. Forman, "East Timor: Exchange and Political Hierarchy," 101; Janet Hoskins, *The Play of Time: Kodi Perspectives on Calendars, History, and Exchange* (Berkeley: University of California Press, 1993), 35; Hägerdal, *Lords of the Land,* 64.

34. Elizabeth G. Traube, *Cosmology and Social Life: Ritual Exchange among the Mambai of East Timor* (Chicago: University of Chicago Press, 1986).

35. C. C. Macknight, *The Voyage to Marege': Macassan Trepangers in Northern Australia* (Melbourne: Melbourne University Press, 1976); Fox, "Notes on the Southern Voyages and Settlements of the Sama-Bajau"; Stacey, *Boats to Burn;* Sarah Yu, "Broome Creole: Aboriginal and Asian Partnerships along the Kimberley Coast," *Queensland Review, Special Edition,* ed. Regina Ganter, *Asians in Australian History* 6, no. 2 (1999): 59–73.

36. Athol Chase, "'All Kind of Nation': Aborigines and Asians in Cape York Peninsula," *Aboriginal History* 5, no. 1 (1981); James Urry and Michael Walsh, "The Lost 'Macassar' Language of Northern Australia," *Aboriginal History* 5, no. 2 (1981); Alan Walker and R. David Zorc, "Austronesian Loanwords in Yolngu-Matha of Northeast Arnhem Land," *Aboriginal History* 5, no. 2 (1981): 109–134; Yu, "Broome Creole."

37. Pierre-Yves Manguin, "Trading Ships of the South China Seas: Shipbuilding Techniques and Their Role in the History of the Development of Asian Trade Networks," *Journal of the Economic and Social History of the Orient* 36, no. 3 (1993): 266n25.

38. Manguin, "Trading Ships," 266–267.

39. Clifford W. Hawkins, *Praus of Indonesia* (London: Nautical Books, 1982); Graeme Henderson and Ian Crawford, "Sampans, Belangs and Junkos: The Pearling Boats of the Aru Islands," *Expedition* 28, no. 1 (n.d.); G. Adrian Horridge, *The Prahu: Traditional Sailing Boat of Indonesia* (Singapore: Oxford University Press, 1981).

40. Wellfelt, "Diversity and Shared Identity," 6.

41. Barnes, *Sea Hunters,* 20.

42. Barnes, *Sea Hunters;* R. H. Barnes, "Lamalerap: A Whaling Village in Eastern Indonesia," *Indonesia* 17 (April 1974): 141.

43. Barnes, "Lamalerap," 152.

44. Roy F. Ellen, *On the Edge of the Banda Zone: Past and Present in the Social Organisation of a Moluccan Trading Network* (Honolulu: University of Hawai'i Press, 2003), 12.

45. Barnes, *Sea Hunters,* 333.

46. Barnes, *Sea Hunters.*

47. Anthony J. S. Reid, Introduction, in *Slavery, Bondage and Dependency in Southeast Asia,* ed. Anthony J. S. Reid (St. Lucia: University of Queensland Press, 1983).

48. Hoskins, *The Play of Time,* 47.

49. James Francis Warren, *The Sulu Zone, 1768–1898: Dynamics of External Trade, Slavery, and Ethnicity in the Transformation of a Southeast Asian Maritime State* (Singapore: Singapore University Press, 1981).

50. Patricia Spyer, *The Memory of Trade: Modernity's Entanglements on an Eastern Indonesian Island* (Durham, NC: Duke University Press, 2000), 1–3.

51. Ellen, *On the Edge of the Banda Zone*, 139–141; Rodney Needham, *Sumba and the Slave Trade*, vol. 31, Working Paper (Clayton, VIC: Monash University Centre of Southeast Asian Studies, 1983).

52. Barnes, *Sea Hunters*, 15.

53. Rik van Welie, "Patterns of Slave Trading and Slavery in the Dutch Colonial World, 1596–1863," in *Dutch Colonialism, Migration and Cultural Heritage*, ed. Gert Oostindie (Leiden: KITLV Press, 2008), 197.

54. Needham, *Sumba and the Slave Trade*, 20–23.

55. Barnes, *Sea Hunters*, 15.

56. Ellen, *On the Edge of the Banda Zone*, 103; Peter Boomgaard, "Resources and People of the Sea in and around the Indonesian Archipelago, 900–1900," in *Muddied Waters: Historical and Contemporary Perspectives on Management of Forests and Fisheries in Island Southeast Asia*, ed. David Henley, Manon Osseweijer, and Peter Boomgaard (Leiden: KITLV Press, 2005), 109.

57. Boomgaard, "Resources and People of the Sea."

58. Alfred Russel Wallace, "On the Arru Islands," Charles H. Smith, "The Alfred Russel Wallace Page," archival materials, Unpublished Diaries S41: 1858, http://people.wku.edu/charles .smith/index1.htm, accessed April 12, 2012.

59. Spyer, *The Memory of Trade*, 8.

60. Manon Osseweijer, "Taken at the Flood: Marine Resource Use and Management in the Aru Islands (Maluku, Eastern Indonesia)" (PhD diss., University of Leiden, 2001).

61. Patricia Spyer, "The Eroticism of Debt: Pearl Divers, Traders, and Sea Wives in the Aru Islands, Eastern Indonesia," *American Ethnologist* 24, no. 3 (1997); Osseweijer, "Taken at the Flood," 125.

62. Spyer, "The Eroticism of Debt."

63. Spyer, "The Eroticism of Debt," 530.

64. Spyer, "The Eroticism of Debt," 530; Spyer, *Memory of Trade;* Riedel, *De Sluik- en Kroesharige Rassen*, 253.

Chapter 4. Master Pearlers on Both Sides of the Frontier

1. Report cited in "Pearl Fishing," *Western Mail*, August 30, 1902, 19.

2. "The Pearling Industry," *The Advertiser (Adelaide)*, January 31, 1903, 7. This figure is more than the bond figure given in Dutch sources cited in the previous chapter, which was more like £16, later £8. The present-day equivalent to £30 would be approximately AUD\$3,360.

3. Henry Hilliard's son Robin was agent in Kupang for Victor Clark's Darwin-based business, "Local Court," *Northern Territory Times*, February 21, 1928, 4. While there is a clear record of Abdoel Gafoer being on the *Gascoyne* in 1923, the records of his citizenship papers refer to all his trips back and forward between Kupang and Australia, recording him coming to Australia in 1921: "ABDOEL Gafoer—Nationality: Indonesian—Arrived Broome per Centaur 22 February 1940," K1331, Indonesian/Abdoel G, Barcode 3504995, NAA, Perth.

4. Patricia Mercer, "Clark, James (1857–1933)," in *Australian Dictionary of Biography*, National Centre of Biography, Australian National University, http://adb.anu.edu.au/biography /clark-james-5664/text9563, published first in hardcopy 1981; Regina Ganter, *The Pearl-Shellers of Torres Strait* (Melbourne: Melbourne University Press, 1994); "Plaster's Boy to Pearl King: The Romantic Life of James Clark, by 'Boorabooriong,'" *Brisbane Courier*, July 12, 1933.

5. Rodney Liddell, *Cape York: The Savage Frontier* (Redbank, QLD: Rodney Liddell, 1996).

6. James Clark providing evidence to the "Pearl-Shell and Beche-de-mer Commission, Report of the Commission" (Brisbane: Queensland State Government, 1908), 28.

7. Steve Mullins, "To Break 'the Trinity' or 'Wipe out the Smaller Fry': The Australian Pearl Shell Convention of 1913," *Journal for Maritime Research* 7, no. 1 (2005): 224.

8. Mullins, "To Break 'the Trinity,'" 224.

9. Steve Mullins, "From TI to Dobo: The 1905 Departure of the Torres Strait Pearl-Shelling Fleets to Aru, Netherlands East Indies," *Great Circle* 19, no. 1 (1997); Steve Mullins, "James Clark and the Celebes Trading Co.: Making an Australian Maritime Venture in the Netherlands East Indies," *Great Circle* 24, no. 2 (2002); Mercer, "Clark, James"; Paul Battersby, *To the Islands: White Australians and the Malay Archipelago since 1788* (Lanham, MD: Lexington Books, 2007). Mullins, the major documenter of the subject, lists the fleets as those of James Clark & Co., E. E. Munro & P. P. Outridge, George Smith & Co., and Reg Hockings, in Mullins, "From Ti to Dobo," 30.

10. John G. Butcher, *The Closing of the Frontier: A History of the Marine Fisheries of Southeast Asia c.1850–2000* (Singapore/Leiden: ISEAS/KITLV, 2004), 128.

11. Steve Mullins, "Australian Pearl-Shellers in the Moluccas: Confrontations and Compromise on a Maritime Frontier," *Great Circle* 23, no. 2 (2001): 13–14.

12. *Fl.*85,300; Mullins, "To Break 'the Trinity,'" 224.

13. Peter Post, "Japanse Bedrijvigheid in Indonesië, 1868–1942: Structurele Elementen van Japan's Vooroorlogse Economische Expansie in Zuidoost Azië" (PhD diss., Vrije Universiteit, 1991), 234.

14. Mullins, "From TI to Dobo," 30.

15. Jeyamalar Kathirithamby-Wells, "'Strangers' and 'Stranger-Kings': The *Sayyid* in Eighteenth-Century Maritime Southeast Asia," *Journal of Southeast Asian Studies* 40, no. 3 (2009).

16. Des Alwi, *Friends and Exiles: A Memoir of the Nutmeg Isles and the Indonesian Nationalist Movement,* ed. Barbara S. Harvey (Ithaca, NY: Cornell Southeast Asia Program Publications, 2008), 11–13.

17. Manon Osseweijer, "Taken at the Flood: Marine Resource Use and Management in the Aru Islands (Maluku, Eastern Indonesia)" (PhD diss., University of Leiden, 2001), 123. Osseweijer notes that Baadilla had complained to the Dutch in 1905 that the Australians were depleting the pearling beds. William Gervase Clarence-Smith, "The Economic Role of the Arab Community in Maluku, 1816 to 1940," *Indonesia and the Malay World* 26, no. 74 (1998): 38, dates the Baadilla concession to 1902, and observes that the sources give the impression that the Baadilla brothers had sold their interests to Clark for 132,000 but were clearly active on Dobo in 1905–1908, with warehouses there. For this figure as buy-in, see "De Parelvisscherij in Indië," *Sumatra Post,* March 16, 1934.

18. Butcher, *Closing of the Frontier*, 130; Alwi, *Friends and Exiles*, 16–17.

19. Alwi, *Friends and Exiles,* 16–17.

20. Mullins, "From TI to Dobo," 34.

21. "The Pearling Industry: Mr James Clark Interviewed," *Queenslander*, November 18, 1905.

22. Mullins, "From TI to Dobo," 35.

23. Post, "Japanse Bedrijvigheid."

24. Cited in Mullins, "To Break 'the Trinity,'" 217, 229.

25. Mullins, "From TI to Dobo," 35–36.

26. Mullins, "To Break 'the Trinity,'" 228.

27. "The Pearl-Shelling Industry: Important Decision," *Morning Post*, February 23, 1906.

28. Mullins, "To Break 'the Trinity,'" 227.

29. Mullins, "To Break 'the Trinity,'" 230.

30. "Shell Sales," *Townsville Daily Bulletin*, July 9, 1912.

31. Post, "Japanse Bedrijvigheid," 234.

32. Mullins, "From TI to Dobo"; see also "Pearlshell: Broome Master Pearlers Discuss Proposed Agreement for Marketing It," *Northern Times*, August 2, 1913.

33. Mullins, "To Break 'the Trinity,'" 234.

34. Mullins, "To Break 'the Trinity,'" 234; "Clark," Barcode 42915, NAA, Canberra.

35. "In Equity (before Mr Justice Harvey) A Pearl Industry Agreement," *Sydney Morning Herald*, September 11, 1915.

36. NAN XL-12, Memorie van Overgave van den aftredenden Gezaghebber der Aroe–Eilanden A. Balk, 1937, Juli. Schmidt and Jeandel were described as the "directors"; "De Parelvisscherij in Indië," *Sumatra Post*, March 16, 1934. Around 1924 the firm was already called Schmidt & Jeandel, as shown by a photograph of their offices on Wihelminastraat in Makassar in the Tropen Museum collection, http://commons.wikimedia.org/wiki/File:COLLECTIE_TROPENMUSEUM_De_Wilhelminastraat_te_Makassar_op_Celebes._TMnr_60013045.jpg; see also http://kitlv.pictura-dp.nl/all-images/indeling/detail/form/advanced/start/1?q_searchfield=Jeandel; Jeandel was also French consul at Makassar.

37. "Plaster's Boy to Pearl King"; Mullins, "James Clark and the Celebes Trading Co."

38. "The Pearling Industry," *Northern Territory Times and Gazette*, May 31, 1927.

39. Stephen G. Bloom, *Tears of Mermaids: The Secret Story of Pearls* (New York: St. Martin's Griffin, 2011), 250–253.

40. "Pearling: Difficulties of Industry at Broome," *Northern Times*, April 14, 1932.

41. NAN XL-12, Memorie van Overgave Balk, 1937; see also "Dobo Items," *Northern Standard*, May 8, 1936.

42. A. G. H. van Sluys, "Dobo-ervaringen," *Koloniaal Tijdschrift* 5, no. 2 (1916), [attribution of authorship by G. Telkamp, according to Clarence-Smith, "The Economic Role of the Arab Community in Maluku"].

43. J. D. F Hardenberg, "De Parelmoervisscherij in het Oosten van den Indischen Archipel," *Indische Gids* 2 (1939); NAN XL-12, Memorie van Overgave Balk, 1937.

44. Post, "Japanse Bedrijvigheid," 232.

45. Butcher, *Closing of the Frontier*, 232; Post, "Japanse Bedrijvigheid."

46. Sluys, "Dobo-ervaringen."

47. "Northern Territory," *Register*, April 9, 1906.

48. Post, "Japanse Bedrijvigheid," 233.

49. Hiroshi Shimizu, "Rise and Fall of the Karayuki-san in the Netherlands Indies from the Late Nineteenth Century to the 1930s," *RIMA* 26, no. 2 (1992).

50. Sluys, "Dobo-ervaringen."

51. Shimizu, "Rise and Fall of the Karayuki-san."

52. Sluys, "Dobo-ervaringen."

53. Sluys, "Dobo-ervaringen"; also NAN XL-12, Memorie van Overgave Balk, 1937.

54. Sluys, "Dobo-ervaringen."

55. Sluys, "Dobo-ervaringen."

56. Patricia Spyer, *The Memory of Trade: Modernity's Entanglements on an Eastern Indonesian Island* (Durham, NC: Duke University Press, 2000); "Singapore v Aru Islands," *Northern Standard*, March 10, 1936; also NAN XL-12, Memorie van Overgave Balk, 1937.

57. "Pearling Seas: The Japanese Invasion," *Townsville Daily Bulletin*, September 2, 1936.

58. Mullins, "To Break 'the Trinity,'" 216; "Lugger Lost in Storm," *Barrier Miner*, September 19, 1935; "Dobo Items," *Northern Standard*, May 8, 1936; "Pearling Luggers Struck by Waterspout," *Northern Standard*, December 31, 1936; "Aroe Island Pearling Area: Diver's Death," *Townville Daily Bulletin*, September 14, 1937.

59. Reference from the *Townsville Daily Bulletin* in Battersby, *To the Islands*, 34; also "Rubber-cultuur op het Eiland Ceram," *Sumatra Post*, September 4, 1918.

60. Elsewhere, *gezaghebber* was used for indigenous officials, but not in this case. See also NAN XL-12, Memorie van Overgave Balk, 1937.

61. NAN XL-12, Memorie van Overgave Balk, 1937; "Landbouwondernemingen op Ceram," *Nieuwe Rotterdamsche Courant*, June 24, 1921; "Vrijheidsberooving en Mishandeling," *Nieuws van den Dag*, May 31, 1920.

62. "The Pearling Industry," *Northern Territory Times and Gazette*, May 31, 1927.

63. "£1400 Pearl Secured by Darwin Pearler," *Western Argus*, March 6, 1934, "Round About," *Northern Standard*, February 27, 1934; "Darwin Notes," *Townsville Daily Bulletin*, January 31, 1934.

64. "Pearling Industry, Northern Territory," Department of the Interior to Cabinet, 1933, A1/15 33/938 PT 2, NAA, Canberra.

65. *Northern Standard*, January 3, 1936.

66. "Schooner Sinks in Timor Sea," *Townsville Daily Bulletin*, April 20, 1939; "Lugger Lost during Timor Crossing," *Central Queensland Herald*, April 27, 1939.

67. "Connors v Clark: Pearl King Declared Bankrupt," *Northern Standard*, September 29, 1936; "Clark Bankruptcy Case," *Northern Standard*, March 9, 1937.

68. "Bankruptcy Examination," *Northern Standard*, February 26, 1937.

69. "Aroe Island Notes," *Northern Standard*, February 26, 1937.

70. Noreen Jones, *Number Two Home: A Story of Japanese Pioneers in Australia* (Fremantle: Fremantle Arts Centre, 2002), 26–32; Prisoner of War/Internee: Muramats, Jiro, MP1103/1, DJ18118, 8600397, NAA; "Pearling Industry, Northern Territory."

71. A1/1 34/2165, E. J. McKay, Pearling Master, Saumlaki, to J. Muramats, July 26, 1933, NAA.

72. "The Pearling Industry: What the Restrictions Are Doing," *Northern Standard*, January 10, 1933.

73. John Bailey, Acting Consul-General, Batavia, July 9, 1932, A1/15 34/ 2165, NAA. The luggers in question were the *Dulcy*, the *Alpha*, and the *Broome*.

74. H. N. Nelson, "Carpenter, Sir Walter Randolph (1877–1954)," in *Australian Dictionary of Biography*, National Centre of Biography, Australian National University, http://adb.anu.edu .au/biography/carpenter-sir-walter-randolph-5510/text9379, published first in hardcopy 1979.

75. A1/1 34/2165, J.W.G. Aitken, Melville Island, to Carpenter, August 22, 1933, NAA.

76. "Passing of the Pioneers: Death of Mr Frank Jardine," *Brisbane Courier*, March 20, 1919.

77. Liddell, *Cape York*, 183–84; "'Bulletin' Pars," *Northern Standard*, February 25, 1936; K. C. Hardy, "Men of Iron: Hardships of Pearlers," *Sydney Morning Herald*, January 16, 1937. Thanks to Steve Mullins (pers. comm.) for information about Mina; and he notes that theirs "comes across as having been a loving relationship that was widely acknowledged in the town, but official reports probably described her as a 'concubine.'"

78. *Northern Standard*, January 3, 1936.

79. Liddell, *Cape York*, 184.

80. "Dobo Items," *Northern Standard*, May 8, 1936.

81. "'Bulletin' Pars," *Northern Standard*, January 7, 1936, and January 3, 1936.

82. Liddell, *Cape York*, 184; NAN XL-12, Memorie van Overgave Balk, 1937, refers to the CTC having four European employees: C. A. and N. P. Monsted, Young, and Jessup.

83. "Secret Service Agent Dies. Mr R. Hockings, Pearler, Helped Britain," *Northern Standard*, June 28, 1932; Norman S. Pixley, "Pearlers of North Australia: The Romantic Story of the Diving Fleets," Presidential Address Read at the Annual Meeting of the Royal Historical Society of Queensland, September 23, 1971; Regina Ganter, *Mixed Relations: Asian-Aboriginal Contact in North Australia* (Crawley: University of Western Australian Press, 2006), 193, shows Tommy Loban in a photograph, probably from the 1920s, with other Thursday Island workers from Timor and Ambon. http://espace.library.uq.edu.au/eserv/UQ:209190/s00855804_1971_1972_9_3_9.pdf, accessed 3rd July 2012; A432 1940/317; A1608 B15/1/1 1915—1938 Secret Intelligence Services, NAA.

84. Post, "Japanse Bedrijvigheid," 234.

85. "Aroe Island Notes," *Northern Standard*, September 10, 1937, "Aroe Islands News Items," *Townsville Daily Bulletin*, January 4, 1940.

86. Andy Müller, *Cultured Pearls: The First Hundred Years* (Lausanne: Andy Müller for Golay Buchel, 1997).

87. "The Pearling Industry: What the Restrictions Are Doing," *Northern Standard*, January 10, 1933.

88. "Supervision of Pearling Industry Urged," *Central Queensland Herald*, August 22, 1935; "Aroe Island Notes," *Northern Standard*, September 10, 1937; "Aroe Islands News Items," *Townsville Daily Bulletin*, January 4, 1940.

89. "Pearling Seas: The Japanese Invasion," *Townsville Daily Bulletin*, September 2, 1936.

90. "Japanese Pearlers, Ousting Australians," *Cairns Post*, January 4, 1937; NAA, A1 1935/4880, letter from Aitken to Bliss, January 4, 1934.

91. NAN XL-12, Memorie van Overgave Balk, 1937, naming Kitano Ambon, Otake Hiramatzu, and Jimpe Nakamichi as resident owners.

92. NAN XL-12, Memorie van Overgave Balk, 1937.

93. "Aroe Islands Area," *Townsville Daily Bulletin*, March 17, 1938; "Aroe Island Notes," *Townsville Daily Bulletin*, April 25, 1939.

94. Natasha Stacey, *Boats to Burn: Bajo Fishing Activity in the Australian Fishing Zone*, Asia-Pacific Environment Monograph Series (Canberra: ANU E Press, 2007), 63.

95. Stacey, *Boats to Burn*, 65.

96. Ernestine Hill, *The Great Australian Loneliness* (Melbourne: Robertson and Mullens, 1943), 37–41.

97. "A Pearler's Wife: Old Broome Days Recalled," *Western Mail*, June 13, 1935.

98. Possibly called the British Trading Company at an earlier stage; Christine Choo, "Asian Men on the West Kimberley Coast, 1900–1940," in *Asian Orientations: Studies in Western Australian History*, ed. Jan Gothard (Perth: University of Western Australia, 1995), 107.

99. "A Trustful Partner," *West Australian,* February 24, 1927; "Elusive Pearls: When 'Time Doesn't Count,'" *Western Mail,* March 3, 1927. Chamberlain was one of those mentioned in reports of the 1908 and 1910 Broome cyclones, and two other men of the same surname, perhaps brothers, were mentioned in 1908.

100. Stacey, *Boats to Burn,* 65.

101. "Local Court," *Northern Territory Times,* February 21, 1928, 4.

102. Stevens is also mentioned as a co-owner. "Pearling Fleet in Squall," *West Australian,* June 5, 1929.

103. Stacey, *Boats to Burn,* 65.

104. Stacey, *Boats to Burn,* 65.

105. Lawrence Griswold, *Tombs, Travel and Trouble* (New York: Hillman-Curl, 1937), 315–316; Timothy P. Barnard, "Chasing the Dragon: An Early Expedition to Komodo Island," in *Lost Times and Untold Tales from the Malay World,* ed. Jan van der Putten and Mary Kilcline Cody (Singapore: National University of Singapore Press, 2009).

106. Griswold, *Tombs, Travel and Trouble,* 316.

107. "Schooner Sinks in Timor Sea," *Townsville Daily Bulletin,* April 20, 1939. "Aroe Islands News Items," *Townsville Daily Bulletin,* January 4, 1940.

108. Griswold, *Tombs, Travel and Trouble,* 315–316.

109. Information from George Hilliard, Robin's son. George was born in Labuan Bajo in 1938. See also Stacey, *Boats to Burn,* 65.

110. Information from George Hilliard. See also Stacey, *Boats to Burn,* 65.

Chapter 5. Labor Migration to North Australia, 1901–1941

1. J. Crosby, British Consul-General, Batavia, to General Secretary, Netherlands East Indies, January 24, 1924; Resident Koepang to General Secretary, January 2, 1924, Mailrap-porten 348, Ministerie van Koloniën, Nationaal Archief, Den Haag.

2. *Singapore Free Press and Mercantile Advertiser,* March 21, 1923.

3. A. T. Yarwood, *Asian Migration to Australia: The Background to Exclusion 1896–1923* (Melbourne: Melbourne University Press, 1964), 96; Lorraine Philipps, "Plenty More Little Brown Man! Pearlshelling and White Australia in Queensland 1901–1918," in *Essays in the Political Economy of Australian Capitalism,* vol. 4, ed. E. L. Wheelwright and K. Buckley (Sydney: Australia & New Zealand Book Company, 1980), 58, 62.

4. "Pearl Fishing," *Western Mail,* August 30, 1902, 19.

5. "Alien Immigration Restriction Act," *West Australian,* June 25, 1907, 7.

6. Report by Mr. Warton, Sub-Collector of Broome, A1 1903/641, Barcode 23, NAA, Canberra. The State Library of Victoria, "What It Used to Cost," gives the figure of £2 2s 10d as the average weekly earnings of a bread-maker in Victoria in 1903, with other tradesmen earning around half that amount, http://guides.slv.vic.gov.au/whatitcost, accessed April 20, 2013; the figure for bread-makers is close to the basic wage set by the Harvester Judgment of 1904, which established the principle in Australia of a basic wage.

7. Stuart Macintyre, *The Oxford History of Australia, Volume 4, 1901–1942: The Succeeding Age* (Melbourne: Oxford University Press, 1986), 103.

8. Philipps, "Plenty More Little Brown Man!," 63.

9. "Pearl-Shell and Bêche-de-mer Commission, Report of the Commission" (Brisbane: Queensland State Government, 1908).

10. See David Northrup, *Indentured Labor in the Age of Imperialism, 1834–1922* (New York: Cambridge University Press, 1995); Julia T. Martínez, "The End of Indenture? Asian Workers in the Australian Pearling Industry, 1901–1972," *International Labor and Working Class History* 67 (2005): 125–147.

11. Kay Saunders, "The Workers' Paradox: Indentured Labour in the Queensland Sugar Industry to 1920," in *Indentured Labour in the British Empire, 1834–1920,* ed. Kay Saunders (London: Croom Helm, 1984), 237.

12. "Aliens at Queensland Mills, 1916," Colonial Sugar Refining Company Papers, CSR 142/1479, Noel Butlin Archives, Canberra.

13. Different sources give slightly lower figures. Our Broome data are taken from the tables of Lois P. Anderson, "The Role of Aboriginal and Asian Labour in the Origin and Development of the Pearling Industry, Broome, Western Australia, 1862–1940" (B.A. honors thesis, Murdoch University, 1978); copy of the table kept in the Broome Historical Museum.

14. "Report of the Administrator of the Northern Territory, 1911," *Commonwealth Parliamentary Papers* (Melbourne: Government Printer, 1912), 54.

15. Rosemarijn Hoefte, "A Passage to Suriname? The Migration of Modes of Resistance by Asian Contract Laborers," *International Labor and Working Class History,* 54 (1998): 20.

16. Maureen De Silva, "Javanese Indentured Labourers in British North Borneo, 1914–1932" (PhD diss., School of Oriental and African Studies, University of London, 2009), 58.

17. "Pearling Crews," *Northern Territory Times and Gazette,* March 20, 1908, 3.

18. "Java-Australia Line," *Sydney Morning Herald,* October 1, 1908.

19. Joseph Norbert Frans Marie à Campo, *Engines of Empire: Steamshipping and State Formation in Colonial Indonesia* (Hilversum: Uitgeverij Verloren, 2002), 283; "Sydney to Singapore," *Sydney Morning Herald,* April 6, 1904, 1.

20. "Norddeutscher Lloyd Bremen," *Straits Times,* July 23, 1900.

21. "Eastern and Australian SS Company's Fleet," *Sydney Morning Herald,* December 13, 1904 6.

22. Sub-Collector of Customs Broome, to Collector of Customs, Fremantle, January 13, 1903, in "Report by Mr. Warton, Sub-Collector Broome re Procedure Adopted in Connection with Introduction of Labourers for Pearling Fleets in WA," A1 1903/641, Barcode 23, NAA, Canberra.

23. "The Pearling Lugger Orion, Recovered from the Malays," *West Australian,* February 14, 1907, 4.

24. Sub-Collector of Customs, Broome, to Collector of Customs, Fremantle, January 13, 1903, in "Report by Mr. Warton," NAA, Canberra.

25. "Nor-West Pearling, Malays Instead of Japanese," *Register,* September 16, 1913, 6; "The Pearling Industry," *West Australian,* September 15, 1913, 7.

26. "Preponderance of Japanese in Pearling. Question of Employment of Other Races. Decision re Ratio of Nationality," A1 1938/2336, 46430, NAA, Canberra.

27. "White Divers at Broome," *Sydney Morning Herald,* July 9, 1912, 8.

28. "The Pearling Industry and the War," *Advertiser (Adelaide),* December 14, 1914.

29. "Pearling Industry," *Nor'West Echo,* July 11, 1914.

30. "Pearling Industry Malay Divers," *Nor'West Echo,* April 4, 1914.

31. "Goldstein, Leon," Barcode 4770726, NAA, Canberra.

32. "Clark," Barcode 42915, NAA, Canberra.

33. "The Pearling Industry, a Master Pearler's Complaint," *West Australian,* April 22, 1915, 6.

34. "Better Pearlshell Sought," *Register,* January 24, 1928, 9.

35. Susan Sickert, *Beyond the Lattice: Broome's Early Years* (Fremantle: Fremantle Arts Centre Press, 2003), 177.

36. "De Parelvisschers van Broome. Goede Betaling maakt Dienst-neming Zeer Populair," *Nieuws van den Dag,* February 5, 1938.

37. A. B. Paterson, "The Pearl Diver," in *Rio Grande's Last Race and Other Verses* (Melbourne: Angus & Robertson, 1902), located at http://www.poetrylibrary.edu.au/poets/paterson-a-b-banjo /the-pearl-diver-0004006, accessed January 20, 2013.

38. Philipps, "Plenty More Little Brown Man!," 76.

39. Anderson, "The Role of Aboriginal and Asian Labour," appendix 4, but listing these as coming from "Dutch East Indies, Timor, Java, Sumatra and Celebes."

40. Henry Taunton, *Australind: Wanderings in Western Australia and the Malay East* (London: Edward Arnold, 1903); also cited at length in Hugh Edwards, *Port of Pearls: Broome's First 100 Years* (Swanbourne: Hugh Edwards, 1984), 35–41.

41. Deb Whitmont and Lisa McGregor, "The Price of Pearl," *4 Corners,* ABC Television, July 10, 2012, http://www.abc.net.au/4corners/stories/2012/07/05/3539781.htm, accessed January 14, 2013.

42. Adrian Cunningham, "On Borrowed Time: The Australian Pearlshelling Industry, Asian Indentured Labour and the White Australia Policy, 1946–1962" (M. Litt. thesis, Australian National University, 1992), 18.

43. A. R. Nasoetion, "Perdjalanan dan Pemandangan di West Australie," *Pewarta Deli,* October 11, 1926. Many thanks to Paul Tickell for this valuable source.

44. "Wages of Divers," *Advertiser (Adelaide),* September 30, 1912, 10.

45. Anderson, "The Role of Aboriginal and Asian Labour," appendix 2.

46. "Report of the Administrator of the Northern Territory, 1911," *Commonwealth Parliamentary Papers,* Melbourne: Government Printer, 1912, 52.

47. Elsie Masson, *An Untamed Territory* (London: Macmillan & Co., 1915), 53–54.

48. Regina Ganter, *The Pearl-Shellers of the Torres Strait* (Melbourne: Melbourne University Press, 1994), 114; Pearling Conditions, A1/15 1914/12612, NAA, Canberra.

49. "Minutes of Evidence of the Progress Report of the Royal Commission on the Pearl-Shelling Industry," *Commonwealth Parliamentary Papers,* 1913, vol. 3, cited in Philipps, "Plenty More Little Brown Man!," 77.

50. Crown Solicitor, Opinion, to Secretary, Attorney-General's Department, March 1, 1916, "Koepang Pearling Indents," A1 1916/10463, Barcode 34425, NAA, Canberra.

51. "5,000 Miles Tour, Ministerial Trip to the North," *West Australian,* June 26, 1920, 6.

52. F. J. Quinlan to Sub-Collector of Customs, Darwin, August 31, 1925, "Sub-Collector of Customs Darwin—Instructions re Pearling," A1 1930/880, Barcode 44862, NAA, Canberra.

53. Six were permitted if there were two divers; Instructions Regarding Employment of Coloured Indentured Labour in the Pearling Industry, 1925, "Sub-Collector of Customs Darwin," NAA, Canberra.

54. "Coolies from Timor," *Western Argus,* February 28, 1928, 31.

55. "NAWU, Constitution and General Rules," Rule 6, Mitchell Library, State Library of NSW, Sydney.

56. "N.A.W.U. Annual General Meeting," *Northern Standard,* September 2, 1930, 2.

57. "Pearl Shell Price," *Sun,* Sydney, February 1, 1929; "Broome Pearler's Committee," A1 28/11303, Barcode 83431, NAA, Canberra.

58. Kepert to Dept. of Home and Territories, January 25, 1929; "Broome Pearler's Committee," NAA, Canberra.

59. "Broome Pearling Fleet," *West Australian,* May 17, 1929, 20.

60. "Report of the Administrator," *Commonwealth Parliamentary Papers* (Melbourne: Government Printer, 1928).

61. Sub-Collector of Customs, Broome to Secretary, Home and Territories Dept., February 5, 1929, "Broome Pearler's Committee."

62. Broome Pearlers' Committee to Home and Territories, December 21, 1928, "Broome Pearler's Committee."

63. "Pearl Industry, Restricted Output Suggested, Darwin Protest," *Advocate,* February 24, 1931, 2.

64. V. R. Kepert, Leura NSW to Home and Territories, January 21, 1929; Quinlan, Ass. Secretary, Home Affairs, to Kepert, January 25, 1929, "Broome Pearler's Committee."

65. Memo, "Pearling—Employment of Malay Labour," May 12, 1933, "V. J. Clark Pearling Appn. Darwin," A1 1935/7697, Barcode 45881, NAA, Canberra.

66. Department of Home and Territories to Sub-Collector of Customs, Darwin, August 31, 1925, "Instructions regarding employment of coloured indentured labour in the pearling industry," "Sub-Collector of Customs Darwin."

67. Customs and Excise Office, Darwin to Department of Home Affairs, March 26, 1929, "Indentured Seamen, Darwin Refusal Duty," A1 1929/1132, Barcode 44703, NAA, Canberra.

68. Toupein, NAWU to Minister of Home Affairs, January 11, 1930, "Sub-Collector of Customs Darwin."

69. "Boko," *Northern Standard,* February 13, 1934.

70. McDonald, "Indentured Labor in Darwin, White Australia Policy Flouted," *Northern Standard,* January 24, 1936.

71. McDonald, "Indentured Labor in Darwin."

72. "Indentured Laborers Obtain Their Wages," *Northern Standard,* April 14, 1931, 5.

73. "Report on the Administration of the Northern Territory, Year Ended 30th June 1934," *Commonwealth Parliamentary Papers* (Canberra: Commonwealth Government, 1934–1937), 20.

74. A try-diver was a novice diver or apprentice diver. Secretary of TPC, B. Morgan to Nylander, May 26, 1937, Applying for Licences, "VJ Clark, Pearler," F1 1938/726, Barcode 332117, NAA, Darwin.

75. Gregory and Co. to Chief Pearling Inspector, May 7, 1938, "Gregory A.C. and Co.—Pearlers," F1 1938/402, Barcode 331755, NAA, Darwin.

76. "Karl W. Nylander Naturalization," A1 1915/10445, Barcode 33020, NAA, Canberra; "Farewell to Contingent," *Northern Territory Times and Gazette,* April 29, 1915.

77. Nylander to Territory Pearling Company, December 10, 1938, "VJ Clark, Pearler."

78. Hermanus, Chasim, Abde, Arnold, Alexsander and Simson, Letter to the editor, "The N.A.W.U. Thanked," *Northern Standard,* December 23, 1938, 14.

Chapter 6. Challenging Social Segregation

1. A. R. Nasoetion, "Perdjalanan dan Pemandangan di West Australie," *Pewarta Deli,* October 6, 1926.

2. Ion L. Idriess, *Forty Fathoms Deep: Pearl Divers and Sea Rovers in Australian Seas* (Sydney: Angus and Robertson, 1937); the 1947 edition states that it is the "fourteenth edition," and there have been subsequent republications.

3. Idriess, *Forty Fathoms Deep,* 334.

4. Idriess, *Forty Fathoms Deep,* 338–343.

5. Warwick Anderson, *The Cultivation of Whiteness: Science, Health, and Racial Destiny in Australia* (Durham, NC: Duke University Press, 2006), 76.

6. Marilyn Lake and Henry Reynolds, *Drawing the Global Colour Line: White Men's Countries and the Question of Racial Equality* (Melbourne: Melbourne University Press, 2008).

7. Idriess, *Forty Fathoms Deep,* 14.

8. Alfred Searcy, *In Australian Tropics* (London: George Robertson & Co., 1909), 363.

9. The term "Capricornia" was used to describe the Northern Territory by novelist Xavier Herbert in his *Capricornia* (Sydney: The Publicist, 1938).

10. Census figures for Darwin, five-mile radius, "Northern Territory. Taking of the Census of the N.T.," A1 1911/16191, Barcode 11760, NAA, Darwin.

11. Staniforth Smith, cited in Henry Reynolds, *North of Capricorn: The Untold Story of Australia's North* (Sydney: Allen & Unwin, 2003), 128–129.

12. See Regina Ganter, with contributions from Julia Martínez and Gary Lee, *Mixed Relations: Asian-Aboriginal Contact in North Australia* (Crawley: University of Western Australian Press, 2006).

13. Susan Sickert, *Beyond the Lattice: Broome's Early Years* (Fremantle: Fremantle Arts Centre Press, 2003), 60.

14. Hugh Edwards, *Port of Pearls: Broome's First 100 Years* (Swanbourne: Hugh Edwards, 1984), esp. 116–23; Noreen Jones, *Number Two Home: A Story of Japanese Pioneers in Australia* (Fremantle: Fremantle Arts Centre, 2002), 105.

15. Mary Albertus Bain, "Male, Arthur (1870–1946)," in *Australian Dictionary of Biography,* National Centre of Biography, Australian National University, http://adb.anu.edu.au/biography /male-arthur-7469/text13013, published first in hardcopy 1986.

16. Edwards, *Port of Pearls,* 117.

17. Sarah Yu, "Broome Creole: Aboriginal and Asian Partnerships Along the Kimberley Coast," *Queensland Review, Asians in Australian History* 6, no. 2 (1999): 60.

18. "Pleasing All Colours. Movies in Nth Australia," *Barrier Miner,* July 31, 1936, 4.

19. C. Price Conigrave, *North Australia* (London: Jonathan Cape, 1936), 120.

20. "Pearling Industry. Prospects of Revival," *Sydney Morning Herald,* July 12, 1932, 8.

21. Julia Martinez, "Ethnic Policy and Practice in Darwin," in Ganter, *Mixed Relations,* 122–139.

22. Ganter, *Mixed Relations,* 193, 200; Anna Shnukal, "'They Don't Know What Went on Underneath': Three Little-Known Filipino/Malay Communities of Torres Strait," in *Navigating Boundaries: The Asian Diaspora in Torres Strait,* ed. Anna Shnukal, Guy Ramsay, and Yuriko Nagata (Canberra: Pandanus Books, 2004), 102.

23. "Malaytown," *Brisbane Courier,* March 28, 1904, 7.

24. David Thomas, catalogue essay in *Works from the Donald Friend Collection* (auction catalogue) (Sydney: Deutscher and Hackett, 2013), http://www.deutscherandhackett.com /node/31500015/, accessed May 28, 2014.

25. Christine Choo, "Asian Men on the West Kimberley Coast, 1900–1940," in *Asian Orientations: Studies in Western Australian History,* ed. Jan Gothard (Perth: University of Western Australia, 1995), 103–104.

26. "Preponderance of Japanese in Pearling. Question of Employment of Other Races," A1 1938/2336, Barcode 46430, NAA, Canberra.

27. "Colour Problem in North-West," *Argus,* March 12, 1921, 5.

28. "Racial Riot, Malay Clubbed and Stabbed," *West Australian,* January 6, 1920, 6.

29. "Broome News," *West Australian,* January 28, 1920, 7.

30. "Colonial Secretary's Comments," *West Australian*, December 22, 1920, 6; "The Broome Riots," *West Australian*, December 23, 1920, 7; "Interesting Details," *West Australian*, December 23, 1920, 7; "Warship for Broome," *West Australian*, December 25, 1920, 7; "Rioting of Japanese and Malays at Broome," *Queenslander*, January 1, 1921, 28.

31. Sickert, *Beyond the Lattice*.

32. "The Week at a Glance," *Queenslander*, October 9, 1920, 25. Before his long sojourn on Buton, Hockings had returned from the Aru Islands in 1908 with the Wanetta fleet. In 1911 he was joined by his nephews Harold and Frank Hockings, who were later to join him in Buton, and in 1912 was granted a lease to set up a pearling base on Darnley Island; "The Week at a Glance," *Queenslander*, January 27, 1912, 9.

33. Idriess, *Forty Fathoms Deep*, 328–329.

34. Idriess, *Forty Fathoms Deep*, esp. 15.

35. Keith Windschuttle, *The White Australia Policy* (Sydney: Macleay Press, 2004), 209.

36. Anna Shnukal and Guy Ramsay, "Tidal Flows: An Overview of Torres Strait Islander–Asian Contact," in *Navigating Boundaries: The Asian Diaspora in Torres Strait,* ed. Anna Shnukal, Guy Ramsay, and Yuriko Nagata (Canberra: Pandanus Books, 2004), 40.

37. Census figures for Darwin, 1911, A1/15 11/16191, NAA, Canberra; Census figures, April 4, 1921, A1/15 1927/7835, NAA, Canberra.

38. Report of the Chief Pearling Inspector, K. Nylander, in Report of the Administrator, *Commonwealth Parliamentary Papers,* 1936–1937 (Canberra: Commonwealth Government, 1937).

39. Clifford Pierce, Sub-Collector of Customs, Memo to Home and Territories Department, October 29, 1928, A1/15 30/880, NAA, Canberra.

40. *Northern Standard*, January 7, 1936.

41. Jones, *Number Two Home*, 27–30, 77, 133–135.

42. Edwards, *Port of Pearls*, 67.

43. Jones, *Number Two Home*, 49–55.

44. Ganter, *Mixed Relations*, 60–61; also mentioned in Idriess, *Forty Fathoms*.

45. Jones, *Number Two Home*, 164.

46. Gregory & Co. for Darwin Pearlers' Committee to Administrator, October 28, 1936, F1 1937/600, NAA, Darwin.

47. Report of the Chief Pearling Inspector, K. Nylander.

48. *Northern Standard*, March 9, 1937.

49. In this context "coloured" is used in place of "half-caste." The gambling house was owned by a man called Sato, according to reporter Jessie Litchfield, "Press Collect," Litchfield Manuscript, NLA MS132, National Library of Australia, Canberra, 48.

50. "Police Court," *Northern Standard*, January 17, 1936.

51. A. E. Koop, Sgt, to Superintendent of Police, Stretton, Darwin, October 18, 1936, F1 1936/220, NAA, Darwin.

52. Report of the Chief Pearling Inspector, K. Nylander.

53. "V. D. Epidemic Scandal," *Northern Standard*, March 2, 1937.

54. "Gossip and Grumbles," *Northern Standard*, March 11, 1938.

55. "Singapore Luggermen," *Northern Standard*, March 6, 1936.

56. "Singapore v Aru Islands," *Northern Standard*, March 10, 1936.

57. "Soccer," *Northern Standard*, January 8, 1937.

58. Henry Lee, Transcript of interview by S. Saunders, 1981, 14–15, TS 261, NTRS 226, NTAS, Darwin.

59. *Northern Standard,* January 22, 1937.

60. "Aroe Island Notes," *Northern Standard,* February 26, 1937.

61. Middleton, Chief of Native Affairs, 1949, cited in Yu, "Broome Creole," 62.

62. Nasoetion, "Perdjalanan dan Pemandangan di West Australie."

63. Memo, Department for Home and Territories, Employment of Indentured Labourers on Shore at Thursday Island, "Sub-collector of customs, Darwin—Instructions re pearling," A1 1930/880, Barcode 44862, NAA, Canberra.

64. Shnukal and Ramsay, "Tidal Flows," 44.

65. Ganter, *Mixed Relations,* 83–90.

66. Samantha Faulkner and Ali Drummond, *Life Belong Ali Drummond: A Life in the Torres Strait* (Canberra: Aboriginal Studies Press, 2007), 6–7.

67. Yu, "Broome Creole," 62.

68. Yu, "Broome Creole," 63.

69. Jeremy Beckett, "The Torres Strait Islanders and the Pearling Industry: A Case of Internal Colonialism," *Aboriginal History* 1, no. 1 (1977): 85.

70. Ganter, *Mixed Relations,* 160–176.

71. Ganter, *Mixed Relations,* from an interview with Philip Dolby.

72. "The Undeclared War," *Northern Standard,* December 3, 1937.

73. Ganter, *Mixed Relations,* 160–176.

Chapter 7. War on the Pearl Frontier

1. "Japanese Consul Not Advised of War, Sydney," *Canberra Times,* December 9, 1941, 3.

2. Yuriko Nagata, '"Certain Types of Aliens': The Japanese in Australia, 1941–1952," in *Relationships: Japan and Australia, 1870s–1950s,* ed. Paul Jones and Vera Mackie (Melbourne: History Department, University of Melbourne, 2001), 218.

3. Pamela Oliver, *Empty North: The Japanese Presence and Australian Reactions, 1860s to 1942* (Darwin: Charles Darwin University Press, 2006), 166.

4. Cited in Hugh Edwards, *Port of Pearls: Broome's First 100 Years* (Swanbourne, WA: Hugh Edwards, 1984), 124–125.

5. Noreen Jones, *Number Two Home* (Fremantle, Western Australia: Fremantle Arts Centre Press, 2002), 176.

6. "Prisoner of War/Internee: Imura, Yasukichi," MP1103/1, QJ16283, Barcode 8610803, NAA, Melbourne; "Imura Yasukichi—Japanese specialist—ex Darwin—M and W Scott," E601, 1955/82, Barcode 3360187, NAA, Darwin.

7. "Prisoner of War/Internee: Kawakami, Takakazu," MP1103/1, DJ18134, Barcode 8611232, NAA, Melbourne.

8. "Prisoner of War/Internee: Muramatsu, Jiro," MP1103/1, DJ18118, Barcode 8600397, NAA, Melbourne.

9. Jones, *Number Two Home,* 178–179; "Prisoner of War/Internee: Muramatsu, Hatsu," MP1103/1, DJF18119, Barcode 8600398, NAA, Melbourne.

10. "Thursday Island Luggers, Diver Difficulty," *Townsville Daily Bulletin,* December 30, 1941, 2.

11. "U.S. Soldiers' Thrilling Timor Deeds," *Courier-Mail* (Brisbane), April 22, 1942, 4.

12. "U.S. Soldiers' Thrilling Timor Deeds."

13. Douglas Lockwood, *Australia's Pearl Harbour, Darwin 1942* (Melbourne: Cassell Australia, 1966), 1.

14. "Koepang Occupied, Japanese Claim," *Argus,* March 2, 1942, 1.

15. John Harcourt, "No White Australia at Broome, Raiders May Have Been Residents," *Argus,* March 4, 1942, 2.

16. Cees Nooteboom, "The Netherlands' Own Dunkirk," in *Broome, 3 March 1942–3 March 2012,* ed. Emma Verheijke (Canberra: Embassy of the Kingdom of the Netherlands and Western Australian Museum, 2012), 16.

17. Nonja Peters, "The Broome Air Battle, 3 March 1942," in Verheijke, *Broome,* 7.

18. "Broome Today, Almost a Ghost Town," *West Australian,* April 14, 1942, 2.

19. "Luggers Smashed by Cyclone," *Daily News,* April 11, 1942, 11.

20. "Broome Gaol Closes," *Daily News,* May 9, 1942, 4.

21. Alan Powell, *The Shadow's Edge: Australia's Northern War* (Melbourne: Melbourne University Press, 1988), 97.

22. Jan Lingard, *Refugees and Rebels: Indonesian Exiles in Wartime Australia* (North Melbourne, VIC: Australian Scholarly Publishing, 2008), 10–22.

23. "KATO Thomas: Nationality—Koepanger," B6531, SEAMEN/KOEPANGER/KATO THOMAS, Barcode 6560883, NAA, Melbourne.

24. "TOLA Noladoe: Nationality—Koepanger," B6531, SEAMEN/KOEPANGER/TOLA NOLADOE, Barcode 6560903, NAA, Melbourne; "LEDA Tobo: Nationality—Koepanger," B6531, SEAMEN/KOEPANGER/LEDA TOBO, NAA, Melbourne.

25. Lingard, *Refugees and Rebels,* 27–32.

26. "Club for Indonesians," *Argus,* June 24, 1942, 5; C. F. Brown, Broome, Memo to CMO, Perth, December 17, 1954, E601, 1951/64, Barcode 3354282, NAA, Darwin.

27. Elizabeth Osborne, *Torres Strait Islander Women and the Pacific War* (Canberra: AIATSIS, 1997), 16.

28. *Townsville Daily Bulletin,* May 12, 1942, 2.

29. Osborne, *Torres Strait Islander Women,* 31–35.

30. Thank you to Anna Shnukal for this family information.

31. Deputy Director of Native Affairs, June 24, 1942, IF/44, QSA.

32. Dewis to Sergeant Holly, May 19, 1942, IF/44, QSA.

33. Ruth Hergarty, *Is That You Ruthie?* (St. Lucia: Queensland University Press, 1999); Thom Blake, *A Dumping Ground: A History of the Cherbourg Settlement* (St. Lucia: University of Queensland Press, 2001).

34. Deputy Director of Native Affairs, May 22, 1942, IF/44, QSA.

35. Reports by Constable 3142 Red Hill Station, July 29, 1943; Constable 3295, Rosalie Station, Brisbane, July 26, 1943; Constable 3063 Farleigh Station August 14, 1943, "Bora Bin Juda," J25 1957/4689, Barcode 1644216, NAA, Brisbane.

36. "Evacuation Coloured People Other than Islanders and Aboriginals," IF/44, QSA.

37. Nulty, November 20, 1959, "Hassan Bin Awel," J25 1957/12548, Barcode 1653523, NAA, Brisbane.

38. Lingard, *Refugees and Rebels,* 26.

39. "Prisoner of War/Internee: Ahmat, Anima," MP1103/1 and MP1103/2, QJF16645, Barcodes 8602330 and 9890610, NAA, Melbourne.

40. "Prisoner of War/Internee; Barba, Leah," MP1103/2, QJF16642, Barcode 9890609, NAA, Melbourne; "Prisoner of War/Internee; Woodhead, May," MP1103/2, QJF16285, Barcode 9890286.

41. "Prisoner of War/Internee; Shibasaki, Jena," MP1103/2, QJF16581, 9890582, NAA, Melbourne. The family were Muslims, but some converted to Christianity; see Peta Stephenson, *Islam Dreaming: Indigenous Muslims in Australia* (Sydney: UNSW Press, 2010), 54.

42. Lingard, *Refugees and Rebels*, 23.

43. Lingard, *Refugees and Rebels*, 35–44.

44. Lingard, *Refugees and Rebels*, 51–52.

45. Lingard, *Refugees and Rebels*, 77–101.

46. Vanessa Seekee, "Island Defenders," http://www.anzacday.org.au/history/ww2/bfa /island_defenders.html, accessed July 12, 2012.

47. Seekee, "Island Defenders."

48. "Amboinese at T'Ville to Be Deported," *Townsville Daily Bulletin*, February 3, 1949.

49. "Cassine, Tamsie," J25 1960/1572, Barcode 1668082, NAA, Brisbane.

50. James G. Fox, Memo to Sec. Department of the Interior, October 25, 1944, "United States Army Transport Service—Small Ships Section Personnel," A433, 1944/2/3043, Barcode 74105, NAA, Canberra.

51. Powell, *The Shadow's Edge*, 132; Lingard, *Refugees and Rebels*, 17.

52. Rodney Liddell, *Cape York: The Savage Frontier* (Redbank, QLD: Rodney Liddell, 1996), 186.

53. Liddell, *Cape York*, 188–189.

54. Liddell, *Cape York*, 188.

55. Adrian Vickers would like to thank the Hilliard family, particularly George, for his story.

56. PR84/119, AWM, Canberra lists Alias Bin Hadje Amat, Amen Bin Ali, Amin Bin Yahya, Amen Bin Taib, Bado Bin Mayo, Djaman Bin Nat, Hassan Bin Ali, Hassan Bin Amat, Hassan Bin Osman, Ismail Bin Yakim, Johare Bin Mat [Johare Bin Matalin], Mami Bin Amat, Omar Jabin Kinang, Rizkie Bin Noor, Sallik Bin Sallum, and Samsam Bin Hessien. These all came from Malaya/Singapore, and most signed up in Claremont, WA; from Indonesia were Delas Adoe from Rote, Diampoon bin Dole, Enak Fai of Timor, Hassan Likoer, Hidjoe Lomi of Timor, Nitti Manis of Kupang, Natoen Neno of Kupang, and Koan Seo of Bestali, Kupang.

57. Film interview with Rowan Waddy (*When the War Came to Australia*), F04022, AWM, Canberra.

58. Lingard, *Refugees and Rebels*, 17; Alan Powell, *War by Stealth: Australians and the Allied Intelligence Bureau 1942–1945* (Melbourne: Melbourne University Press, 1996); "Fairview" no longer exists; it burned down in the late twentieth century.

59. Powell, *The Shadow's Edge*, 132; Lingard, *Refugees and Rebels*, 17.

60. Powell, *The Shadow's Edge*, 132.

61. Ronald McKie, *The Heroes: Daring Raiders of the Pacific War* (Sydney: Angus and Robertson, 1961); Powell, *War by Stealth*, 66.

62. Jack Wong Sue, *Blood on Borneo* (Perth: AKR/L. Smith, 2001).

63. There is some confusion about his identity, and two separate records seem to have become merged. A revised memorial plaque names him as Bin Shalid, but he is also named in war service file B883, WX41467, NAA, Canberra, as born in Ulu Klang (Malaysia), on July 23, 1923. All the other SRD records refer to him as "Bin Said," also sometimes as "Ma'Errof"; see AWM PR 84/119 and AWM Alan Wood (Correspondence, Index Cards, Original Papers and Research Notes Collated in Preparation for the Writing of the Services Reconnaissance Department (Srd) History. Includes Material on Various Srd Operations, Including Semut I And II) (PR85/325), notes 419/118/30. For the revised citation, see http://www.awm.gov.au/research /people/roll_of_honour/person.asp?p=531059, accessed February 25, 2012.

64. Powell, *War by Stealth*, 311.

65. Sue, *Blood on Borneo*, 111, 253, 269. Also in Agas II was Sergeant Kanun bin Garfu from Melbourne, with whom Sue had kept up some contact into the twenty-first century. When Sue

was evacuated to Morotai for medical treatment, he also ran across Mandor Bin Ali, a local recruit who had been part of an operation at Palawan, although Sue did not know what happened to Bin Ali after that. Ali Bin Salleh's files list him as being born in Singapore in 1919, and his next of kin as Salleh Assan. His wife was Victoria, and they had three children. E601 1951/58, Barcode 3358292, NAA, Darwin, & WX36797, B883, Barcode 6369024, NAA, Canberra.

66. Sometimes his name is spelled "Saleh"; Powell, *War by Stealth*, 304.

67. Ooi Keat Gin, "Prelude to Invasion: Covert Operations before the Re-occupation of Northwest Borneo, 1944–45," *Journal of the Australian War Memorial* 37 (2002), http://www.awm.gov.au/journal/j37/borneo.asp, accessed May 31 2014.

68. Anon., "G. S. Carter," *Wikipedia*, which cites his "Sarawak Adventure," *New Zealand Surveyor* (Institute of New Zealand Surveyors) 19, no. 3 (December 1946): 246–257, http://en.wikipedia.org/wiki/G._S._Carter, accessed May 31, 2014.

69. AWM PR 84/119 and Wood Notes (Z Special Unit, AIF) (PR85/325).

70. B883, WX36796, service record, NAA, Melbourne; Gin, "Prelude to Invasion," 296; Powell, *War by Stealth*.

71. The Soen Hin service record B883, WX36793, Barcode 6369020, NAA, Canberra.

72. Special Forces Roll of Honour, http://www.specialforcesroh.com/awards-5960.html, accessed 30 December 2011, but his name does not appear on the AWM list of Military Medal recipients, possibly because that lists only "Australians on active service with Australian forces." Note that his name is recorded as "Teh Soen Hin" in the first part of this listing, but there is a cross reference to the more regular spelling of his name and his correct service number. His service files say only that he was awarded the Pacific Star, the War Medal, and Australian Service medals in 1956.

73. Sue, *Blood on Borneo*, 356.

74. Sue, *Blood on Borneo*.

75. The Soen Hin service record B883, WX36793, Barcode 6369020, NAA, Canberra.

76. Abu Kassim's archival files list his full name as Abu Kassim Bin Marah, and as being born in Berauang Ulu, Malaysia, in 1916 or 1917 and married to Djiween Patricia. WX36796, B883, Barcode 6369023, NAA, Canberra. Simeon Bin Said had also been in Z Force according to his daughter, Sally Bin Demin, who was also at the Broome meeting, but he had served in New Guinea. He does not appear in the other lists related to SRD, so he may have been in a different part of the military such as the Small Ships. He is listed in the National Archives as Smeyon bin Said, born Singapore, service number W87108, B884, NAA, Melbourne.

77. "Deportee Will March in Perth on Anzac Day," *Daily News*, April 21, 1949.

78. "Timor Surrendered on HMAS Moresby," *Argus*, September 12, 1945, 6.

79. According to one newspaper report, five American airmen who had been washed ashore on Tanimbar Island after their plane ran out of fuel were nursed by Japanese remaining on the island. The Japanese radioed for help to the RAAF and a plane was sent to bring the men back to Darwin. "Five US Airmen Rescued from Tanimbar Islands," *Argus*, September 24, 1945, 7.

Chapter 8. Disputed Borders on the Pearl Frontier

1. Jan Lingard, *Refugees and Rebels: Indonesian Exiles in Wartime Australia* (North Melbourne, VIC: Australian Scholarly Publishing, 2008), 77–122.

2. Heather Goodall, "Uneasy Comrades: Tuk Subianto, Eliot V. Elliott and the Cold War," *Indonesia and the Malay World* 40, no. 117 (2012): 209–230.

3. Lingard, *Refugees and Rebels*, 77–122.

4. Lingard, *Refugees and Rebels,* 123–141.

5. Heather Goodall, "Port Politics: Indian Seamen, Australian Unionists and Indonesian Independence 1945–1947," *Labour History* 94 (2008): 43–68.

6. Lingard, *Refugees and Rebels,* 143–267.

7. "Islands North of Darwin. 'Occupied' by Indonesians," *Cairns Post,* August 17, 1950.

8. "USI Blockade Cuts Islander's Rations," *Daily News* (Perth), August 15, 1950, 5.

9. Edwards, Telegram draft, Dossier on *Tiki,* Inv Nr 22109 (Geheim), 2.05.117, Ministerie van Buitenlandse Zaken 1945–1954, NAN, Den Haag.

10. Interview with Bill Edwards, 225, TS601, four tapes recorded in 1989, Northern Territory Archives Service, Darwin.

11. Interview with Bill Edwards, 225, TS601.

12. "Voyage of the Tiki—Top Secret Documents," A1838, TS383/6/5, Barcode 272002, NAA, Canberra.

13. Interview with Bill Edwards, 225, TS601.

14. "Japan Puts Ban on Pearl Divers," *West Australian,* January 7, 1953, 4.

15. L. F. E. Goldie, "Australia's Continental Shelf: Legislation and Proclamations," *International and Comparative Law Quarterly* 3, no. 4 (1954): 539.

16. "Pearl Shell Price May Drop £140 Ton," *Argus,* June 29, 1949, 7.

17. "Pearl Shell Price," *Cairns Post,* October 9, 1952, 5; Stephen G. Bloom, *Tears of Mermaids: The Secret Story of Pearls* (New York: St. Martin's Griffin, 2011), 250–253.

18. Susan Sickert, *Beyond the Lattice: Broome's Early Years* (Fremantle: Fremantle Arts Centre Press, 2003), 178.

19. "Ten Men Lost in Gale at Sea," *Northern Standard,* December 10, 1948, 3.

20. Gwenda Tavan, *The Long Slow Death of White Australia* (Melbourne: Scribe Publications, 2005).

21. Sickert, *Beyond the Lattice,* 178.

22. T. R. Sullivan, A/Commonwealth Migration Officer, Darwin to CMO Perth, March 26, 1956, "Employment of Japanese in Pearling Industry," E601 1953/7, Barcode 833894, NAA, Darwin.

23. "Lamadoe Salawatoes, Indonesian under Scope of WRR Act," E601 1957/58, Barcode 3366744, NAA, Darwin.

24. David Northrup, *Indentured Labor in the Age of Imperialism, 1834–1922* (Cambridge: Cambridge University Press, 1995); Kay Saunders, ed., *Indentured Labour in the British Empire, 1834–1920* (Canberra: Croon Helm, 1984).

25. Peter Stalker, *The Work of Strangers: A Survey of International Labour Migration* (Geneva: International Labor Organisation, 1994), 13.

26. Bruno Lasker, *Human Bondage in Southeast Asia* (Chapel Hill: University of North Carolina Press, 1950), 244–252.

27. Margaret Wilson, Clive Moore, and Doug Munro, "Asian Workers in the Pacific," in *Labour in the South Pacific,* ed. Clive Moore, Jacqueline Leckie, and Doug Munro (Townsville: James Cook University, 1990), 88.

28. "Profits Big but Wages and Conditions Poor in Perilous Pearling Industry," *Northern Standard,* August 13, 1948, 3.

29. Adrian Cunningham, "On Borrowed Time: The Australian Pearlshelling Industry, Asian Indentured Labour and the White Australia Policy, 1946–1962" (M. Litt. thesis, Australian National University, 1992), 37.

30. Cunningham, "On Borrowed Time," 46.

31. Cunningham, "On Borrowed Time," 47; see also Hanifa Deen, "The Pearl Diver," *Muslim Journeys,* Uncommon Lives, National Archives of Australia, http://uncommonlives.naa.gov.au/muslim-journeys/stories/the-pearl-diver.aspx, accessed May 18, 2014.

32. Cunningham, "On Borrowed Time," 49.

33. Arthur Calwell, House of Representatives, *Hansard,* March 3, 1948.

34. Cunningham, "On Borrowed Time," 51–52.

35. Cunningham, "On Borrowed Time," 55.

36. Cunningham, "On Borrowed Time," 62.

37. "Second Diving Fatality in a Week," *Northern Standard,* August 6, 1948, 5.

38. "Death of Pearler," *Northern Standard,* October 14, 1949, 12.

39. "Profits Big but Wages and Conditions Poor," 3.

40. Cunningham, "On Borrowed Time," 63.

41. "Pearling Industry May Take a Dive," *Northern Standard,* January 13, 1950, 1.

42. "Re-establishment of Pearling Industry—Northern Territory", A452 150/77 PART 2, Barcode 3108696, NAA, Canberra.

43. Cunningham, "On Borrowed Time," 76–77.

44. Cablegram Australian Embassy, Djakarta, to Department of External Affairs (hereafter DEA), March 15, 1952, "Immigration—Admission of Asiatics and Others for Pearling," A1838/2 1531/49, NAA, Canberra.

45. Memo, Department of Immigration (hereafter DI), "Pearling Indents—Question of Permitting Them to Leave Their Base During Lay-up Season," December 1, 1952, "Indonesians Engaged in Pearling Industry," A6980 T1, S250243, NAA, Canberra.

46. Julia Martínez, "The End of Indenture? Asian Workers in the Australian Pearling Industry, 1901–1972," *International Labor and Working Class History* 67 (2005): 125–47.

47. DEA to Sec. Dept. of Territories, June 29, 1954, "Visit of Mr Hamzah to Broome and Darwin," A452 53/598, Barcode 3435186, NAA, Canberra.

48. F. E. Wells, August 5, 1954, "Visit of Mr Hamzah."

49. Confidential submission to Cabinet, Australian Pearling Industry, G. McLeay, Acting Minister for Commerce and Agriculture, November 26, 1954, "Pearling—Admission of Japanese Indentured Labour—Part 3," A6980 S250205, Barcode 896173, NAA, Canberra.

50. Record of conversation, Dr Tamzil, Indonesian Ambassador with J. P. Quinn, Acting Secretary, DEA, February 28, 1955, A609 520/1/32, NAA, Canberra.

51. F. S. Wise, Administrator, to Secretary, Dept. of Territories, April 4, 1955, "Re-establishment of Pearling Industry—Northern Territory," A452 1950/77 Part 3, Barcode 3108706, NAA, Canberra.

52. Cunningham, "On Borrowed Time," 93–94.

53. Frank Galbally chaired the committee that produced the *Galbally Report* recommending that Australia turn from a policy of assimilation to one of multiculturalism. *Review of Post Arrival Programs and Services for Migrants, Migrant Services and Programs* (Canberra: Department of Immigration and Ethnic Affairs, 1978).

54. Cunningham, "On Borrowed Time," 106.

55. P. R. Heydon, DI, Report to the Minister, Specialists and Employees for the Pearling Industry, September 26, 1969. Approved September 30, 1969, "Pearling Industry—Employment Conditions—Part 3," A446 1969/72528, Barcode 1975470, NAA, Canberra.

56. P. A. Haynes to Senator P. Sim, May 8, 1970, "Pearling Industry—Employment Conditions—Part 3."

57. W. K. Brown, DI, Conversation with Keith Dureau of Pearls Pty. Ltd. and Haynes of A.C. Morgan Pty. Ltd., Western Australia, April 8, 1970, "Pearling Industry—Employment Conditions—Part 3."

58. P. H. Cook, Secretary of the Department of Labour and National Service to Secretary, DI, May 19, 1970, "Pearling Industry—Employment Conditions—Part 3."

59. Present Structure of the Industry, December 1970, "Pearling Industry—Employment Conditions—Part 3."

60. Admission of Non-Europeans for Employment in the Pearling Industry, Citizenship and Travel Branch, DI, "Pearling Industry—Employment Conditions—Part 3."

61. B. H. Barrenger, DI, February 9, 1971, "Pearling Industry—Employment Conditions— Part 3."

62. "Immigration—Migrants in employment in Australia—Nick Paspaley, from Greece," A12111, 1/1963/16/89, Barcode 7450583, NAA, Canberra.

63. Bloom, *Tears of Mermaids*, 250–253; Ben Hills, "Pearl Jam," *Good Weekend, Sydney Morning Herald*, September 7, 2013, http://www.smh.com.au/action/printArticle?id=4711619, accessed February 5, 2014.

64. "Pearl of a Tower in Lustrous Darwin Setting for Paspaley Family," *Australian*, June 23, 2012.

65. Deb Whitmont and Lisa McGregor, "The Price of Pearl," *Four Corners*, ABC, July 10, 2012, http://www.abc.net.au/4corners/stories/2012/07/05/3539781.htm, accessed March 4, 2013.

66. Hills, "Pearl Jam."

Chapter 9. Marriage and Australian Citizenship

1. Andrew Markus, *Australian Race Relations, 1788–1993* (Sydney: Allen & Unwin, 1994), 171.

2. Markus, *Australian Race Relations*, 172.

3. "ABDOEL Gafoer—Nationality: Indonesian—Arrived Broome per Centaur 22 February 1940," K1331, Indonesian/Abdoel G, Barcode 3504995, NAA, Perth.

4. "Indentured Labor Face Deportation after 27 Years," *Northern Standard*, December 10, 1948, 1.

5. "Abdoel Gafoer," E601 1961/181, Barcode 3371549, NAA, Darwin.

6. Press statement released by Arthur Calwell, "Australian Immigration Policy. Deportation of 14 Malay Seamen," A4968 25/10/2, Barcode 635471, NAA, Canberra.

7. Gwenda Tavan, *The Long Slow Death of White Australia* (Melbourne: Scribe Publications, 2005), 55.

8. "Malay Feeling Running High," *Townsville Daily Bulletin*, February 5, 1949, 1; also cited in Sean Brawley, *The White Peril: Foreign Relations and Asian Immigration to Australasia and North America, 1919–1978* (Sydney: University of New South Wales Press, 1995), 248.

9. Brawley, *White Peril*, 253, 248.

10. Tavan, *Long Slow Death*, 55.

11. Arthur Calwell, Second Reading Speech on War-Time Refugees Removal Act in House of Representatives, "Australian Immigration Policy. Deportation of 14 Malay Seamen."

12. War-Time Refugees Removal Act, No. 32 of 1949, *Commonwealth Parliamentary Papers* (Canberra: Commonwealth of Australia, 1949), 135–138.

13. P. Kersley to Commonwealth Migration Officer (CMO), Brisbane, "Pearling, Indentured Labour, Admission of Policy," J25 1958/850, Barcode 1541063, NAA, Brisbane.

14. G. G. Collins, Department of Agriculture and Stock, to Senator Courtice, March 26, 1950, "Pearling, Indentured Labour, Admission of Policy," J25 1958/850, Barcode 1541063, NAA, Brisbane.

15. C. W. Kirk, A/Sub-Collector of Customs to CMO Brisbane, June 19, 1950, "Pearling, Indentured Labour, Admission of Policy," J25 1958/850, Barcode 1541063, NAA, Brisbane.

16. A. L. Nutt, Acting Secretary, Department of Immigration (DI) to CMO Brisbane, August 29, 1952, "Pearling, Indentured Labour Admission of Policy," J25 1958/850, Barcode 1541063, NAA, Brisbane.

17. "Broome or Deportation for 8 Darwin Pearlers," *West Australian,* December 13, 1948.

18. Julia Martínez, "The 'Malay' Community in Pre-War Darwin," *Asians in Australian History: Queensland Review* 6, no. 2 (1999): 45–58.

19. "Death of C. J. Pon," *Northern Standard,* April 11, 1930, 5.

20. "Symbol of People's Struggles," *Northern Standard,* February 11, 1949, 8.

21. "POELING OER Theios born 8 February 1912; Catherine Ann (née Outram and Marshall) born 28 September 1913—Indonesian," A446, 1958/64356, Barcode 7773923, NAA, Canberra.

22. Arthur Calwell, Address by the Minister for Immigration to Diplomatic Representatives of Neighbour Countries, June 2, 1949, "Australian Immigration Policy. Deportation of 14 Malay Seamen," A4968 25/10/2, Barcode 635471, NAA, Canberra.

23. "MacArthur Plea for Calwell," *Free Press,* March 26, 1949; "Australian Immigration Policy. Deportation of 14 Malay Seamen," A4968 25/10/2, Barcode 635471, NAA, Canberra.

24. Speech by Arthur Calwell, *Official Hansard,* House of Representatives, Federal Parliament of Australia, Immigration Bill 1949, Second Reading, July 5, 1949, http://parlinfo.aph.gov.au/parlInfo/search/display/display.w3p;query=Id%3A%22hansard80%2Fhansardr80%2F1949-07–05%2F0075%22, accessed December 12, 2012.

25. Brawley, *White Peril,* 253.

26. E. A. Membery, Acting CMO, Perth, to Secretary DI, August 28, 1951, "The Soin [*sic*] Hin—Indonesian under Scope of W R R Act—Bond Form 15," E601, I1957/67, Barcode 3366760, NAA, Darwin.

27. Townsend Memo, August 17, 1951, "The Soin [*sic*] Hin—Indonesian under Scope of W R R Act—Bond Form 15," E601, I1957/67, Barcode 3366760, NAA, Darwin.

28. "The Soen Hin," B883 WX36793, Barcode 6369020, NAA, Canberra; "The Soin [*sic*] Hin," E601, I1957/67, NAA, Darwin.

29. "Jeskial Mesak," A516 NE 28, No Barcode, NAA, Darwin.

30. "Deport Orders, 2 Pearlers May Stay," *Courier-Mail,* August 27, 1954, 7.

31. Sally Bin Demin, *Once in Broome* (Broome: Magabala Books, 2007), 43.

32. "Application for Naturalisation—RIWU Beri born 12 July 1901," A446 1956/63700, Barcode 8364136, NAA, Canberra.

33. Mavis E. Wright to Harold Holt, June 12, 1951, "Beri Riwu—Indonesian under Scope Wartime Refugees Removal Act—Bond Form 15," E601, 1951/64, Barcode 3354282, NAA, Darwin.

34. C. F. Brown, Broome, Memo to CMO, Perth, December 17, 1954, E601, 1951/64, Barcode 3354282, NAA, Darwin.

35. Solomon, Sub-Collector, Broome, Memo, August 19, 1955, "Bernardus Senge," A516 NE229, NAA, Darwin.

36. L. H. Townsend, Sub-Collector, Broome, Memo, June 22, 1951, "Bernardus Senge," A516 NE229, NAA, Darwin.

37. Mrs V Senge to Sub-Collector, Broome, September 13, 1954; Hardwick, Gibson and Gibson Solicitors to Officer in Charge, DI, Perth, July 21, 1955, "Bernardus Senge," A516 NE229, NAA, Darwin.

38. K. Walsh A/Sub-Collector, Broome to DI, January 15, 1955, "Bernardus Senge," A516 NE229, NAA, Darwin.

39. Application for Naturalization, "Bernardus Senge," A516 NE229, NAA, Darwin.

40. "Adam Hari Bin—Indonesian," E37 1966/871, Barcode 5310928, NAA, Darwin.

41. Tavan, *Long Slow Death*, 90.

42. Cited in Tavan, *Long Slow Death*, 94.

43. Keiko Tamura, "The Entry of Japanese War Brides into Australia," in *Relationships: Japan and Australia, 1870s–1950s*, ed. Paul Jones and Vera Mackie (Melbourne: History Department, University of Melbourne, 2001), 249.

44. *Argus*, July 11, 1952, 1.

45. Tavan, *Long Slow Death*, 95–98.

46. Tamura, "The Entry of Japanese War Brides," 250.

47. "Esek, Anaktotote," J25 957/3859, Barcode 1642452, NAA, Brisbane.

48. Kersley to Sub-Collector, Thursday Island, January 7, 1948, "Esek Anaktotote," J25 957/3859, Barcode 1642452, NAA, Brisbane.

49. Report, July 22, 1957, "Esek Anaktotote," J25 957/3859, Barcode 1642452, NAA, Brisbane.

50. Tavan, *Long Slow Death*, 99.

51. Andrew Markus, "Heyes, Sir Tasman Hudson Eastwood (1896–1980)," *Australian Dictionary of Biography*, National Centre of Biography, Australian National University, http://adb.anu.edu.au/biography/heyes-sir-tasman-hudson-eastwood-10497/text18623, accessed February 3, 2013; Tavan, *Long Slow Death*, 102.

52. Alexander Batfini to Minister for Immigration, March 10, 1960, "Alexander Batfini," A516 NE1, NAA, Darwin.

53. L. Liveris, CMO, Darwin to Secretary, DI, November 29, 1954, "Alexander Batfini," A516 NE1, NAA, Darwin.

54. H. C. Giese, Director of Welfare to CMO, Darwin, Received December 2, 1959, "Alexander Batfini," A516 NE1, NAA, Darwin.

55. L. Liveris to Sec. DI, June 21, 1960. "Alexander Batfini," A516 NE1, NAA, Darwin.

56. Speech by Jim Cairns, Member for Yarra, *Official Hansard*, House of Representatives, Federal Parliament of Australia, Migration Bill 1958, Second Reading, August 5, 1958, http://parlinfo.aph.gov.au/parlInfo/search/display/display.w3p;db=HANSARD80;id=hansard80%2Fhansardr80%2F1958-08-05%2F0066;query=Id%3A%22hansard80%2Fhansardr80%2F1958-08-05%2F0065%22, accessed December 12, 2012.

57. A. L. Nutt, Acting Secretary, DI to Cairns, December 23, 1960, "Jeskial Mesak, Indonesian," A516 NE 28, NAA, Darwin.

58. His father was Tola Toeloe and his mother Leten Bado. L. Liveris to Regional Director, ASIO, May 26, 1960, "Noladoe Toeloe," A516 NE44, NAA, Darwin.

59. Elizabeth Marshall, East-West Committee, September 5, 1960, "Noladoe Toeloe," A516 NE44, NAA, Darwin.

60. Application for Naturalization, "Noladoe Toeloe," A516 NE44, NAA, Darwin.

61. Elizabeth Marshall to Nutt, DI, June 13, 1961, "Alexander Batfini," A516 NE1, NAA, Darwin.

62. L. Liveris to Sec. DI, August 21, 1961, "Alexander Batfini," A516 NE1, NAA, Darwin.

63. Leslie Bury, Acting Minister for Immigration to J. N. Nelson, Alice Springs, May 31, 1962, "Alexander Batfini," A516 NE1, NAA, Darwin.

64. Nulty to Director of Native Affairs, June 27, 1961, "Herwawa, Albert," J25 1959/641, Barcode 1656198, NAA, Brisbane.

65. "Herwawa Albert: Service number Q116089," B884 Q116089, Barcode, 4863988, NAA, Brisbane.

66. Radke, April 10, 1961, "Herwawa, Albert," J25 1959/641, NAA, Brisbane.

67. Cavanagh, Senior Sergeant, June 1, 1961, "Herwawa, Albert," J25 1959/641, NAA, Brisbane.

68. Nulty to Director of Native Affairs, June 27, 1961, "Herwawa, Albert."

69. Thank you to Anna Shnukal for providing this information.

70. Allen to CMO Brisbane, August 18, 1960, "Titisay Henry," J25 1959/1420, Barcode 1656560, NAA, Brisbane.

71. Bruce to Nulty, September 4, 1957, Nulty to Secretary, November 20, 1959, "Bora Bin Juda," J25 1957/4689, Barcode 1644216, NAA, Brisbane; Draney, December 10, 1952, "Doraho Salen Bin," J25 1958/2442, Barcode 1657702, NAA, Brisbane.

72. "Kaprisi Karel," J25 1959/156, Barcode 1050504, NAA, Brisbane.

73. Raima was Saia Bin Awal's sister. Thank you to Anna Shnukal for providing the details of the name and age recorded on his tombstone.

74. Nulty to Adair, July 13, 1960, "Bagu Bin Amat," J25 1958/3085, Barcode 967426, NAA, Brisbane.

75. "LEBA Taba—Nationality: Indonesian—Arrived Broome per Centaur 1924," K1331, 1964/1965/LEBA T, Barcode 3364896, NAA, Perth.

76. "Ole (Oel) Hati, (Indonesian Pearling Operative)," W1956/3661, PP105/1, NAA, Perth.

Conclusion

1. "Bodah Salem—Indonesian," E37 1966/996, Barcode 5425348, NAA, Darwin.

2. "The Soin [sic] Hin," E601, I1957/67, Barcode 3366760, NAA, Darwin.

3. Regina Ganter, in Regina Ganter, with contributions from Julia Martínez and Gary Lee, Mixed Relations: Asian-Aboriginal Contact in North Australia (Crawley: University of Western Australia Press, 2006), 244–254.

4. Jessica Mauboy, interviewed by Ray Martin, "From Darwin to the World," September 27, 2010, http://sixtyminutes.ninemsn.com.au/stories/8020466/from-darwinto-the-world, accessed February 3, 2013.

5. Trent Dalton, "Jessica Mauboy on Her Music Salvation, and Her Australian Idol Secret," Australian Magazine, August 10, 2013, http://www.theaustralian.com.au/news/features/little -big-voice/story-e6frg8h6-1226693678142, accessed February 5, 2014.

6. Samantha Faulkner and Ali Drummond, Life Belong Ali Drummond: A Life in the Torres Strait (Canberra: Aboriginal Studies Press, 2007), 81–82.

7. Faulkner, Life Belong Ali Drummond, 68.

8. Faulkner, Life Belong Ali Drummond, 5–12.

9. Faulkner, *Life Belong Ali Drummond*, 65. Note that Muslim-raised Jamel Shibasaki also converted to Catholicism on marriage; see Peta Stephenson, *Islam Dreaming: Indigenous Muslims in Australia* (Sydney: UNSW Press, 2010), 54; for a discussion of Filipino descendants on Thursday Island, see Anna Shnukal, "A Double Exile: Filipino Settlers in the Outer Torres Strait Islands, 1870s–1940s," *Aboriginal History* 35 (2011): 161–178.

10. Sally Bin Demin, *Once in Broome* (Broome: Magabala Books, 2007), 5–11.

11. Bin Demin, *Once in Broome*, 31, 37–40.

12. Bin Demin, *Once in Broome*, 28, 47, 55.

Bibliography

Archives

Archives nationale d'outre-mer (ANOM), Aix-en-Provence.
Australian War Memorial (AWM), Canberra.
Koninklijk Instituut voor Taal-, Land- en Volkenkunde (KITLV), Royal Institute for Linguistics and Anthropology, Leiden.
KITLV Picture Archives. http://kitlv.pictura-dp.nl/.
Litchfield, Jessie Manuscript "Press Collect," NLA MS132, National Library of Australia, Canberra.
Nationaal Archief, National Archives of the Netherlands (NAN) (before 2002, Algemeen Rijksarchive, ARA).
National Archives of Australia (NAA), Canberra and State branches.
Noel Butlin Archive Centre, Canberra.
Northern Territory Archives Service (NTAS), Darwin.
Queensland State Archives (QSA), Brisbane.
State Records Office of Western Australia (SROWA), Perth.
Tropen Museum Picture Archives. http://commons.wikipedia.org/wiki/File:COLLECTIE_TROPENMUEUM.
Wallace Papers. Unpublished Diaries S41: 1858, http://people.wku.edu/charles.smith/index1.htm.

Newspapers

Most Australian newspapers accessed online via Trove, National Library of Australia, https://trove.nla.gov.au/newspaper.
Dutch newspapers accessed via Historische Kranten, Koninklijke Bibliotheek, http://kranten.kb.nl/.
Singapore newspapers accessed via National Library of Singapore, http://newspapers.nl.sg/.
Advertiser (Adelaide)
Advocate
Argus
Australian
Barrier Miner
Brisbane Courier
Cairns Post
Canberra Times

Central Queensland Herald
Courier-Mail
Daily News
Inquirer & Commercial News
Kalgoolie Western Argus
Morning Bulletin
Morning Post
Nieuw Rotterdamsche Courant
Nieuws van den Dag
Nor'West Echo
Northern Miner
Northern Standard
Northern Territory Times
Northern Territory Times and Gazette
Northern Times
Perth Gazette and West Australian Times
Pewarta Deli
Queenslander
Register
Singapore Free Press and Mercantile Advertiser
South Australian Register
Straits Times
Sumatra Post
Sun
Sydney Morning Herald
Townsville Daily Bulletin
West Australian
Western Argus
Western Mail

Government Publications

Commonwealth of Australia. "Galbally, Report." *Review of Post Arrival Programs and Services for Migrants, Migrant Services and Programs.* Canberra, 1978.
Koloniaal Verslag, The Hague. http://www.statengeneraaldigitaal.nl/.
Northern Territory Annual Reports. *Commonwealth Parliamentary Papers,* various years.
Official Hansard, various years. http://www.aph.gov.au/Parliamentary_Business/Hansard.
Queensland State Government. "Pearl-Shell and Beche-de-mer Commission, Report of the Commission." Brisbane, 1908.
Staatsblad van Nederlandsch-Indië over het jaar 1816–. http://babel.hathitrust.org/cgi/pt?id=mdp.35112105251930;seq=744;view=1up

Secondary Sources

Aljunied, Syed Muhd Khairudin. *Colonialism, Violence and Muslims in Southeast Asia.* Abingdon: Routledge, 2009.

Alwi, Des. *Friends and Exiles: A Memoir of the Nutmeg Isles and the Indonesian Nationalist Movement*, edited by Barbara S. Harvey. Ithaca, NY: Cornell Southeast Asia Program Publications, 2008.

Andaya, Leonard Y. *Leaves of the Same Tree: Trade and Ethnicity in the Straits of Melaka.* Honolulu: University of Hawai'i Press, 2008.

Anderson, Warwick. *The Cultivation of Whiteness: Science, Health, and Racial Destiny in Australia.* Durham, NC: Duke University Press, 2006.

Anon. "G. S. Carter." *Wikipedia.* http://en.wikipedia.org/wiki/G._S._Carter.

Bain, Mary Albertus. *Full Fathom Five.* Perth: Artlook Books, 1982.

———. "Male, Arthur (1870–1946)." In *Australian Dictionary of Biography,* National Centre of Biography, Australian National University, http://adb.anu.edu.au/biography/male-arthur-7469/text13013, published first in hardcopy 1986.

Balint, Ruth. "Aboriginal Women and Asian Men: A Maritime History of Color in White Australia." *Signs* 37, no. 3 (Spring 2012): 544–554.

———. *Troubled Waters: Border, Boundaries and Possession in the Timor Sea.* Crows Nest, NSW: Allen & Unwin, 2005.

Barnard, Timothy P. "Chasing the Dragon: An Early Expedition to Komodo Island." In *Lost Times and Untold Tales from the Malay World,* edited by Jan van der Putten and Mary Kilcline Cody, 41–53. Singapore: National University of Singapore Press, 2009.

Barnes, R. H. "Lamalerap: A Whaling Village in Eastern Indonesia." *Indonesia* 17 (April 1974): 136–159.

———. *Sea Hunters of Indonesia: Fishers and Weavers of Lamalera.* Oxford: Clarendon Press, 1996.

Barnes, Ruth. "The Bridewealth Cloth of Lamalera, Lembata." In *To Speak with Cloth: Studies in Indonesian Textiles,* edited by Mattiebelle Gittinger, 43–55. Los Angeles: Museum of Cultural History, University of California, 1989.

Barraud, Cécile. *Tanebar-Evav: Une société de maisons tournée vers le large.* Cambridge: Cambridge University Press, 1979.

Battersby, Paul. *To the Islands: White Australians and the Malay Archipelago since 1788.* Lanham, MD: Lexington Books, 2007.

Beckett, Jeremy. "The Torres Strait Islanders and the Pearling Industry: A Case of Internal Colonialism." *Aboriginal History* 1, no. 1 (1977): 77–104.

Bin Demin, Sally. *Once in Broome.* Broome: Magabala Books, 2007.

Blake, Thom. *A Dumping Ground: A History of the Cherbourg Settlement.* St. Lucia: University of Queensland Press, 2001.

Bloom, Stephen G. *Tears of Mermaids: The Secret Story of Pearls.* New York: St. Martin's Griffin, 2011.

Boomgaard, Peter. "Resources and People of the Sea in and around the Indonesian Archipelago, 900–1900." In *Muddied Waters: Historical and Contemporary Perspectives on Management of Forests and Fisheries in Island Southeast Asia,* edited by David Henley, Manon Osseweijer, and Peter Boomgaard, 97–120. Leiden: KITLV Press, 2005.

Braddon, Russel. *Thomas Baines and the North Australian Expedition.* Sydney: Collins, 1986.

Brawley, Sean. *The White Peril: Foreign Relations and Asian Immigration to Australasia and North America, 1919–1978.* Sydney: UNSW Press, 1995.

Butcher, John G. *The Closing of the Frontier: A History of the Marine Fisheries of Southeast Asia c.1850–2000*. Singapore: ISEAS/KITLV, 2004.

Campo, Joseph Norbert Frans Marie à. *Engines of Empire: Steamshipping and State Formation in Colonial Indonesia*. Hilversum: Uitgeverij Verloren, 2002.

"Characters of Broome, Episode 1: Donnelly McKenzie." Australian National Indigenous Television, August 7, 2013. http://www.nitv.org.au/fx-program.cfm?pid=6185D122 -A8DE-482B-38CDEFD7429165A7&pgid=61AF0DB6-0A5F-9010-AF7519DC0 E1E9607.

Chase, Athol. "All Kind of Nation: Aborigines and Asians in the Cape York Peninsula." *Aboriginal History* 5 (1981): 7–20.

Chesterman, John, and Brian Galligan. *Citizens without Rights: Aborigines and Australian Citizenship*. Cambridge: Cambridge University Press, 1997.

Conigrave, C. Price. *North Australia*. London: Jonathan Cape, 1936.

Choo, Christine. "Asian Men on the West Kimberley Coast, 1900–1940." In *Asian Orientations: Studies in Western Australian History*, edited by Jan Gothard, 89–111. Perth: University of Western Australia, 1995.

———. *Mission Girls: Aboriginal Women on Catholic Missions in the Kimberley, Western Australia, 1900–1950*. Crawley: UWA Press, 2001.

Clarence-Smith, William Gervase. "The Economic Role of the Arab Community in Maluku, 1816 to 1940." *Indonesia and the Malay World* 26, no. 74 (1998): 32–49.

Collins, Ben. "The History of Indonesians in Broome." ABC Kimberley, July 8, 2010. http://www.abc.net.au/local/stories/2010/07/08/2947883.htm?site=kimberley.

D'Albertis, L. M. *New Guinea: What I Did and What I Saw*. London: Sampson Low, Marston, Searle, & Rivington, 1880.

Dalton, Trent. "Jessica Mauboy on Her Music Salvation, and Her Australian Idol Secret." *Australian Magazine, Australian*, August 10, 2013. http://www.theaustralian.com.au /news/features/little-big-voice/story-e6frg8h6-1226693678142.

Dashwood, C. J. *Pearl-shelling Industry in Port Darwin and Northern Territory*. Melbourne: Government Printer, 1902.

Deen, Hanifa. "The Pearl Diver." In *Muslim Journeys*. Uncommon Lives, National Archives of Australia. http://uncommonlives.naa.gov.au/muslim-journeys/stories/the-pearl -diver.aspx.

Dickson, Rod. *The Price of a Pearl*. Perth: Hesperian Press, 2002.

Donegan, Jacqui, and Raymond Evans. "Running Amok: The Normanton Race Riots of 1888 and the Genesis of White Australia." *Journal of Australian Studies* 25 (2001): 83–98.

Drabbe, P. *Het Leven van den Tamembarees: Ethnografische Studie over het Tamembaree-sche Volk*. Internationales Archiv Fur Ethnographie. Leiden: Brill, 1940.

DuBois, Cora. *The People of Alor: A Social-Psychological Study of an East Indian Island*, 2 vols. New York: Harper, 1944.

Earl, George Windsor. *The Eastern Seas, Voyages and Adventures in the Indian Archipelago, in 1932-33-34, Comprising a Tour of the Island of Java–Visits to Borneo, the Malay Peninsula, Siam*. London: W. H. Allen, 1837.

Edmonds, Carl. "Pearl Diving: The Australian Story." *Supplement to South Pacific Underwater Medicine Society Journal* 26, no. 1 (1996): 4–10.

Edwards, Hugh. *Port of Pearls: Broome's First 100 Years.* Swanbourne: Hugh Edwards, 1984.

Eisler, William, and Bernard Smith. *Terra Australis: The Furthest Shore.* Sydney: Art Gallery of New South Wales, 1988.

Ellen, Roy. *On the Edge of the Banda Zone: Past and Present in the Social Organisation of a Moluccan Trading Network.* Honolulu: University of Hawai'i Press, 2003.

Elson, Robert E. *The Idea of Indonesia: A History.* Cambridge: Cambridge University Press, 2008.

Emmer, P. C., and R. Shlomowitz. "Mortality and Javanese Labour in Surinam (1890–1936) and Malaya (1912–1933)." *Working Papers in Economic History.* Adelaide: Flinders University, 1995.

Faulkner, Samantha, and Ali Drummond. *Life Belong Ali Drummond: A Life in the Torres Strait.* Canberra: Aboriginal Studies Press, 2007.

Favenc, Ernest. *The Moccasins of Silence.* Sydney: Robertson, 1895.

Ford, Michele, and Lenore Lyons. "Travelling the Aspal Route: Grey Labour Migration through an Indonesian Border Town." In *The State and Illegality in Indonesia,* edited by E. Aspinall and G. van Klinken, 107–122. Leiden: KITLV, 2011.

Forman, Shepard. "East Timor: Exchange and Political Hierarchy at the Time of the European Discoveries." In *Economic Exchange and Social Interaction in Southeast Asia: Perspectives from Prehistory, History, and Ethnography,* edited by Karl L. Hutterer, 97–111. Ann Arbor: Center for South and Southeast Asian Studies, University of Michigan, 1977.

Fox, James J. *Harvest of the Palm: Ecological Change in Eastern Indonesia.* Cambridge, MA: Harvard University Press, 1977.

———. "Notes on the Southern Voyages and Settlements of the Sama-Bajau." *Bijdragen tot de Taal-, Land- en Volkenkunde* 133, no. 4 (1977): 459–465.

Ganter, Regina. *The Pearl-Shellers of Torres Strait.* Melbourne: Melbourne University Press, 1994.

Ganter, Regina, with contributions from Julia Martínez and Gary Lee. *Mixed Relations: Asian-Aboriginal Contact in North Australia.* Crawley: University of Western Australian Press, 2006.

Gibbney, H. J. "D'Albertis, Luigi Maria (1841–1901)." In *Australian Dictionary of Biography,* National Centre of Biography, Australian National University, http://adb.anu.edu.au/biography/dalbertis-luigi-maria-3351/text5045, published first in hardcopy 1972.

Gin, Ooi Keat. "Prelude to Invasion: Covert Operations before the Re-Occupation of Northwest Borneo, 1944–45." *Journal of the Australian War Memorial* 37 (2002). http://www.awm.gov.au/journal/j37/borneo.asp.

Goldie, L. F. E. "Australia's Continental Shelf: Legislation and Proclamations." *International and Comparative Law Quarterly* 3, no. 4 (1954): 535–575.

Gomang, Syarifuddin R. "Muslim and Christian Alliances: 'Familial Relationships' between Inland and Coastal Peoples of the Belagar Community in Eastern Indonesia." *Bijdragen tot de Taal-, Land- en Volkenkunde* 162, no. 4 (2006): 468–489.

Goodall, Heather. "Port Politics: Indian Seamen, Australian Unionists and Indonesian Independence 1945–1947." *Labour History* 94 (2008): 43–68

———. "Uneasy Comrades: Tuk Subianto, Eliot V. Elliott and the Cold War." *Indonesia and the Malay World* 40 (2012): 209–230.

Griswold, Lawrence. *Tombs, Travel and Trouble.* New York: Hillman-Curl, 1937.

Hägerdal, Hans. "Cannibals and Pedlars." *Indonesia and the Malay World* 38, no. 111 (2010): 217–246.

——. *Lords of the Land, Lords of the Sea: Conflict and Adaptation in Early Colonial Timor, 1600–1800*. Leiden: KITLV Press, 2012.

Hägerdal, Hans, trans. "Memorie van Overgave van den Fundgeerend Controleur van Alor G.A.M. Galen, dated 15 December 1946. Collectie Losse Aanwinsten Bestuursambtenaren No.26, Nationaal Archief, Den Haag." *HumaNetten* 25 (2010): 14–44, and 27 (2011): 53–96. http://lnu.se/polopoly_fs/1.24684!HumaNetten%2C%20 Nr%2025%2C%20v%C3%A5ren%202010.pdf (part 1); and http://lnu.se/polopoly _fs/1.61220!Nr_27%2C_hosten_2011.pdf (part 2).

Hardenberg, J. D. F. "De Parelmoervisscherij in het Oosten van den Indischen Archipel." *Indische Gids* 2 (1939): 827–833.

Hau'ofa, Epeli. *A New Oceania: Rediscovering Our Sea of Islands*. Suva: University of the South Pacific, 1993.

Hawkins, Clifford W. *Praus of Indonesia*. London: Nautical Books, 1982.

Henderson, Graeme, and Ian Crawford. "Sampans, Belangs and Junkos: The Pearling Boats of the Aru Islands." *Expedition* 28, no. 1 (n.d.): 36–46.

Herbert, Xavier. *Capricornia*. Sydney: The Publicist, 1938.

Hergarty, Ruth. *Is That You Ruthie?* St. Lucia: Queensland University Press, 1999.

Hill, Ernestine. *The Great Australian Loneliness*. Melbourne: Robertson and Mullens, 1943.

Hills, Ben. "Pearl Jam." *Good Weekend, Sydney Morning Herald*, September 7, 2013. http:// www.smh.com.au/action/printArticle?id=4711619.

Ho, Engseng. *The Graves of Tarim: Genealogy and Mobility across the Indian Ocean*. Berkeley: University of California Press, 2006.

Hoefte, Rosemarijn. "A Passage to Suriname? The Migration of Modes of Resistance by Asian Contract Laborers." *International Labor and Working Class History* 54 (1998): 19–39.

Honniball, J. H. M. "E.H. Laurence, Stipendiary Magistrate." *Early Days: Journal of the Royal Western Australian Historical Society* 7, no. 7 (1975): 19–24.

Horridge, G. Adrian. *The Prahu: Traditional Sailing Boat of Indonesia*. Singapore: Oxford University Press, 1981.

Hoskins, Janet. *The Play of Time: Kodi Perspectives on Calendars, History, and Exchange*. Berkeley: University of California Press, 1993.

Houben, Vincent J. H. "Javanese Labour Migration into Southeast Asia, the Pacific and Australia." In *Proceedings of the University of Queensland History Research Group, No. 5*, edited by Paul Crook, 16–30. Brisbane: University of Queensland, 1994.

Howard, John. "Australia in the World." *Address by the Prime Minister, the Hon. John Howard MP, to the Lowy Institute for International Policy*. Sydney: The Lowy Institute, 2005.

Hussainmiya, B. A. *Orang Rejimen: The Malays of the Ceylon Rifle Regiment*. Kuala Lumpur: Universiti Kebangsaan Malaysia, 1990.

Idriess, Ion L. *Forty Fathoms Deep: Pearl Divers and Sea Rovers in Australian Seas*. Sydney: Angus and Robertson, 1937.

Jones, A. M. *Africa and Indonesia: The Evidence of the Xylophone and Other Musical and Cultural Factors*. Leiden: E. J. Brill, 1964.

Jones, Noreen. *Number Two Home: A Story of Japanese Pioneers in Australia.* Fremantle: Fremantle Arts Centre, 2002.

Jones, Sidney. *Making Money off Migrants: The Indonesian Exodous to Malaysia.* Hong Kong and Wollongong: ASIA 2000 and the Centre for Asia Pacific Social Transformation Studies, University of Wollongong, 2000.

Jones, Timothy G. *The Chinese in the Northern Territory.* 3rd ed. Darwin: Charles Darwin University Press, 2005.

Jonge, Nico de, and Toos van Dijk. *Forgotten Islands of Indonesia: The Art and Culture of the Southeast Moluccas.* Singapore: Periplus, 1995.

Kampen, P. N. van. "De Paarl- en Parelmoervisscherij langs de Kusten der Aroe-Ielanden." *Mededeelingen van het Visscherij-Station te Batavia* 2 (1908): 1–30.

Kana, Nico L. *Dunia Orang Sawu.* Jakarta: Sinar Harapan, 1983.

Kathirithamby-Wells, Jeyamalar. "'Strangers' and 'Stranger-Kings': The *Sayyid* in Eighteenth-Century Maritime Southeast Asia." *Journal of Southeast Asian Studies* 40, no. 3 (2009): 567–591.

Kerr, Alan. *A Federation in These Seas: An Account of the Acquisition by Australia of Its External Territories.* Barton, ACT: Attorney General's Department, Commonwealth of Australia, 2009.

Lake, Marilyn, and Henry Reynolds. *Drawing the Global Colour Line: White Men's Countries and the Question of Racial Equality.* Melbourne: Melbourne University Press, 2008.

Lasker, Bruno. *Human Bondage in Southeast Asia.* Chapel Hill: University of North Carolina Press, 1950.

Liddell, Rodney. *Cape York: The Savage Frontier.* Redbank, QLD: Rodney Liddell, 1996.

Lingard, Jan. *Refugees and Rebels: Indonesians in Wartime Australia.* North Melbourne, VIC: Australian Scholarly Publishing, 2008.

Lockard, Craig A. "The Javanese as Emigrant." *Indonesia* 11 (1971): 41–62.

Lockwood, Douglas. *Australia's Pearl Harbour, Darwin 1942.* Melbourne: Cassell Australia, 1966.

——. *The Front Door: Darwin, 1869–1969.* London: Angus & Robertson, 1969.

Lockwood, Rupert. *Black Armada.* Sydney South: Australasia Book Society, 1975.

Loveband, Ann. "Positioning the Product: Indonesian Migrant Women Workers in Taiwan." *Journal of Contemporary Asia* 34, no. 3 (2004): 336–348.

Macintyre, Stuart. *The Oxford History of Australia, Volume 4, 1901–1942: The Succeeding Age.* Melbourne: Oxford University Press, 1986.

Macknight, C. C. "Outback to Outback: The Indonesian Archipelago and Northern Australia." In *Indonesia: Australian Perspectives,* edited by R. G. Garnaut, J. J. Fox, P. T. McCawley, and J. A. C. Mackie, 137–148. Canberra: Research School of Pacific and Asian Studies, Australian National University, 1980.

——. *The Voyage to Marege': Macassan Trepangers in Northern Australia.* Melbourne: Melbourne University Press, 1976.

Manguin, Pierre-Yves. "Trading Ships of the South China Seas: Shipbuilding Techniques and Their Role in the History of the Development of Asian Trade Networks." *Journal of the Economic and Social History of the Orient* 36, no. 3 (1993): 253–280.

Markus, Andrew. *Australian Race Relations, 1788–1993.* Sydney: Allen & Unwin, 1994.

——. "Heyes, Sir Tasman Hudson Eastwood (1896–1980)." In *Australian Dictionary of Biography,* National Centre of Biography, Australian National University, http://adb.anu.edu.au/biography/heyes-sir-tasman-hudson-eastwood-10497/text18623, published first in hardcopy 1996.

Martínez, Julia. "The End of Indenture? Asian Workers in the Australian Pearling Industry, 1901–1972." *International Labor and Working Class History* 67 (2005): 125–147.

——. "The 'Malay' Community in Pre-War Darwin." *Queensland Review: Asians in Australian History* 6, no. 2 (1999): 45–58.

Masson, Elsie. *An Untamed Territory.* London: Macmillan, 1915.

Mauboy, Jessica, interviewed by Ray Martin. "From Darwin to the World," September 27, 2010. http://sixtyminutes.ninemsn.com.au/stories/8020466/from-darwinto-the-world.

Maurer, Jean Luc, in collaboration with Marcel Magi, and with a contribution by Marie-Jo Siban. *Les Javanais du Caillou: Des affres de l'exil aux aléas de l'intégration.* Paris: Association Archipel, 2006.

Maxwell, Robyn. "Textiles and Tusks: Some Observations on the Social Dimensions of Weaving in East Flores." In *Five Essays in the Indonesian Arts: Music, Theatre, Textiles, Painting and Literature,* edited by Margaret J. Kartomi, 43–62. Clayton, VIC: Monash University, 1981.

——. *Textiles of Southeast Asia: Tradition, Trade and Transformation.* Melbourne: Oxford University Press, 1990.

McCarthy, Mike. "Before Broome." *Great Circle* 16, no. 2 (1994): 76–89.

McKie, Ronald. *The Heroes: Daring Raiders of the Pacific War.* Sydney: Angus and Robertson, 1961.

McKinnon, Susan. *From a Shattered Sun: Hierarchy, Gender, and Alliance in the Tanimbar Islands.* Madison: University of Wisconsin Press, 1991.

McPhee, Ewen. "Archaeology of the Pearl Shelling Industry in Torres Strait." *Memoirs of the Queensland Museum, Cultural Heritage Series* 3, no. 1 (2004): 363–377.

Mercer, Patricia. "Clark, James (1857–1933)." In *Australian Dictionary of Biography,* National Centre of Biography, Australian National University, http://adb.anu.edu.au/biography/clark-james-5664/text9563, published first in hardcopy 1981.

Ministry of Trade of the Republic of Indonesia. *Indonesian South Sea Pearls* (n.d., n.p.).

Moor, J. H. *Notices of the Indian Archipelago and Adjacent Countries.* London: Frank Cass, 1837.

Moore, Ronald. "The Management of the Western Australian Pearling Industry, 1860 to the 1930s." *Great Circle* 16, no. 2 (1994): 121–138.

Mudie, Ian. "Cadell, Francis (1822–1879)." In *Australian Dictionary of Biography,* National Centre of Biography, Australian National University, http://adb.anu.edu.au/biography/cadell-francis-3136/text4675, published first in hardcopy 1969.

Muljono-Larue, Fidayanti. *Histoire de l'immigration des Javanais sous contrat en Nouvelle-Calédonie, 1896–1950.* Noumea: Centre territorial de recherche et de documentation pedagogiques, 1996.

Müller, Andy. *Cultured Pearls: The First Hundred Years.* Lausanne: Andy Müller for Golay Buchel, 1997.

Mullins, Steve. "Australian Pearl-Shellers in the Moluccas: Confrontations and Compromise on a Maritime Frontier." *Great Circle* 23, no. 2 (2001): 3–23.

——. "The Costa Rica Packet Affair: Colonial Entanglements and Tests of Empire in Pre-Federation New South Wales." *Journal of the Royal Australian Historical Society* 87, no. 2 (2001): 268–285.

——. "From TI to Dobo: The 1905 Departure of the Torres Strait Pearl-Shelling Fleets to Aru, Netherlands East Indies." *Great Circle* 19, no. 1 (1997): 30–39.

——. "James Clark and the Celebes Trading Co.: Making an Australian Maritime Venture in the Netherlands East Indies." *Great Circle* 24, no. 2 (2002): 22–52.

——. "To Break 'the Trinity' or 'Wipe Out the Smaller Fry': The Australian Pearl Shell Convention of 1913." *Journal for Maritime Research* 7, no. 1 (2005): 215–244.

Nagata, Yuriko. "'Certain Types of Aliens': The Japanese in Australia, 1941–1952." In *Relationships: Japan and Australia, 1870s–1950s,* edited by Paul Jones and Vera Mackie, 217–240. Melbourne: History Department, University of Melbourne, 2001.

Needham, Rodney. *Sumba and the Slave Trade.* Working Paper, vol. 31. Clayton, VIC: Monash University Centre of Southeast Asian Studies, 1983.

Nelson, H. N. "Carpenter, Sir Walter Randolph (1877–1954)." In *Australian Dictionary of Biography,* National Centre of Biography, Australian National University, http://adb .anu.edu.au/biography/carpenter-sir-walter-randolph-5510/text9379, published first in hardcopy 1979.

Nooteboom, Cees. "The Netherlands' Own Dunkirk." In *Broome, 3 March 1942–3 March 2012,* edited by Emma Verheijke, 14–25. Canberra: Embassy of the Kingdom of the Netherlands and Western Australian Museum, 2012.

Northrup, David. *Indentured Labor in the Age of Imperialism, 1834–1922.* Cambridge: Cambridge University Press, 1995.

Oliver, Pamela. *Empty North: The Japanese Presence and Australian Reactions, 1860s to 1942.* Darwin: Charles Darwin University Press, 2006.

Oosterzee, Penny van. *Where Worlds Collide: The Wallace Line.* Kew, Victoria: Reed, 1997.

Osborne, Elizabeth. *Torres Strait Islander Women and the Pacific War.* Canberra: AIATSIS, 1997.

Pannell, Sandra. "Of Gods and Monsters: Indigenous Sea Cosmologies, Promiscuous Geographies and the Depths of Local Sovereignty." In *A World of Water: Rain, Rivers and Seas in Southeast Asian Histories,* edited by Peter Boomgard, 72–102. Leiden: KITLV Press, 2007.

Paterson A. B. "The Pearl Diver." In *Rio Grande's Last Race and Other Verses* (Melbourne: Angus & Robertson, 1902). http://www.poetrylibrary.edu.au/poets/paterson-a-b -banjo/the-pearl-diver-0004006.

Peters, Nonja. "The Broome Air Battle, 3 March 1942." In *Broome, 3 March 1942–3 March 2012,* edited by Emma Verheijke, 6–8. Canberra: Embassy of the Kingdom of the Netherlands and Western Australian Museum, 2012.

Philipps, Lorraine. "Plenty More Little Brown Man! Pearlshelling and White Australia in Queensland 1901–1918." In *Essays in the Political Economy of Australian Capitalism,* vol. 4, edited by E. L. Wheelwright and K. Buckley, 58–84. Sydney: Australia & New Zealand Book Company, 1980.

Pixley, Norman S. "Pearlers of North Australia: The Romantic Story of the Diving Fleets." Presidential Address Read at the Annual Meeting of the Royal Historical Society of

Queensland, September 23, 1971. http://espace.library.uq.edu.au/eserv/UQ:209190
/s00855804_1971_1972_9_3_9.pdf.

Powell, Alan. *Far Country: A Short History of the Northern Territory,* 5th ed. Darwin: Charles
Darwin University Press, 2009.

———. *The Shadow's Edge: Australia's Northern War.* Melbourne: Melbourne University
Press, 1988.

———. *War by Stealth: Australians and the Allied Intelligence Bureau 1942–1945.* Melbourne: Melbourne University Press, 1996.

Pratt, Ambrose. *The Big Five.* London: Ward, Lock & Co, 1910.

Preston, Diana, and Michael Preston. *A Pirate of Exquisite Mind: The Life of William Dampier, Explorer, Naturalist and Buccaneer.* London: Doubleday, 2004.

Reid, Anthony J. S. Introduction to *Slavery, Bondage and Dependency in Southeast Asia,*
edited by Anthony J. S. Reid, 1–25. St. Lucia: University of Queensland Press, 1983.

———. *Southeast Asia in the Age of Commerce 1450–1680,* 2 vols. New Haven, CT: Yale
University Press, 1987, 1993.

Reynolds, Henry. *North of Capricorn, The Untold Story of Australia's North.* Sydney: Allen &
Unwin, 2003.

Riedel, Johan Gerard Friedrich. *De Sluik- en Kroesharige Rassen tusschen Selebes en Papua.*
's-Gravenhage: Martinus Nijhoff, 1886.

Roever, Arend de. *De Jacht op Sandelhout: De VOC en de Tweedeling van Timor in de Zeventiende Eeuw.* Zutphen: Alberg Pers, 2002.

Roosman, R. S. "A Shadow over a Silent New Caledonia Community." *Pacific Islands
Monthly* 49, no. 3 (March 1978): 21–30.

Saunders, Kay, ed. *Indentured Labour in the British Empire, 1834–1920.* Canberra: Croon
Helm, 1984.

Schaper, Michael. "The Broome Race Riots of 1920." In *Asian Orientations: Studies in Western Australian History 16,* edited by Jan Gothard, 112–132. Perth: Department of History, University of Western Australia, 1995.

Searcy, Alfred. *In Australian Tropics.* London: George Robertson & Co., 1909.

Seekee, Vanessa. "Island Defenders." http://www.anzacday.org.au/history/ww2/bfa/island
_defenders.html.

Shimizu, Hiroshi. "Rise and Fall of the Karayuki-san in the Netherlands Indies from the
Late Nineteenth Century to the 1930s." *Review of Indonesian and Malaysian Affairs*
26, no. 2 (1992): 17–43.

Shineberg, Dorothy. *The People Trade: Pacific Island Laborers and New Caledonia, 1865–
1930.* Honolulu: University of Hawai'i Press, 1999.

Shnukal, Anna. "A Double Exile: Filipino Settlers in the Outer Torres Strait Islands, 1870s–
1940s." *Aboriginal History* 35 (2011): 161–178.

———. "'They Don't Know What Went on Underneath': Three Little-Known Filipino/
Malay Communities of Torres Strait." In *Navigating Boundaries: The Asian Diaspora
in Torres Strait,* edited by Anna Shnukal, Guy Ramsay, and Yuriko Nagata, 81–122.
Canberra: Pandanus Books, 2004.

Shnukal, Anna, and Guy Ramsay. "Tidal Flows: An Overview of Torres Strait Islander–
Asian Contact." In *Navigating Boundaries: The Asian Diaspora in Torres Strait,* ed-

ited by Anna Shnukal, Guy Ramsay, and Yuriko Nagata, 33–51. Canberra: Pandanus Books, 2004.

Sickert, Susan. *Beyond the Lattice: Broome's Early Years*. Fremantle: Fremantle Arts Centre Press, 2003.

Sissons, David. "The Japanese in the Australian Pearling Industry." *Queensland Heritage* 3, no. 10 (1979): 9–27.

———. "*Karayuki-San:* Japanese Prostitutes in Australia, 1887–1916—I." *Historical Studies* 17 (1977): 323–341.

Sluys, A. G. H. van. "Dobo-ervaringen," *Koloniaal Tijdschrift* 5, no. 2 (1916): 299–317.

Spaan, Ernst. "Taikongs and Calos: The Role of Middlemen and Brokers in Javanese International Migration." *International Migration Review* 28, no. 1 (1994): 93–113.

Spyer, Patricia. "The Eroticism of Debt: Pearl Divers, Traders, and Sea Wives in the Aru Islands, Eastern Indonesia." *American Ethnologist* 24, no. 3 (1997): 515–538.

———. *The Memory of Trade: Modernity's Entanglements on an Eastern Indonesian Island*. Durham, NC: Duke University Press, 2000.

Stacey, Natasha. *Boats to Burn: Bajo Fishing Activity in the Australian Fishing Zone*. Asia-Pacific Environment Monograph Series. Canberra: ANU E Press, 2007.

Stalker, Peter. *The Work of Strangers: A Survey of International Labour Migration*. Geneva: ILO, 1994.

State Library of Victoria. "What It Used to Cost." http://guides.slv.vic.gov.au/whatitcost.

Stephenson, Peta. *Islam Dreaming: Indigenous Muslims in Australia*. Sydney: UNSW Press, 2010.

———. *The Outsiders Within. Telling Australia's Indigenous-Asian Story*. Sydney: University of New South Wales Press, 2007.

Streeter, Edwin W. *Pearls and Pearling Life*. London: George Bell and Sons, 1886; repr. Carlisle, WA: Hesperian Press, 2006, and Harlow: Matching Press, 2006.

Sue, Jack Wong. *Blood on Borneo*. Perth: AKR/L. Smith, 2001.

Swadling, Pamela. *Plumes from Paradise: Trade Cycles in Outer Southeast Asia and Their Impact on New Guinea and Nearby Islands until 1920*. Boroko: Papua New Guinea National Museum in association with Robert Brown and Associates (Qld.), 1996.

Tagliacozzo, Eric. "Navigating Communities: Race, Place, and Travel in the History of Maritime Southeast Asia." *Asian Ethnicity* 10, no. 2 (2009): 97–120.

———. *Secret Trades, Porous Borders: Smuggling and States along a Southeast Asian Frontier, 1865–1915*. New Haven, CT: Yale University Press, 2005.

Tamura, Keiko. "The Entry of Japanese War Brides into Australia." In *Relationships: Japan and Australia, 1870s–1950s*, edited by Paul Jones and Vera Mackie, 242–264. Melbourne: History Department, University of Melbourne, 2001.

Taunton, Henry. *Australind: Wanderings in Western Australia and the Malay East*. London: Edward Arnold, 1903.

Tavan, Gwenda. *The Long Slow Death of White Australia*. Melbourne: Scribe Publications, 2005.

Termorshuizen, Thio. "Indentured Labour in the Dutch Colonial Empire 1800–1940." In *Dutch Colonialism, Migration and Cultural Heritage*, edited by Gert Oostindie, 261–314. Leiden: KITLV Press, 2008.

Thomas, David. Catalogue essay. In Deutscher and Hackett, *Works from the Donald Friend Collection* (auction catalogue). Sydney: Deutscher and Hackett, 2013. http://www .deutscherandhackett.com/node/31500015/.

Traube, Elizabeth G. *Cosmology and Social Life: Ritual Exchange among the Mambai of East Timor.* Chicago: University of Chicago Press, 1986.

Urry, James, and Michael Walsh. "The Lost 'Macassar' Language and Culture of Northern Australia." *Aboriginal History* 5, no. 2 (1981): 109–134.

Vickers, Adrian. "The Country and the Cities." *Journal of Contemporary Asia* 34, no. 3 (April 2004): 304–317.

———. "From Bali to Lampung by Way of the Pasisir." *Archipel* 45 (1993): 55–76.

———. "'Malay Identity': Modernity, Invented Tradition, and Forms of Knowledge." *Review of Indonesian and Malaysian Affairs* 31, no. 1 (1997): 173–212.

———. "A Paradise Bombed." *Griffith Review* 1 (Spring 2003): 105–113.

Walker, Alan, and R. David Zorc. "Austronesian Loanwords in Yolngu-Matha of Northeast Arnhem Land." *Aboriginal History* 5, no. 2 (1981): 109–134.

Walker, David. *Anxious Nation: Australia and the Rise of Asia 1850–1939.* St. Lucia: University of Queensland Press, 1999.

Wallace, Alfred Russel. *The Malay Archipelago. The Land of the Orang-utan and the Bird of Paradise: A Narrative of Travel, with Studies of Man and Nature.* London: Macmillan & Co., 1869.

Warren, James Francis. *The Sulu Zone, 1768–1898: Dynamics of External Trade, Slavery, and Ethnicity in the Transformation of a Southeast Asian Maritime State.* Singapore: Singapore University Press, 1981.

Welie, Rik van. "Patterns of Slave Trading and Slavery in the Dutch Colonial World, 1596–1863." In *Dutch Colonialism, Migration and Cultural Heritage,* edited by Gert Oostindie, 155–260. Leiden: KITLV Press, 2008.

Whitmont, Deb, and Lisa McGregor. "The Price of Pearl." *4 Corners.* Australian Broadcasting Corporation Television, July 10, 2012. http://www.abc.net.au/4corners/stories/2012/07/05/3539781.htm.

Widodo, Triono, Hendy Sulistiowaty, Noor Yudanto, Andy Johan Prasetyo, Riza Tyas Utami Hirzam, Fadhil Nugroho, Asrianti Mira Anggraeni, and Putu Utami Ardarini Sadha. "Report on National Survey of Remittance Patterns of Indonesian Migrant Workers, 2008." Jakarta: Bank Indonesia, Directorate of Economic and Monetary Statistics, 2009.

Wilson, Margaret, Clive Moore, and Doug Munro. "Asian Workers in the Pacific." In *Labour in the South Pacific,* edited by Clive Moore, Jacqueline Leckie, and Doug Munro, 78–107. Townsville: James Cook University, 1990.

Williams, Catharina Purwanti. *Maiden Voyages: Eastern Indonesian Women on the Move.* Singapore: ISEAS, 2007.

Windschuttle, Keith. *The White Australia Policy.* Sydney: Macleay Press, 2004.

Yarwood, A. T. *Asian Migration to Australia: The Background to Exclusion 1896–1923.* Melbourne: Melbourne University Press, 1964.

Yu, Sarah. "Broome Creole: Aboriginal and Asian Partnerships along the Kimberley Coast." *Queensland Review,* special issue edited by Regina Ganter, *Asians in Australian History* 6, no. 2 (1999): 59–73.

Dissertations and Theses

Anderson, Lois P. "The Role of Aboriginal and Asian Labour in the Origin and Development of the Pearling Industry, Broome, Western Australia, 1862–1940." B.A. honors thesis, Murdoch University, 1978.

Cunningham, Adrian. "On Borrowed Time: The Australian Pearlshelling Industry, Asian Indentured Labour and the White Australia Policy, 1946–1962." M.Litt. thesis, Australian National University, 1992.

De Silva, Maureen. "Javanese Indentured Labourers in British North Borneo, 1914–1932." PhD diss., School of Oriental and African Studies, University of London, 2009.

Farram, Steven. "From 'Timor Koepang' to 'Timor NTT': A Political History of West Timor, 1901–1967." PhD diss., Charles Darwin University, 2003.

Gomang, Syarifuddin R. "The People of Alor and Their Alliances in Eastern Indonesia: A Study in Political Sociology." Master's thesis, University of Wollongong, 1993.

Martínez, Julia. "Plural Australia: Aboriginal and Asian Labour in Tropical White Australia, Darwin, 1911–1940." PhD diss., University of Wollongong, 1999.

Nicolspeyer, Martha M. "De Sociale Structuur van een Aloreesche Bevolkingsgroep." PhD diss., Leiden University, 1940.

Osseweijer, Manon. "Taken at the Flood: Marine Resource Use and Management in the Aru Islands (Maluku, Eastern Indonesia)." PhD diss., University of Leiden, 2001.

Post, Peter. "Japanse Bedrijvigheid in Indonesië, 1868–1942: Structurele Elementen van Japan's Vooroorlogse Economische Expansie in Zuidoost Azië." PhD diss., Vrije Universiteit, 1991.

Wellfelt, Emilie. "Diversity and Shared Identity: A Case Study of Interreligious Relations in Alor, Eastern Indonesia." Master's thesis, Göteborg University, 2007.

Index

Page numbers in italics indicate figures.